A PRIEST TO TURN TO

Dedicated to
Archbishop Philip M. Hannan
who is a
priest and bishop
to turn to.

A Priest to turn to

**Biblical and Pastoral Reflections
on the Priesthood**

Rev. William F. Maestri

ALBA · HOUSE   NEW · YORK

SOCIETY OF ST. PAUL, 2187 VICTORY BLVD., STATEN ISLAND, NEW YORK 10314

Library of Congress Cataloging-in-Publication Data

Maestri, William.
      A priest to turn to: Biblical and pastoral reflections on the
priesthood / by   William F. Maestri.
          p. 252   cm. 21 × 14
      Bibliography: p.
      ISBN 0-8189-0546-8
      1. Priesthood.   2. Catholic Church — Clergy.   3. Clergy — Office.
4. Catholic Church — Clergy — Religious life.   I. Title.
    BX1912.M217   1989
    262'.142—dc19   88-31418
                                                  CIP

Nihil Obstat:
Rev. J. Emile Pfister, S.J.
Censor Librorum

Imprimatur:
† Archbishop Francis B. Schulte
Archdiocese of New Orleans
February 28, 1989

Designed, printed and bound in the United States of
America by the Fathers and Brothers of the
Society of St. Paul, 2187 Victory Boulevard,
Staten Island, New York 10314, as part of their
communications apostolate.

Printing Information:

Current Printing · first digit 1 2 3 4 5 6 7 8 9 10 11 12

Year of Current Printing - first year shown
 1989   1990   1991   1992   1993   1994   1995   1996

TABLE OF CONTENTS

INTRODUCTION

The title of this book is not my own creation. In the summer of '72 (my rather mundane version of the Summer of '42), I was a college seminarian taking a course in history at Loyola University in New Orleans. Before going to class, I would visit the Most Holy Name of Jesus Church which is located on the campus (I was surrounded by Jesuits!). As I was surveying the book rack, a title caught my imagination: *A Future to Hope In*, by Father Andrew M. Greeley. One of the chapters was entitled, "A Priest to Turn to." Father Greeley wrote:

> The priest's role, therefore, is to be what the role of the religious functionary has always been — to be God's man — to be the one others can "turn to" for care and love. . .
>
> To be the man of God to whom others turn, to be the man whose relationships are the most important in the world, to be the one who is held ex-officio to display models of friendship for others to imitate, may be terrifying, but it is hardly dull. And if men turn away from the possibility of assuming such a role, it is not because there are not risk-takers in the human race — there still are — but because stupidity and apathy and inertia and stubbornness and immaturity have allowed the role to become obscured, dehumanized, and buried within the wall of the rectory. But the man of faith and hope is quite confident that the walls are going to come tumbling down. (pp. 266, 276)

These stirring words sealed my fate as a "Greeley fan" (he even penned a Foreword to a book I wrote for Alba House). I can only throw myself on the mercy of the Lord and ask forgiveness! Anyway, what struck me as essential about Father Greeley's words was his presentation of the priest as the man of God proclaiming the good news of hope. I would be hard pressed to find a better story for the Catholic priest than being God's man of hope. For the Catholic Story is one long narrative of God's unbounded love for us. And this passionate, Divine Love made visible in Jesus is the cause of our hope. The priest is the man of God who embodies the Divine Love and evokes hope in others. The priest proclaims the here and now presence of God and, at the same time, assures us that the best is yet to be. The Apostle Paul knew of what he wrote: eye has not seen, nor ear heard, what God has waiting for us. This God who is madly in love with us, and wants us to respond in love, can't wait to reveal more and more of what is yet to be.

No doubt to some this talk of hope seems childish, unreal and far removed from the world of today's church, priest and society. It would seem that all this talk of hope (a kind of false consciousness) does not take seriously the shortage of vocations to the priesthood, the number of priests who have left and the increasing pain of those who stay. Reality would seem to demand a less tender-hearted and a more tough-minded assessment of the situation.

While not wanting to minimize any of the above-mentioned problems, I am simply convinced that the Really Real is on the side of hope. During times of transition, uncertainty, and a general loss of nerve, the message of hope is crucial. In fact, the message of hope calls for great courage. Little is required to join the chorus of doom and gloom. In the end, each of us (and priests are *not* excluded) must make a decision; a Pascal type wager, if you will, about the meaning of our existence. We will either accept the stories about Yahweh and Jesus or we will accept the pessimistic stories told by contemporary philosophers such as Martin Heidegger. We will either live the stories of the God who makes all things new; who liberates and redeems; who pours out the Spirit so as to renew the face of the earth; who rises from the dead and holds out the

vision of a new heaven and a new earth; or we will tell the
stories of an absurd, unfeeling cosmos in which we find
ourselves "thrown without a thrower." For the Christian and for
God's man of hope (the priest), the decision is clear. We wager
everything on the hopeful stories of Yahweh and Jesus.

If there is a persistent theme which runs through these
reflections on the priesthood, it is this: today's priests are
important for today's Church. The laity want and value priests.
The laity want their priests to be men of holiness, competence,
love, care, encouragement, challenge, and hope. This is the
priest people turn to. Horror stories notwithstanding, priests
are very important in the Church and in the lives of the faith
community.

Is the above nothing more than an empty assertion lacking in that much prized litmus test of truth — statistics?
Hardly. No one has studied, sociologically, the American
priesthood with greater professional competence and insight
than Father Andrew Greeley. His massive research, along with
the research of his colleagues at the National Opinion Research Center, supports the importance of the priest. Two brief
citations deserve mention.

In *A Church to Come Home to* (co-authored by his sister,
Dr. Mary Durkin), concerning the importance of the priest,
they write:

> The Catholic priest is an important person in the church.
> He always has been and he still is, despite the resentment
> caused by his well-publicized resignation and despite the
> often self-pitying "identity crisis." . . . Priests matter.
> Priests matter more than anyone in the church except the
> spouse. Poor priestly ministry may drive people to the
> fringes; the ministry of a good minister makes them long
> to come home; and the hope that they might encounter
> priestly leadership with vision, taste, sensibility and
> courage provides powerful motivation to come home . . .
> (pp. 71-72)

The priest is not only important for those who return but
for those who stay. Again, Father Greeley:

> . . . one of the most striking findings of both the 1974
> study of the adult Catholic population and the 1979 study
> of young Catholics was that priests are still of enormous
> importance to Catholics. Indeed, the strongest correlate
> of church attendance and Catholic identification for both
> the young people and for the general population were not
> issues of sex, birth control, abortion and the ordination of
> women. Rather, the strongest predictor of Catholic be-
> havior and identification was the quality of the Sunday
> sermon preached in the respondent's parish church.
> (*American Catholics Since the Council*, pp. 112-13)

Unfortunately, the laity's valuing of the priest is not
shared by a number of priests. The experience of more than a
few priests is one of self-doubt, uncertainty, loss of meaning,
and a general sense that one is not making a difference in the
lives of people. The so-called vocation crisis is not merely one
of numbers. It is much more serious and tragic. The real crisis
concerning vocations and priesthood is with priests themselves. Can we really expect the young to follow Jesus and
serve in the Church as priests if we present priesthood without
joy, humor, enthusiasm, imagination, zest, and a deep sense
of having found the pearl of great price for which we have
wagered everything? None of this is said in order to deny the
challenges and burdens. Yet the priest of Jesus Christ, the
man of hope, lives in such a way as to say that hope, not
despair; life, not death; light, not darkness have the last word.
Such a story of priesthood is *awe*-fully attractive.

How are we to account for the drastic changes in the
contemporary priesthood? How did we move from Bishop
Fulton Sheen to Father Ralph of *The Thorn Birds*? The answer
to these questions is complex. In Chapter One, I will offer
some reflections. For now, we can say that fundamental
changes in the Catholic population in general and fundamental
changes which emerged from the Second Vatican Council
played a crucial role.

The traditional immigrant Church ended to a large extent
with the election of John F. Kennedy as President of the United

States. (The "browning of the Catholic Church" is offering new challenges and opportunities. A new immigrant Church is well underway.) Beginning in the 50's and continuing down to the present, the Catholic population has come of age in American society. The social portrait of the contemporary Catholic is painted something like this: Catholics are attending college and professional schools in great numbers; the income of Catholics has risen in corresponding fashion; and politically, the American Catholic population remains loyal to the Democratic Party and is progressive concerning social and economic justice issues. All of this means that the priest is no longer the most educated member of the parish. The types of services rendered by today's parish are vastly different than in years past. The styles of leadership in today's parish call for more than the pastor merely giving orders. Finally, the way(s) of being a Catholic have greatly changed. Many Catholics make their own decisions about cult, code, and creed. The traditional modes of respect for and esteem shown to the priest are things of the past.

Changes were taking place not only in American society, but within the Catholic Church as well. The Second Vatican Council ushered in enormous changes in the Church. The Council provided Catholics with an exciting new vision of church, the role of the laity, and the ministry of the episcopacy. Unfortunately, there was a general failure at renewal of the Catholic priesthood. Our understanding of the Church, the laity, and the bishops was changed. However, the role of the priest was largely ignored. In his excellent article on the priesthood, "Jesuits as Priests: Crisis and Charism," J. William Harmless, S.J. writes concerning the Council's failure to spiritually renew the priesthood:

> Vatican II was a massive success . . . Nonetheless, the council had its weaknesses and blind spots . . . one of which was its failure to renew the priesthood. That is not to say that Vatican II did not change the shape and understanding of priesthood. It certainly did. But it failed

to renew it, at least in the way that it renewed the
ministries of the bishops and of the laity . . . (p. 26)

In general, the council gave much less attention to
the role of priests than it did to that of bishops and of the
laity. In *Lumen Gentium*, for example, the role of the
bishops receives some nine paragraphs (nos. 20-28) and
the role of the laity also nine (nos. 30-38), the role of the
priest only one (no. 28). (p. 22)

Hence, changes in the American Catholic population as
well as changes within the Church profoundly affected the role
and self-image of the priest.

The following essay is organized in three major sections
with each section addressing four aspects of priesthood. Section One, *The Fundamentals*, will concern itself with the priest
as a man of faith, a man of mystery and a disciple, and with the
self-image of the priest. Section Two, *Pastoral Ministry*, will
address the issue of work as it relates to the priesthood. This
section will open with a spiritual reflection on work (ministry)
in light of our theology of creation. We will then proceed to
three major areas of priestly ministry or work: preaching,
liturgical celebration, and pastoral care. The final section,
Toward a Priestly Spirituality, will center on the priest as a
man of holiness. We will reflect on the nature of priestly
holiness as revealed in the life of Mary, the Mother of Jesus.
The priest is called to be a spiritual leader for the community.
We will use the ministry of Peter as our guide for spiritual
leadership or ministry. The spirituality of the priest is greatly
enhanced by friendship with women. And the priest as friend
has much to contribute to women and the spirituality of the
family. Finally, the Person of Jesus is at the heart of the
priestly ministry. This presentation will conclude and com-
mence with a reflection on Jesus as the Man for Others, the
Eternal High Priest; and the Priest to Turn to. A list for further
reading will be included at the end of this essay.

A brief methodological word about coming attractions is
in order. What follows is a series of reflections on the Catholic
priesthood within the American context. These reflections do

not claim to be scholarly tracts. These reflections are just that — reflections. They are grounded in the witness of Scripture, the witness of the Catholic Story, and the witness of this priest who is grateful for having been called to serve. Naturally each reader will add his (and hopefully, her) witness and experience to what follows. In so doing, the reader makes up what is lacking in the writer.

A word of gratitude is also called for. I am grateful to God for my vocation and all who nurtured that vocation. The Monks of St. Joseph Abbey, the seminarians of St. Joseph Seminary College, and the faith community at Mercy Academy are very special gifts of grace. I am indebted to Fathers Victor, Timothy, and Edmund of the Society of St. Paul and the entire community at Alba House Publishing. A special word of appreciation is extended to Patricia E. Regan for all her help in preparing this book.

William F. Maestri
St. Joseph Abbey
St. Benedict, Louisiana

The Fundamentals

CHAPTER ONE

ABRAHAM:
The Priest as Man of Faith

The call of Abraham in the book of Genesis (12:1-9) serves as the model for the biblical experience of vocation. We see in the relationship between the Lord and Abraham the three fundamental elements of vocation: call, challenge, and care. We have disclosed to us in the call of Abraham the basic aspects of following the Lord in faith. Priestly existence is one such journey of faith in the Lord. By exploring the story of Abraham, we can gain valuable insight into the priestly vocation and the priest as a man of faith for the community of faith.

The Call (Gn 12:1-9)

The call to Abraham comes in a very uncomplicated manner: the Lord simply tells him to take his family and move to a land the Lord will provide. Abraham does not engage in a great deal of soul-searching. His response of faith is as simple as the call itself. Abraham goes where the Lord directs him.

The reality of being called by the Lord today is not quite as simple or direct. Few, if any, of us have been called to the priestly life in so direct a fashion as the Lord God's encounter with Abraham. If we were to ask Abraham what motivated his move to a new land, his answer would go something like this: "The Lord God came to me and told me what he wanted done. He made me an offer I would have been crazy to refuse."

We modern Abrahams have a more difficult time. Most of us would respond to the question, how or why did you become a priest? in a fashion quite different from Abraham. No doubt we would respond in terms of what St. Thomas Aquinas called secondary causes. That is, we would respond to the nurturing of our priestly vocation in terms of a significant other — mother, nun, or priest. All of us who are priests are able to name those secondary causes and significant others who spoke about the priesthood and gave witness to the priestly life as one of joy, happiness, holiness, and humor. We can name a Father Pat, a Sister Mary Kevin, and a mother (especially important if she is blessed enough to be Irish!) who cooperated with God's grace by planting the idea of being a priest in our hearts. The vocation director was not to be found only in the chancery, but in the home, classroom, and parish.

We must be very clear on this point: God's call to the ordained priestly ministry comes to us through human beings. We human beings are the sacraments, the revelation, and encouragement of God's call to serve as priests, to those whom the Lord God makes an offer they would be crazy to refuse. And the parish priest is one of the most powerful sacraments or revelations of God's call to others to preach the Gospel, celebrate the Eucharist, and serve the needs of the community. There are few things as humanly attractive to the young as observing an elder engaged in a vocation to which he or she is committed. The happy, holy, humorous, and competent priest is the best invitation to follow the Lord through the priestly life. The young will want to see just what is it (and who is it) that turns us on and lights up the life of the priest.

Unfortunately (tragically would not be too strong a word), a significant number of priests simply refuse to be sacraments of God's call to the young to serve as priests. Why does such a destructive attitude exist among the clergy? Father Andrew M. Greeley offers the following troubling assessment based on his research:

The numerical decline of the priesthood, which may be the most serious problem facing the church in the wake of the Second Vatican Council, does not seem to be properly attributable to a spiritual decline among young Catholics, a very considerable proportion of whom are interested in social and religious problems and even (ten percent) would be willing to consider a life of dedication to the church. . .

The vocation problem, in other words, is a priestly problem and not a young person problem . . . The clergy are in the process of committing collective suicide because they do not have enough confidence in themselves and their work to actively recruit young men to follow them into the priesthood. (*American Catholics Since the Council*, pp. 118, 120, 122)

Vocations to the priesthood do not fall unmediated from the heavens. The Catholic family, parish, and school are crucial places for inviting young men to become priests. The young are open, spiritual, and ready for a challenge. The Lord God continues to call and invite the young to dream dreams and see visions. The Lord God continually pours out the Spirit into the hearts of the young, preparing them for generous service in the name of Jesus and the Gospel. Yet God's call and Spirit work through poor, limited, and redeemed human flesh. The same flesh which Jesus took on continues to be a sacrament of God's call to serve as a priest. The call to priesthood becomes flesh. And that enfleshed call looks very much like the mother down the street, the parish priest, and the nun in the school. Through "ordinary lives," God does his extraordinary work.

The Challenge

God's call to the priesthood does not come by way of cheap grace. The call to priestly existence bespeaks a challenge. The challenge of a priestly vocation is present at the beginning and throughout the whole of one's priestly commitment.

The Lord's call to Abraham was simple and direct. The challenge to accept the call required the courage of faith. Not the faith of intellectual assent, but the courageous faith which moves one on a lifelong journey with the Lord. Such a faith involves risk-taking and the wagering of one's whole life on the call of God. The Lord calls for Abraham to leave the land of his heritage and venture forth into a new situation. The security, safety, and leisure that is awaiting Abraham will be laid aside. The God of surprises is calling and challenging this seventy-five years young man to start anew. With the simple courage that characterizes the man of faith, the Bible tells us, "Abram went as the Lord directed him . . ." (Gn 12:4).

The call to a priestly life is a challenge to enter a new situation. The new is always exciting and appealing — from a distance. At the same time, we know that the new also carries with it the unknown. There is always the tension between the forward lure of the new and the backward pull of the familiar.

In one of my first year formation classes at the seminary, a young man asked the following question: "How can I be sure that I am doing what God wants by coming to the seminary? How can I have that inner peace which tells me that I made the right decision?" This young seminarian's concerns are not uncommon. His questions could have been asked by Abraham, the fishermen in Galilee, the zealous Saul, and every person who desires to do the will of the Lord.

How to respond to this seminarian's questions? A vocation to the priesthood does not lend itself to the clear and distinct analysis we expect from solving a mathematical problem. There is always a zone of uncertainty and a degree of probability about a priestly vocation. Simply put: we do not enjoy absolute certainty; rather we must struggle with the tension of God's dream for our lives. At no point in the vocation process do we enjoy total certainty. We must resist the temptation to become self-satisfied and complacent like the foolish landowner in the Gospels. The tension and uncertainty experienced by the seminarian never really leaves the priest and his ministry. This is not a sign of divine displeasure. The tension and uncertainty are a sign of the human condition and they remind us of the continuing need to live the examined, prayerful, priestly life.

Our young seminarian finds much in common with Abraham. There are a number of significant issues which face seminarians: sexuality, celibacy, authority, relationships in general, loneliness, work satisfaction, and the future shape of the priesthood itself. In addition, seminarians may find that their decision to enter the seminary is not supported by home, school, or parish as it once was in the past. Also there are simply not as many seminarians as in former times. The academic and formation faculties of the seminary are placed under enormous pressure to provide support, nurturing, and guidance for the seminarian desiring to follow the Lord. In the midst of such a challenging situation, the seminarian must be willing to risk and wager. He must be willing to come and see what the Lord has in mind. There are no guarantees. The seminarian of today must follow the example of Abraham and simply journey in faith into that new situation which is both exciting and threatening; attractive and evokes fear and trembling.

The Catholic priest of today finds himself in a new situation as well. The immigrant canopy which once provided security, meaning, status, and esteem is a thing of the past. The image, role, and ministry of the priest have undergone profound changes. The sacred canopy which proclaimed the priest *in persona Christi* has waned. Perhaps the most challenging aspect of this new situation in which the priest finds himself concerns the loss of being distinctive. That is, the Second Vatican Council spoke eloquently of the role of the laity and the notion of the common priesthood of all the baptized. Unfortunately, the priesthood of all believers became confused in such a way that it seemed to diminish the priesthood of the ordained minister. James A. Fisher, in his excellent book on the priesthood, *Priests: Images, Ideals, and Changing Roles*, writes:

> Vatican Council II was very conscious of reviving this ancient tradition of the common priesthood of all the faithful . . . However, despite the Council's efforts to explain how the ministerial priesthood and the common priesthood complement one another, there is still ambiguity.

The passing of the immigrant Church; the failure of the Second Vatican Council to provide a renewal of the priesthood to keep pace with its renewing of the laity, bishops, and Church as a whole; profound changes in the American Catholic population in terms of education and income; the development of the role of the laity; the fostering of ministries at the parish level; and the general decline in morale of the clergy because of an increase in priests leaving and a decrease in those joining have all contributed to the trauma facing the priest in the American context. Yet all the news is not bad.

Unfortunately, we lack sufficient sociological data at present to discuss in detail the state of the priesthood in America. However, what we do know goes something like this: by and large, Catholic priests exhibit a level of emotional maturity compatible with other groups in society. Priests do pray and continue to find meaning and satisfaction in their work. Priests do love the Church and are committed to its identity and mission. There are tensions to be sure: authority; Church structures that seem unresponsive to pastoral needs; some teachings (mostly in the area of sexual ethics) which seem out of touch with the experience of the community priests serve; loneliness continues to be a major problem; and a general level of stress related to ministry, role expectations, and job satisfaction in terms of making a difference in the lives of people. (For a more detailed presentation of the sociological dimensions of the priesthood in America, see the NORC Survey of 1972, *The Catholic Priest in the United States: Sociological Investigations*, ed., A. Greeley. Also see *American Catholics Since the Council*, A. Greeley, 1985, and *The Future of Catholic Leadership: Responses to the Priest Shortage*, D. Hoge, 1987, Sheed & Ward.) What is remarkable is that even in the midst of this priestly discontent, priests do continue to serve with dedication, maturity, competence, and hope.

What remains most painful when considering the priesthood is the number of priests who are in pain. The pain experienced by a number of priests grows out of a lack of confidence, satisfaction from ministry, and a general feeling that what the priest does is unimportant and not appreciated. This pain is not only experienced by priests, but its effects are felt throughout the Church, for priests who find themselves in such a situation often refuse to invite young men to join them in the ministry. Misery may love company, but not where priests are concerned. Commenting on the new situation of American priests since the Council, Father Greeley writes:

> What has gone wrong in the Catholic priesthood in the United States since the Second Vatican Council? Even stated as simply as that last question, the crisis in the priesthood remains to a considerable extent inexplicable. The changes of the Second Vatican Council did something to the priesthood from which it has yet to recover. Until we understand better than we do now why the Council was such a savage blow to the morale, the self-esteem, the self-confidence, and the self-respect of priests, we will have to accept as almost inevitable the continued decline in the number of priests available to minister to the church and the mounting problems for laity and for priests because of that decline. (*The Catholic Priest in the United States: Sociological Investigations*, pp. 127-128)

From all that has been said in this section, are we to despair? The temptation is easy to answer in the affirmative. Yet for a people who proclaim the death and resurrection of Jesus to be their foundational story, despair is ruled out. We are a people of hope and courageous faith. The God who calls and challenges us is also the God who provides a way through the desert, a light that shines in the darkness, and a message of renewal in the midst of a dying world. The God who called

Abraham is the God who challenged him to accept a new situation. The old structure, certainties, and expectations would be no more. Abraham would move to a new land which the Lord God would provide. Priests find themselves called and challenged. The old structure and roles have died and the new have not yet appeared. We are between the evenings. It is a time for a courageous faith and bold action. For the Lord God who calls and challenges does not abandon us. The God of Abraham, our God, cares for and provides us with the nourishment for the journey of faith.

Care

The Lord God requires more of Abraham than moving to a new land. The Lord will ask of Abraham a surrender of what is most precious to him — Isaac. In one of the most poignant passages in Scripture (Gn 22:1-14), Abraham and Isaac make their way to the appointed place of sacrifice. In "fear and trembling," Abraham walks with Isaac ready to do this seemingly irrational thing the Lord requires. Finally the silence is broken when Isaac asks, "Father! Here are the fire and the wood, but where is the sheep for the holocaust?" "Son," Abraham answered, "God himself will provide the sheep for the holocaust." After this brief exchange, the two continue going forward.

The response of Abraham, "the Lord will provide," is at the center of the biblical witness concerning God's ways with his people. God not only calls and challenges; God *cares* for his people. Even in the midst of great trials, desperate hours, and seemingly irrational situations, God is at work caring for and providing all that is needed so the journey of faith can continue forward. The courageous faith of Abraham allowed him to see that even in the midst of this new situation, God was still providing and caring for him. It was easy to experience the presence of God in the richness of the new land. It was a joyful voice which praised the Lord at the birth of Isaac. Could Abraham still see the Lord at work now that Isaac was required? The answer is yes. Abraham was confident that God does not abandon those he has called and challenged. Even in the midst of what seem like death, rejection, and God playing a cruel joke, Abraham was able to see the light. Abraham was still able to proclaim that the God who gave him this new land and a son in his old age, was going to provide a way out of the darkness. Father George A. Maloney, S.J. writes:

> [Faith] is a vision that takes man from darkness and places him fully in the light of God's loving presence as the Ground of all being. It is a true "unconcealment," an uncovering of what is always there but our lack of faith keeps us from communicating with the ever-present and ever-loving God . . . In a gentle security of knowing we are loved by the all-perfect God, we let go of our need to interpret events or happenings according to our darkened ideas that we entertain . . . we fashion opinions of ourselves and the world around us that are simply a lie and do not present the "really real" as God sees it. (*Nesting in the Rock*, p. 77)

The priest today has much to learn from Abraham. Abraham has much to teach us about God's care in the midst of a challenging situation. And what he teaches us is timely and timeless: God cares. God's caring, committed love is at work even in the most desperate and tragic of situations. The priest today finds himself in a new situation. The once viable forms of ministry and identity have had to be renewed, transformed, and, in many instances, replaced. In other words, the priesthood has undergone a kind of dying. No dying is without pain, and death always bring a sense of loss. But for the Christian, dying holds the promise of rising and every death contains the hope of new life. In what seems to be the eclipse of God, a courageous faith proclaims, "God will provide. God will continue to care and to love; to call and to challenge." Father Karl Rahner, S.J. puts it in the following way:

> In the midst of all this history, at a thousand different times and places, in a thousand forms, the one thing

occurs which produces and sustains it all: the silent
coming of God. This can happen. But whether it really
does, and where, is the unfathomable secret of God, and
of man's fundamental freedom. (*Servants of the Lord*, p.
70)

The temptation is great to believe that the silence of God
is not a coming but a withdrawal. Yet faith offers a different
vision. The vision of faith allows us to see the "signals of
transcendence" and the "rumor of angels." The laity do value
and appreciate their priests. The laity do not want to diminish
or devalue the priesthood, but they want to work with men of
faith and hope and love. The young are still being called by
Jesus to follow him through priestly ministry. In the words of
Archbishop Rembert Weakland, O.S.B.:

> There is no reason . . . not to mention the importance for
> the community of the priestly vocation. I would not want
> to minimize the many difficulties today which a young
> person has in accepting a calling that is for life, and
> especially one that involves a celibate commitment; but,
> surely, we should not exaggerate those difficulties nor be
> wanting in our faith in a provident God who also looks
> after those whom he calls. (*All God's People*, p. 48)

It cannot be emphasized enough that confidence in God's
care does not mean being excused from our responsibility to
foster vocations and live the priestly life in confident hope. We
are desperately in need of priestly men with the courage and
conviction of their calling to follow the Lord. We need priestly
men of humor, hope, holiness, and integrity who are models of
God's calling, challenging, and caring grace. We need
families, parishes, and schools which nurture the grace of
God's call to serve as a priest. God's caring, committed love
must continually become incarnate—in the Church and in the
life of the priest.

A Concluding Word

When Sarah finds out that she is to have a son at her age, she does a wonderfully human thing — she laughs. (Sarah must have been Irish!) The incongruity of the situation calls for laughter. God is doing something hilarious. Human expectations and sensibilities are being turned upside down. Women as old as Sarah simply do not have children. This situation is funny. The Lord asks Abraham why Sarah laughed. Abraham tells the Lord that it is rather amusing that he and Sarah are expecting a child. Sarah becomes afraid because she laughed. Sarah even lies by saying she didn't laugh. That's the way it is with fear — it stops the laughter. Fear drives us to lying and prevents us from seeing the hilarity of the human condition. Yet Sarah does regain her sense of humor. After all, she names the child Isaac, a name which means "from one who laughed." Sarah's words at the circumcision of Isaac are crucial: "God has given me cause to laugh, and all who hear of it will laugh with me" (Gn 21:6). Abraham held a great feast. (And I would like to think that God in his heaven laughed and celebrated as well.)

As with Abraham, we priests have much to learn from Sarah. We must once again learn the importance of laughter and the grace of good humor. I am not talking about the laughter of the cynic or the crude humor of the adolescent. I am speaking about the laughter and humor which allows us to be serious but never desperate; to admit our problems but never allow them to become our excuses; to acknowledge our limits but to praise more the grace of God at work in us.

No doubt this talk of laughter and humor will trouble those who are comfortable with Calvinism, Puritanism, and the story of an angry God whose hands are full of sinners. The talk of laughter and humor will give comfort to those who believe that we might as well laugh at the present crisis with vocations and the priesthood. Trouble and comfort are not what laughter and humor are about. They are about hope and confidence. Laughter and humor are ways of loving and ways of facing a challenge with courage. For only the strong can laugh. Only the confident can risk humor. Only the person of faith can see the hilarious ways of God with his world.

If Sarah could risk laughter, how much more can we Catholics (and priests) give ourselves over to laughter. We tell, celebrate, and live the most hilarious, comical, loving, and courageous story ever — the Resurrection of Jesus. Sin and death do not have the last words. New life and hope are at the center of the universe. To misuse Mark Twain: the rumors of the death of the priesthood have been greatly exaggerated. Granted, there are problems: the pain of priests who feel devalued and diminished, a shortage of vocations, and the unfortunate situation in which priests are not willing to actively recruit for the priesthood. None of these will be solved by prophets of gloom and doom.

Will they be solved by humor and laughter? Not totally. But the task will be harder for God and those who care about priests without the good red wine of Catholic laughter.

CHAPTER TWO

JOHN THE BAPTIZER:
The Priest as Man of Mystery

In our initial reflection, we considered some of the challenges and opportunities facing today's priest. We affirmed the importance of priests for today's community of faith, the desire of the laity for priestly leadership, and the need for priests to be men of a courageous faith in a time of transition. The priest is one who knows the importance of laughter and the value of humor. We turned to Abraham and Sarah as our biblical disclosure models for insights into a faith which is courageous enough to risk hilarity. The priest as the man of faith proclaims the death and resurrection of Jesus. Beyond the tragedies, uncertainties, and deaths there is the promise and hope of new life.

We now turn our attention to the priest as the man who dwells with mystery. I am not speaking about the mindless mystery which is often evoked when we find ourselves unable to answer a question. It is not the shallow mystery of a grade B movie or thinly veiled detective story. It is not the mystery which is temporarily applied to those things which will later be explained. The mystery of which I speak is, to use the language of Gabriel Marcel, not a problem to be solved but the Really Real to be encountered in our hearts and world.

The mystery in which the priest dwells is the God who is the beyond, yet in our midst; transcends the confines of this

world, yet is active in the marrow of our everyday; lives in
unapproachable light and yet shines in the darkness of our
history; the Logos who is the Divine Word and at the same time
became our poor flesh in Jesus. The mystery in which the
priest dwells cries out with Isaiah, "Woe is me; I am doomed!
For I am a man of unclean lips, living among a people of
unclean lips; yet my eyes have seen the King, the Lord of
hosts!" (Is 6:5), and with Simon Peter, "Depart from me Lord,
for I am a sinful man." The priest is also able to be one with
Jesus in the least of our brothers and sisters. The priest dwells
in the mystery which reveals itself at the edges of life and all
places in between. The priest who dwells in mystery bespeaks
and reveals the God who is Gracious Love.

In this chapter, we will consider the following: The
cultural situation of mystery today. The experience of mystery
and the naming of that mystery have to a large extent been
eclipsed in our scientific and technological culture. The priest
as the man who dwells in mystery must be concerned with
uncovering mystery in the midst of what seems only profane,
mundane, and routine. The witness of Scripture has much to
offer for such a task. We will explore the experience of mystery
through the Hebrew Scriptures and the disclosure of mystery
through the life and death of John the Baptizer. Finally, we will
draw on those biblical insights as they might better help us to
uncover the Gracious Mystery we call God at work in our
world. The priest as the man who dwells in mystery is charged
with the pastoral task of disclosing to the faith community the
Mystery who is behind us, within and around us, and lures us
ever forward in hope.

The Situation of Mystery Today

A priest friend of mine and his teen-aged niece, Maureen, went to see the latest horror movie, *Poltergeist III*.
During the post-movie analysis, my priest friend remarked, "I
don't see why this movie draws such a crowd." I wasn't sure if
he meant *this* particular movie or this particular *form* of movie.

So in my best scholastic voice, I asked him to clarify what he meant. He responded, "I don't see what is so attractive about *this kind* of movie. I just don't understand why people are drawn to watch such a story. Besides, I didn't like *this* film very much."

Maureen, a world class theologian in the making, offered, "It's the mystery, Uncle Tim. There is always the hint of something unseen, unexpected, hidden yet always present, and ready to break into view." The responses of Father Tim and Maureen highlight the situation of mystery in our present condition. My priest friend has vocalized our impaired sense of mystery. The chief reality architects of today's social construction of what is true, beautiful, and good (scientists, technocrats, and other "cultured despisers") assure us that what we see is what we get. And what we see is *all* we get. We must learn to live one-dimensionally and let children and fools speak about enchantment, mystery, imagination, and myth. Reality is reduced to what can be classified, objectified, categorized, quantified, and presented in clear and distinct ideas. Ours is a "world without windows." Life is too short and too serious to busy ourselves with fantasy. Our horizon is restricted to the here and now. All talk of transcendence or the holy is pure escapism. The religious dimension of existence has been termed as nothing more than psychological projection or lingering superstitions from a less enlightened age. Commenting on our diminished sense of mystery, James J. Bacik, in his brilliant book, *Apologetics and the Eclipse of Mystery*, writes:

> . . . I want to isolate one particular problem faced by Christian apologists in dealing with many of their contemporaries: the eclipse of a proper sense of mystery. This is an umbrella phrase which indicates that a sizable number of people in the modern Western world have a diminished or distorted perception of the deeper dimensions of their experience — the mysterious depths that are necessarily present even though temporarily hidden

or misunderstood. This general problem is experienced
by people today in various forms and is best understood
by examining its particular manifestations.

What are the particular manifestations of this diminished
sense of mystery? Dr. Bacik discussed five types of individuals
who experience an eclipse of mystery. First, there are those we
might term secular atheists, for whom God and mystery are
totally meaningless. The method of science and the power of
technology provide one with the only means necessary for
living successfully in this world. There is no reality beyond
that which can be uncovered by science and there is no
ultimate Power to which every knee must bend.

Not all atheists are so confident or self-satisfied. The
second group of people who experience a diminished sense of
mystery are those who must struggle with evil and the tragedies
of existence. In the face of what seems irrational, uncaring,
unloving, and powerless, it seems absurd to proclaim a God
who is all-loving and powerful. Bacik calls these the "troubled
atheists" for whom life is absurd and who believe that all one
can do is be a Sisyphean hero. All one can do is accept one's
situation and continue to push the rock which, at day's end,
will return to where it first began.

We live in a society which is highly pluralistic and
lacking in what sociologist Peter L. Berger calls "the sacred
canopy." There are a number of "plausibility structures"
which claim to be true, beautiful, and good. In the midst of so
many conflicting claims and voices, how is one to know which
story is authentic and which is simply a cruel joke? In the
midst of our knowledge explosion, there is so much to know
that no one person, community, or system can claim to provide
ultimate answers and absolute certainty. Hence, the only
prudent thing to do is to keep one's options open. It is wise not
to become committed. By "hanging loose," and not "burning
our bridges," we remain available for the next (newest) option
or lifestyle. This is the strategy of the skeptic, who simply
refuses to commit to the unknown and the mysterious because
he cannot be sure the wager is worthy of trust.

The eclipse of mystery is also found within the community of faith. Such an eclipse takes two major forms: those who believe it is irreverent to speak of mystery and so remain silent, and secondly, the zealous believers who claim to have a direct line to God. The silent believers reject any attempt at locating mystery within the limits of this world. Mystery is unmediated. That is, the revelation of mystery comes to the individual directly without passing through creation, history, social structures, or human experience. All one can do in the face of the overwhelming mystery is to keep silent. Any attempt to speak aloud the unspeakable is foolish and a scandal. Mystery, however, becomes eclipsed for them since it does not manifest itself in worldly reality.

The final manifestation of this diminished sense of mystery, and the second form to be found in the community of faith, is the zealous believer who claims to have a "pipeline to God." Mystery becomes reduced to a direct manifestation of God's will to the individual or one controls mystery by placing it in neat propositional doctrines. Mystery, the divine or God, becomes a projection of our concepts or needs. We learn to. domesticate the sacred or holy by placing it within a carefully constructed intellectual system. All one need do is simply know (intellectually) the doctrines. Mystery is neutralized. Mystery will be kept at a safe distance so as not to make any demands on us. Whether through direct communication from God, or through a tightly constructed system of doctrines, the goal is the same: mystery is to be controlled and, in the process, reduced to something we can manage.

Yet in the midst of this general diminished sense of mystery, there is a persistence of the sacred and a thirsting for the holy. For all of the talk about secularization, religion does endure. In the words of Maureen, "There is always the hint of something unseen, unexpected, hidden yet always present, and ready to break into view." We find ourselves reading Stephen King, and waiting in line to see *E.T.* and *Poltergeist III*. No matter what today's reality policemen tell us, we search for mystery and the whisper of something (or Someone) lurking just beneath the surface of what seems so ordinary and every-day. Perhaps it would be better to say that mystery is in search of us. It (He/She) is after us and wants to reveal itself. Mystery is all around us. Even in the midst of the computer and the hum of the technical, the mysterious surfaces and is glimpsed. For just a few moments, we find ourselves scared to death by a King novel and charmed into renewal and hope by a Spielberg film. For all too short a time, grace touches our hearts and opens our eyes. We see amid the ordinary, banal, routine, and drab everydayness of our existence the promise of something (Someone?) more. The touch of comfort by a friend; the smile of recognition from a child returning home; a small hand extended in trust; the silent presence of others in moments of deep pain; the power of a summer storm; the beauty that is the month of May; the courage to stand for something and someone against the odds; the refusal to be vanquished or embittered by disappointment; the wonder of birth and the awesome reality of death all speak to us of another dimension and a Reality that is ever present.

The temptation is always present to avoid mystery and live one-dimensionally. Too often, we are willing to trade adventure and zest for safety and the undisturbed life. We can also flee from mystery and its demands by turning to drugs, alcohol, sex, power, and conspicuous consumption. Rather than face the ultimate questions of life (What is the meaning of my existence? Why do the innocent suffer? Why must I die? What is truth, beauty, and goodness? What difference do I make in living?) we rush into a pleasure which distracts us or a power (money, technology, military) which offers us the illusion that we are in control. Mystery confronts us with the issues we would rather not consider; or at least consider at some later and more convenient hour. Mystery reminds us of our radical dependence and the shocking contingency of our existence. Mystery tells us that we are not our own, but we are sustained by a power greater than the self. Dr. Bacik contends that the talk of mystery and ultimate questions can seem silly in a scientific age. Yet the ultimate questions will not go away. This long quotation from Dr. Bacik is worth repeating:

> In fact, all attempts to escape the question [the radical question of my existence and its meaning] amount to a neurotic flight from reality and in the long run cannot succeed. Rather than being haunted by the repressed question, it seems far better to face it directly. This means moving into a realm of mystery where we are forced to admit our contingency, to accept our dependence on a source we do not control, to respond to a summons beyond our familiar world, to submit to a power greater than ourselves. Objections to such a submission can be heard: this kind of talk makes no sense in a scientific age, such a plunge into the unknown is too frightening, it is better not to think or talk about such mysterious matters, more data and certainty are needed before taking this risk, it is not really so mysterious as it first seems. However, others say the question and its demands cannot be forbidden. It is built into our very being. We are persons who combine infinite longings with finite capabilities, and therefore cannot avoid the question of whether our desires will ultimately reach fulfillment or be doomed to frustration. We awake to find ourselves on a journey not of our own choosing and must wonder where it leads and whether it has a final destination. Our daily activities absorb our attention, but periodically we must ask if it is all worthwhile. In fact, the great fundamental question that we are lurks on the edge of our consciousness. It can be eclipsed for a time, at a price, but it always retains the power to claim our attention and drive us again into the realm of mystery. (*Apologetics and the Eclipse of Mystery*, p. 78)

The eclipse of mystery, along with its power to claim our attention, is one of the most important pastoral opportunities facing the Church. Church leadership must find creative ways of enhancing our sense of mystery which envelopes our existence, yet is too often ignored or denied. An important dimension of the Church's pastoral mission is to awaken a sense of mystery among those within the community and those who are far off. In the Church's preaching and teaching, it must relate what is proclaimed, taught, and practiced in love to the fundamental questions of human existence. The total life of the Church must be concerned with disclosing that Mystery Who answers the ultimate questions of life and death and beyond. Even more boldly, the Church dares, in fear and trembling, to proclaim that this Mystery has revealed itself in a definitive way in the person of Jesus of Nazareth. This Mystery who has become visible in Jesus, and surrounds us and seeks us out, is one of total love and gracious presence. For in the midst of our daily dyings, there is also the promise and hope of resurrection. We live in a world in which grace is everywhere. All speaks of the grandeur of God. About our grace-filled existence and world, Father Karl Rahner, S.J. has written:

> The secular world, as secular, has an inner mysterious depth, in all its earthly mysteries from birth to death, through which, by the grace of God, it is open to God and his infinitely incomprehensible love even when it is not, before receiving the explicit message of the gospel, aware of it. . . For whenever its demands and its reality are really met and endured in the whole breadth and depth of natural human existence and in the totality of human life, then, according to Christian teachings, the grace of Christ is already at work and this response and endurance are already something Christian though they may be explicitly only secular and natural. (*Christian in the Market Place*, p. 97)

In attempting to awaken a sense of mystery, we have much to learn from our ancestors in faith. Specifically, we need to explore the Hebrew Scriptures' witness concerning mystery. Then we will turn our attention to John the Baptizer as the man who dwells in mystery. John will serve as our disclosure model for the priest who is called to awaken a sense of mystery and grace in those whom he serves.

Mystery: A Biblical View

The opening pages of the Bible tell us the following: "God looked at everything he had made, and he found it very good" (Gn 1:31). Everything from the beginning proceeds from the creative, powerful love of God. Everything which is, is sustained by God and finds its perfection in the Divine Will. All of reality bespeaks the presence of God. The Spirit and the very life breath of God are continually present in the world. The world, creation, is a sacrament of God's mysterious, loving process. The world is overflowing with God's grace and is alive by his love. The creation proclaims a God who is transcendent, wholly Other, non-reducible, and, at the same time, present in the smallest and most ordinary aspects of existence. In the haunting words of Abraham Heschel, "man is not alone." There is about the most ordinary and taken-for-granted occurrences a signal of transcendence. The philosopher-poet Alfred North Whitehead put it thus: "When you understand all about the sun and all about the atmosphere and all about the rotation of the earth, you may still miss the radiance of the sunset and the glory of the morning sky." What we moderns can too often miss is the spiritual dimension of existence. In our drive to know, control, manipulate, and dominate, we can easily become impoverished concerning the wonder and mystery present in even the most ordinary of events. We can easily become numb to the grandeur.

Not only does nature speak of the mystery and transcendence of existence but the most powerful "rumor of angels" comes from the mystery of human existence. The Psalmist is caught up in the wonder of creation and the special place of the human person:

> When I behold your heavens,
>   the work of your fingers,
>   the moon and the stars
>   which you set in place —
> What is man that you should be
> mindful of him,

or the son of man that you
  should care for him?
You have made him a little less
than the angels,
    and crowned him with glory and honor.
You give him rule over the
works of your hands,
    putting all things under his feet. . .
O Lord, our Lord,
how gracious is your name over all the earth!
                                    (Ps 8:4-7, 10)

The wonder of nature bespeaks a hidden presence and the mystery of human existence fills us with the deep awareness that we are not our own. We did not bring ourselves into existence and we cannot redeem ourselves by ourselves. We are here because of a power greater than ourselves. The very life breath of that power (that Someone?) is at work in us. Hence, the human vocation or calling is to be the shepherd of mystery and bring to unconcealment that gracious, holy presence which causes all to be. That mysterious power which brought all things into existence has entrusted us with *continuing* the story of creation and re-creation.

We humans find ourselves *addressed* in the everydayness of our lives. Such a call reveals the depth and the wonder of our experience. In our search for knowledge, we are unsatisfied with every answer and continue looking for Truth. We keep our commitments long after there is any personal gain, for no other reason than we gave our word. Our fidelity bespeaks of a Faithful One beyond all human commitments and broken promises. We stand on the side of the weak against the strong; we keep company with the fallen; we lift our voices on behalf of those who are rendered invisible and of no account; we continue to find ourselves in love knowing that no earthly love will ever still us completely; and, in the midst of tragedy, we still proclaim a hope which gives us the courage to walk through the rain. In all of these, and in countless other examples, we open ourselves to mystery, respond to that mystery, and we reveal that Mystery shining through our humanity.

The witness of the Bible goes even further. Mystery itself is transcended in its self-revelation; in its being known and in allowing itself to be seen. That is, the witness of Scripture tells us that the Mystery beyond mystery wants to be known by us and loved by us even as that Mystery loves us and seeks us out. The Mystery found in nature and in human existence cares for us and loves us beyond measure. The Mystery beyond mystery is God. God wants to be in relationship with us and wants us to respond to him. This God who is Mystery beyond mystery takes for himself a people who make known his name and experience his gracious presence. This God who entered into covenant with Israel would in the fullness of time reveal himself in a most dramatic way. The God who is Mystery beyond all mystery and provides meaning to all that is, reveals himself with all of the splendor of a child! The God of eternity becomes temporal; the God of power becomes weak; the God of un-approachable distance touches our human heart and history; the God of transcendence becomes imminent; and the God in whose image we are made becomes one like us. The mystery of the Divine Lover becomes visible in the life of Jesus of Nazareth.

John the Baptizer: Herald of Mystery

The atmosphere was electric. Large crowds had come from Jerusalem and the surrounding region of Judea to see and hear this man of the desert and of the water. Many preachers and self-proclaimed prophets had arisen. Many were desperate for deliverance. Many wanted someone in whom to believe and a cause in which to hope. Yet none had captured the imagination of the people like this strange man. His clothes were out of the ordinary — a garment of camel's hair and a leather belt around his waist. Some even reported that his diet was as strange as his dress — grasshoppers and wild honey. News had spread throughout the region that this man was going to make an appearance and preach in the desert.

As the crowds grew in anticipation, a solitary figure appeared on the horizon. There was a collective straining forward to see if it was he. Finally, the people recognized the man walking toward them. It was the one they called the Baptizer. He was John the son of Zechariah and Elizabeth. In addition to the stories of his extraordinary birth, some said that John had received a call from the Lord. The crowd stilled to listen as John prepared to preach.

"The Lord is about to do a new thing," began John, "and each of you must be ready to do a new thing. The old ways of living and valuing will no longer work. Right in your midst the Lord is at work."

The crowds were anything but passive. They were filled with questions. Many wanted to know if John was the Messiah. John was clear in his response.

"I am a herald much like the one spoken of in Isaiah. My vocation is to prepare your hearts and imaginations. I have been sent to open your eyes and ears so you can see and hear the salvation of God."

The crowds who came to hear John were ordinary people — tax collectors, soldiers, fishermen, and merchants. They were an oppressed people who were enmeshed in the daily concerns of survival. Yet John challenged them to be open and receptive to the graciousness of God in their particular situations. John called them to look beyond their roles, duties, anxieties, and brief victories to experience God at work. None of this was easy but it was necessary so that God could work through them. John sought to lift burdens so that liberation would follow. John offered those who were open to grace the message of hope and a new way of living. The past would not have the last word. There was a future in which to hope. Why? Because God was coming to meet them from that future. The heart's deepest longings, its greatest hopes were about to be realized. Beyond their wildest expectations, God was going "to bring glad tidings to the poor, to proclaim liberty to captives, recovery of sight to the blind and release to prisoners, to announce a year of favor from the Lord."

In capturing the imagination of the crowd, John also captured the hostility of those who were comfortable with the way things were. Many of the religious leaders and the respectable folk feared John. All this talk about hope, change, liberation, and new life was threatening to those for whom good news was bad news.

John made frequent appearances at the Jordan to baptize with water. John called the people to repentance and conversion. The reality of sin had to be confronted since the greater reality of God's grace was about to be made visible. One day while John was preaching and baptizing, some Pharisees and Sadducees came to observe. After watching the enthusiasm of the crowd, and being addicted to human respect, the Pharisees and Sadducees came to be baptized as well. John would have none of it.

"You brood of vipers!" his voice boomed out across the water. "Who told you to flee from the wrath to come?" John did not suffer hypocrites gladly. He was not in the people-pleasing business. John was concerned with calling people to authentic conversion and openness to God's grace.

"You have come here so that you can be seen by the people," he continued, "but I see no evidence of a changed heart." At this point, one of the Pharisees spoke up.

"How can you speak to us in such a way?" he indignantly challenged John. "We are the chosen people. We are of the state of Abraham!"

John's face burned with anger at such human arrogance. He responded, "You pride yourselves on your ancestry. Fair enough. However, Abraham would be the first to reject what you are doing and *not* doing. He would be the first to tell you that God could make these very stones his descendants."

"Are you denying the importance of the promise?" retorted the Pharisee.

"Not at all," said John. "What I am telling you is that more than birth is required to be a people of the promise. To be part of God's people is not to be excused from righteousness, but it is a call to live each day in the way of the Lord. You must be reborn. For at this very moment, God is at work clearing the threshing floor and gathering his grain into the barn. You must make an authentic decision before it is too late."

John, the herald of mystery, is one day confronted with the Mystery made visible. At the Jordan, as John had done countless times, he was preaching and baptizing. In what seemed like an ordinary day, the extraordinary become flesh. The Baptizer looked up and saw Jesus.

"I should be baptized by you," said John. Jesus looked at John with great love and responded, "Give in for now. We must do this if we would fulfill all of God's demands."

It was during John's ordinary tasks that Jesus came to him. Because John was found faithfully doing his assigned task, he was confronted by Jesus. John did not journey great distances or attempt to manipulate God into some display of the divine. John simply did what the Lord required. Even though he didn't fully understand what Jesus was asking of him at the Jordan, John did it simply because Jesus asked him.

It ought not surprise us that John was soon arrested by order of Herod, for John had dared to speak truth to power. He publicly denounced the crimes of Herod. He challenged the mighty on their thrones to acknowledge the ultimate power of God. He called on those who were sure of their goodness to repent and experience a change of heart. The forces of this world reacted as they always do when confronted by men and women of imagination — with violence and death. This herald of mystery, this strange man who troubled the comfortable must be silenced. As usual, the powerful failed to see how weak they were. Prison, torture, and death do not silence God's messengers of that other dimension. It is those whom the world considers strange, those who often dwell in the waste-land, who signal the coming of God. They are not luxuriously dressed or found among the rich and famous. The heralds of mystery are not reeds swaying in the wind, but men and women of conviction and hope.

The mission to herald the mystery of the Kingdom is passed to the Church. And it is the priest who continues the work of John — preparing hearts and minds for the revelation of God's saving love made visible in Jesus. The priest is the messenger of mystery. The priest is the man who dwells in mystery.

The Priest: The Man Who Dwells In Mystery

The philosopher George Santayana once said that when we lose sight of the goal, we double the effort. Current research into the state of the priesthood indicates the presence of a crisis of identity and a loss of meaning by priests as to the value of what they do. The temptation is great to double the effort. That is, the priest can come to the conclusion that his worth is defined by the quantity of his work. All he need do is do more. If he does more, he will be *valued* more. If he does more, he will *be* more. If the priest does more the crises of identity and meaning will be solved. Right? Not really. In fact, just the opposite will occur. The workaholic priest too often finds himself physically drained, emotionally depressed, spiritually empty, and fighting feelings of resentment and guilt. The priest experiences the eclipse of mystery and an alienation from the gracious presence of God. The priestly vocation ceases to be a blessing and becomes the heavy burden of a guilt-ridden duty. Father Paul T. Keyes insightfully captures the fundamental issue which all priests must face, that is, do we dwell in mystery or do we become absorbed in the every-day? He writes:

> A functionally oriented priest has the tendency to experi-
> ence life as a series of never-ending problems that must
> be solved when, in reality, life is a mystery. Life is God's
> gift. The gift of life lives within me and beyond me, and,
> consequently, I am called be a wayfarer. The functional
> model of man suggests that man is the center of the
> universe and that it is man who projects meaning upon his
> world. As a pilgrim wayfarer, however, I am a receiver of
> meaning that already exists in my world, placed there by

the generous and caring presence of God. I become
inspired by the meaning of my world, the events, the
people, and the things of such a world, when I learn to let
go of my meaning and let God's meaning emerge. . .

The fundamental question that a parish priest has to
ask is whether he is letting himself be open to a deeper
and more ultimate mystery beyond himself. (*Pastoral
Presence and the Diocesan Priest*, p. 67)

If the priest is to pastor others into the ways of mystery, he
must be a man who dwells in mystery. He must take time to
reflect, pray, read, study, listen, and be open to the mystery of
his existence and the graciousness of his vocation. Granted
that all of this sounds like "wasting time" and being lazy. The
tape in our heads keeps playing, "Do more. Be up and doing.
Be active." That tape must be stilled with the voice of the Spirit
calling to our spirit. Mindless, compulsive, non-reflective
activity only drives us further into a functional mode of
ministry. We become efficient managers and organizers. We
administer the affairs of the parish and keep the books well-
balanced. However, we can easily become blinded to mystery
and deaf to the call of the Spirit. We run a tight ship and give
orders in clear and certain terms. Yet in time, we cease to be
pastors, for we have forgotten how to lead those entrusted to our
care into the ways of mystery.

The priest people turn to is a priest who dwells in mystery
and knows how to lead others into the mystery of their lives.
The priest who dwells in mystery and matters is a man of hope
in the face of the many temptations to despair; a man of light
into the darkness and death which are too much with us; a man
who challenges us to liberty and commitment in an age which
talks freedom but is everywhere in chains. The priest who
matters dwells in mystery and uncovers the mysterious, gracious, loving presence of God in the lives of those to whom he
ministers. The priest people turn to is able to laugh and help
others laugh. And why not? For the priest people turn to is the
man who dwells in the mystery of the Resurrection. Death does
not have the final word. Victory is on the side of life. The

Empty Tomb is a story which invites us to believe, trust, love, and hope. The priest is the storyteller of the Cross, Empty Tomb, and Resurrection. Talk about mystery!

The disclosure model for the priest as the man who dwells in mystery is John the Baptizer. The Fourth Gospel offers us a powerful spiritual reflection on the meaning of John's ministry for the priest as the man who dwells and leads us to mystery. Several aspects of the Fourth Gospel's portrait of the Baptizer deserve mention.

1. *"There was a man named John sent by God, who came as a witness to testify to the light, so that through him all men might believe — but only to testify to the light, for he himself was not the light" (Jn 1:6-8).*

Many people who heard John preach and saw him baptize wanted to know who he was. Expectations for the coming Messiah were high. The people were in need of deliverance. They were vulnerable to anyone who offered them hope. John did not take advantage of their needs. John did not try to become a savior to the people. John clearly knew who he was and what he was about. Namely, John was a witness. His role was to testify and present evidence concerning the Light. Through his witnessing, others would come to experience the Light and know Jesus. Through his testimony, others would come to faith in Jesus as the true Messiah.

The priest is a herald, witness, and one who gives testimony concerning the Light who is Christ. The priest must not preach himself or fall into the trap of being a messiah. Only Jesus saves. Only Jesus is our hope of glory and newness of life. The testimony given by the priest must extend beyond ideas and things read from a book. The testimony given by the priest must be existential and relational. The priest who heralds the Light so that others can believe knows the Light in a personal way. The priest is in relationship with Jesus and wants to invite, challenge, and lure others to know the Light in such a way. All that the priest does points to Jesus as the Light of the world.

2.   *"The next day John was there again with two of his disciples.*
     As he watched Jesus walk by he said, 'Look! There is the
     Lamb of God!' The two disciples heard what he said, and
     followed Jesus" (Jn 1:35-37).

   John knew how to practice tough love. That is, John knew
when it was time to let go of his disciples so that they could
follow the true Master — Jesus. Letting go is always difficult.
Surrendering to another when our time is completed is painful.
Yet John's whole life was one of preparing others to meet the
true Lamb of God. When the time came, he responded with the
directness of faith. Love does not only mean holding on; it
means knowing when and how to let go. John was able to point
to the passing presence of Jesus. John was able to lead his
disciples to that Mystery alone who would take away their sins
and offer them eternal life.
   The priest as pastor who dwells in mystery must also be
able to point to the true Lamb of God. In the lives of those
whom he serves, the priest must be able to lead people to an
experience of Jesus. People turn to the priest who can help
them find the gracious, caring, redeeming presence of God in
the midst of their wasteland. In the midst of what seems so
ordinary and routine, profane and destructive, the priest
points out the hidden presence of Jesus. It is only to such a
priest, a man who dwells in mystery, that people turn for
meaning and hope in times of suffering and loss, birth and
death, and the heroic effort to continue to give and be committed when all seems hopeless. The father who daily works at
a job for his family; a mother who makes a house a home; a
teacher who silently corrects papers; a young person who
rejects peer pressure; a priest in a remote region of the world
preaching the Gospel; all these and countless others need to
see the Lamb of God passing in their midst. For it is in the
office, home, classroom, street, and remote village that Jesus
is to be seen and encountered. The priest helps to provide
meaning to those moments when we are filled with joy and
ecstasy; those moments when we are called out of ourselves by
a Goodness beyond all our deserving and hoping; and those

moments when our souls are filled with the graciousness of existence and the feeling that it is good to be alive. The priest helps those in his care to experience freedom, responsibility, truth, love, joy, sorrow, suffering, death, and life within a larger horizon. The priest who dwells in mystery also dwells with the community of disciples and says, "Look! There is the Lamb of God!"

3. *"When Jesus turned around and noticed them following him, he asked them, 'What are you looking for?' They said to him, 'Rabbi, where do you stay?' 'Come and see,' he answered. So they went to see where he was lodged, and stayed with him that day"* (Jn 1:38-39).

From this brief passage we know that John was faithful to his vocation. He prepared the way of the Lord. The disciples of John now followed Jesus and became his disciples. Again we see that John was not the Light or the Lamb, but one who witnessed to the true Light of the World. It was time for Jesus to shine forth and for John to diminish. The disciples would now follow the One who would free them from sin and reveal the mysteries of the Kingdom of God. The priest must always point to Christ as the One whom people seek. The priest is called to help people seek Jesus and have the courage to stay with him. And where are we to journey in search of the Lord? We are to look into the various situations in which we find ourselves. John found Jesus in the Jordan. The disciples were called as they carried out their ordinary tasks as fishermen. The priest must find Jesus in all of the ordinary and routine aspects of ministry. Each member of the community must see Jesus in his or her daily concerns. The priest cannot force mystery to be disclosed nor can he force people to see the deeper dimensions of life. The priest can only invite, lure, and persuade others to "come and see" where Jesus dwells. The freedom of the other must always be respected. The priest tries to awaken a sense of mystery which is present but often forgotten or ignored.

Where does Jesus stay? Right in the midst of our everyday existence. Jesus is present with the invitation to "come and see."

Jesus invites priest and parishioner to look with the eye of faith beyond the surface to those deep down things. Jesus is inviting priest and parishioner to stay with him and not flee. The wilderness is filled with idols and false lights, each promising to give happiness and peace. However, they are bound to disappoint us and leave us empty. It is only when we see, really see with faith, that the One who asks the question, "What are you looking for?" is also the One who answers that question and the riddle of our existence.

A Concluding Word

In the twelfth chapter of the Fourth Gospel, Jesus entered Jerusalem for the feast of the Passover. Some Greeks approached Philip and asked to see Jesus. This is the timeless request of all Christians through the ages — the desire to see Jesus. We want to live beyond the immediate and see deeper into our existence and the ultimate questions of life. The priest as the man who dwells in mystery is called to minister to those who want to find where Jesus stays. The priest, through his words and actions, helps the community of faith to see Jesus in spirit and truth. The priest helps the community to experience the gracious, loving, demanding, and caring presence of Jesus in the midst of everydayness. We continue to want to see Jesus. The priest continues to be the man who says, "Look! There is the Lamb of God!"

CHAPTER THREE

THE POOR WIDOW:
The Priest as Disciple

From Abraham, we learn the need for a courageous faith during times of transition and subsequent uncertainty. From John the Baptizer, we are invited to experience the gracious, caring, challenging, and loving presence of the God who took on our flesh in Jesus of Nazareth. But what can we possibly learn from "one poor widow"? What can this unnamed woman possibly teach us about priestly ministry? After all, she was without credentials and resources. She had very little means of support and self-sufficiency. This woman was dependent on the chances of life and the good will of the public. And she was dependent on the gracious, providential care of our loving Father who has counted the very hairs of our heads. The cost of her discipleship is the cost of dependency on grace. Her dependency did not breed caution, but exuberance, overflowing generosity, and foolishness by the bookkeeping standards of the world. In the midst of the giving by the rich and famous, this one poor widow put two small copper coins in the treasury. Yet Jesus declared her giving to be more than all of the rest. Why? "They gave from their surplus wealth, but she gave from her want, all that she had to live on" (Mk 12:44). This one poor widow went unnoticed by the crowd, which was impressed with the show of giving. Jesus indicated that real giving often occurs in obscurity and slightly out of view of the main stage. This one poor widow has much to teach the priest about the cost of discipleship, that is, the cost of living, hoping, serving, and loving in obscurity. The world may little note nor long remember what we do in daily ministry, but Jesus does. The cost of discipleship, the daily journey to Jerusalem, and the picking up of one's cross in priestly ministry involves ministering in obscurity. Often we find ourselves placing our meager talents in the service of others. The challenge is to place our all, however small, and trust that the Lord will supply what is lacking.

The story of the one poor widow is found in the Gospel of Mark (12:41-44). It is not unimportant that Mark used the designation "one poor widow." Each of these words is important, for they help set the stage for our reflections and highlight deep truths about the Christian life and priestly existence.

1. *One.* Unlike our own age, which glories in large numbers (the Gallup Poll and the Nielsen Ratings, to name but two examples), Jesus saw great importance in the number "one." Jesus understood the uniqueness of the individual and the special gift that that person is. Furthermore, Jesus was able to see significant aspects of a person's life based on seemingly insignificant things. The crowds and the leaders of Jesus' day would often be impressed by external manifestations of religious zeal, power, and wealth. Not Jesus. Jesus highlighted those actions and words which frequently went unnoticed. The crowd was putting large sums of money in the treasury. No doubt many, even the disciples, were impressed. Yet Jesus held up for imitation the *one* poor widow who gave the two small coins. Jesus called the disciples, and all who could see and hear with faith, to look beyond the surface and see in this one poor widow's generosity a revelation of the generosity of God. God has given to us all that He is in the person of Jesus Christ. This one poor widow is a sacrament, a revelation, of the unbounded, generous love of God.

Throughout his ministry, Jesus called attention to the importance of the seemingly insignificant things. In the parables of Jesus, *one* plays a crucial role. In her insightful little book, *Jesus the Therapist*, Hanna Wolff writes the following concerning Jesus' fascination with the little things and the small number one:

> It is precisely the seemingly little things that Jesus takes so seriously. . . . It is a trustee's failure to take *one* talent seriously, his refusal to put it to work, as if after all nothing need be done with just one talent, that calls his whole mode of existence into question. Similarly, it is the *one* lost sheep that the shepherd goes in search of so tirelessly. It is the *one* lost penny that the housewife turns her house topsy-turvy to find. And it is the *one* refusal to celebrate his brother's home-coming, on the part of the brother who has always stayed home and minded his father, that characterizes the elder brother's whole being. Jesus' habit of appraising the whole on the basis of one small part permeates all his speech and action, as we know. (p. 95)

If we found ourselves in the temple that day, no doubt we would have paused to wonder: Isn't this one poor widow embarrassed at giving such a small amount? Shouldn't she be on the receiving end rather than the giving end? A very instructive aspect of her giving is that she is a woman who is self-accepting. She knows who and what she is. She need make no apologies to any one. It is because she is so self-accepting that she can be so generous and giving. Because she does not hate herself or make excuses, this one poor widow is able to give, not so much the money, but the true gift of herself. Because she has been on the receiving end of God's graciousness in ways we do not know (and she does not fully comprehend), this one poor widow calls for the special praise of God.

2. *Poor.* Not only are the poor always with us, but they are always *invisible*. They live, like Lazarus, outside our houses longing for a share in our bounty. However, the poor do not make an impression. The poor don't count in a meaningful way. The poor do not sell products on television and seldom consume enough to make Madison Avenue take notice. The

poor are of no account. The attention of the crowd in Mark's
Gospel was fixed on the large sums being put in the treasury.
Little note was taken of the poor widow. She and her gift were
not visible to the crowd.

To be poor is to be without means and resources. One's
presence has no effect. It is to be overly dependent on others
for the basic necessities of life. To be poor is to be vulnerable.
For all these reasons, the poor have a special claim for the
special love of God because they are in special need. It is the
Lord who is ever mindful of the poor. It is the Lord who hears
their cries and actively breaks the yoke of slavery and oppression. The special love of the Lord extended to the poor is
beautifully expressed in Psalm 146:

> The Lord sets the prisoners free; the Lord opens the eyes
> of the blind. The Lord lifts up those who are bowed down;
> the Lord loves the righteous. The Lord watches over the
> sojourners, He upholds the widow and the fatherless; but
> the way of the wicked He brings to ruin. (Vs. 7-9)

While the world ignores the poor and continues to live
with the illusions of self-sufficiency, control, and power, the
Bible proclaims a God who cares and acts on their behalf.
Jesus proclaims the poor blessed and says that they shall have
their fill. Those who are poor by the standards of the world are
rich in God's grace. The poor have much to teach us about the
illusion of earthly riches and self-sufficiency. Pastor and
theologian Eugene H. Peterson writes:

> We do not begin life on our own. We do not finish it on our
> own. Life, especially when we experience by faith the
> complex interplay of creation and salvation, is not
> fashioned out of our own genetic lumber and cultural
> warehouses. It is not hammered together with the planks
> and nails of our thoughts and dreams, our feelings and
> fancies. We are not self-sufficient. We enter a world that
> is created by God, that already has a rich history and is
> crowded with committed participants . . . We keep on

being surprised because we are in on something beyond our management, something over our needs. (*Earth & Altar: The Community of Prayer in a Self-Bound Society*, p. 149)

This one poor widow is *both* poor in spirit and poor in terms of material possessions. The poverty of her spirit moves her to be rich in ways beyond measure. She is able to give all that she has knowing that God will never be outdone in generosity. God has acted and will continue to act to sustain those who trust and dare to give from their want, all that they have to live on.

3. *Widow.* In addition to being judged insignificant and poor, this woman was a widow. The social role of a widow was one which afforded little protection and maximum vulnerability to exploitation and injustice. The widow was set apart from the community by being required to wear special clothes which called attention to her condition (Gn 38:14, 19). Also, the widow was severely limited in what she could inherit from her husband. After her husband died, the widow belonged to the eldest son of the family. There were rigid limitations on her options concerning future marriage.

Again, what is most troubling about the social role of the widow is the reality of being left vulnerable to exploitation and injustice. The widow was vulnerable to abuse and she was often powerless in terms of redress. The widow lacked anyone to defend her rights in the courts. She was often beyond the reach of justice. Like the poor, she was invisible and of no account. The Hebrew Scriptures tell us that the widow was frequently a victim of abuse and injustice. The prophets continually spoke out against the unjust treatment shown to the widow. Consider these examples:

> Put away your misdeeds from before my eyes;
>   cease doing evil; learn to do good.
> Make justice your aim: redress the wronged,
>   hear the orphan's plea, defend the widow. (Is 1:16-17)

> Only if you thoroughly reform your ways and your deeds;
> if each of you deals justly with his neighbor; if you no long
> oppress the resident alien, the orphan, and the widow; if
> you no longer shed innocent blood in this place, or follow
> strange gods to your own harm, will I remain with you in
> this place, in the land which I gave your fathers long ago
> and forever. (Jr 7:5-7)

> Do not oppress the widow or the orphan, the alien or the
> poor; do not plot evil against one another in your hearts.
> (Zc 7:10)

The question arises: if the widow is being oppressed and exploited, who will care and rise to defend her? The witness of Scripture is clear: Yahweh will defend the widow. In the words of the prophet Malachi:

> I will draw near to you for judgment,
>   and I will be swift to bear witness
> Against the sorcerers, adulterers,
>   and perjurers,
>   those who defraud the hired man
>   of his wages,
> Against those who defraud widows
>   and orphans;
>   those who turn aside the stranger,
>   and those who do not fear me,
>   says the Lord of hosts. (Ml 3:5)

Jesus was anything but unmindful of, and indifferent to, the exploitation of the widow. In the passage immediately preceding our story of the one poor widow, Jesus took to task the hypocrisy of the scribes who desired human respect for their external acts of holiness. However, their hearts were corrupt since they "devour the savings of widows" (Mk 12:40). Even though the savings of widows are too often devoured (perhaps even *this* widow), some of them still show signs of nobility, generosity, and trust in God. There are many excuses for becoming bitter and self-pitying, but we see in the life of this one poor widow the ability of the human spirit to rise above injustice and point to a better, more generous, and caring way of living. Jesus invites all would-be disciples to see what can happen when the human heart is open to receive God's grace.

The one poor widow singled out by Jesus has much to teach us about the meaning of discipleship: the importance of small things and the value of one; the truth of dependency as a challenge to the illusion of self-sufficiency; and the blessing of being detached so as to be free to love in an unbounded way. The poor widow's mite is not in the quantity of her money but in the abundance of her heart. She can teach the priest of today who often ministers in obscurity to dispel the demon of ambition with the angel of pastoral love, to contend with the demon of success through the angel of fidelity, and to overcome the demon of remorse with the angel of integrity. Each of these three demons and angels are confronted at various ages and stages of priestly ministry. Each stage and age involves its cost of discipleship; its own particular invitation to pick up one's cross and follow Jesus.

The Demon of Ambition v. The Angel of Pastoral Love

The first months and years after ordination are times of zeal, wonder, and the desire to excel. There is no burn-out or rust-out. The oils of ordination are fresh. The words of the prophet Joel capture powerfully the opening pages of one's priestly ministry: "I will pour out my spirit on all mankind. Your sons and daughters shall prophesy . . . your young men shall see visions . . . in those days, I will pour out my spirit" (Jl 3:1-2). The early stages of priestly ministry are times of vision, prophecy, and a rush of the Holy Spirit. Yet it is precisely because of such zeal and the desire to make a difference that we also find at work the demon of ambition. The story of Father Ken will help us to see how such a demon works.

One day a recently ordained priest, let's call him Father Ken, came to see me. He wanted to talk about "my situation as

a newly ordained priest." Father Ken had been very popular in
the seminary. He was an outstanding student as well. After one
year of theology at the local diocesan seminary, Ken was sent
to Rome for further studies and ordination. Everyone had high
expectations for him and his pastoral ministry in the diocese.
Ken had these high expectations of himself as well.

Upon his return from Rome, Ken was assigned to a small
parish with a pastor and an associate. Ken told me that "his
troubles" began almost immediately. He found his ideas were
not immediately accepted. The pastor seemed to value the
pastoral experience of his first associate more than the theology Ken had learned in Rome. The pastor told Ken that he had
the makings of a good preacher, but his sermons tended to be
"too abstract" and "overly intellectual" at times. Ken went on
to indicate that he was beginning to resent his assignment and
the people in the parish. He felt he should be sent to a parish
"that would take advantage" of his talents and training. Ken
felt wasted and unappreciated. He concluded by saying that he
was thinking of seeing the bishop in order to obtain a new
assignment.

Father Ken got his appointment with the bishop who
asked him to be patient and gain some pastoral experience to
help mature his obvious gifts. Ken interpreted the bishop's
response as "ecclesiastical indifference." With a great deal of
resentment and anger, Ken told me that he would "play the
church game" and "do his time" in this parish. Because he was
young, he figured he would eventually get what he wanted. In
the meantime, he would tough it out and "follow the party
line."

No doubt there is a strong feeling to judge Father Ken
harshly. He certainly isn't acting Christ-like. Yet we need to
temper our reaction by keeping in mind that the disciples and
the early Church struggled with the demon of ambition. The
very night on which Jesus shares the Passover with his disciples before he is to be crucified, a dispute breaks out among
the Twelve as to who is the greatest (Lk 22:24). On another
occasion, the disciples engage in talk about greatness and

ambition. Jesus calls forth a little child and says, "the least among you is the greatest" (Lk 9:48). James and John even have their mother asking Jesus to provide her sons with places of honor and power in the kingdom (Mt 20:21). Finally, in the letter of James, we read of favoritism being shown to those who are rich and famous. The poor and ordinary members of the assembly were pushed to the rear (Jm 2:2). The demon of ambition can be likened with the poor — it will be with us always.

The words and the deeds of Jesus call us to overcome the demon of ambition with the angel of pastoral love. When the disciples are debating greatness, Jesus tells them that true greatness comes to the one who knows how to serve, for Jesus is in their midst as the Servant of Yahweh and the servant to the needs of others. To be great in the ways of Jesus means that one serves in love the needs of the community (Lk 22:27). Jesus goes beyond words and provides the disciples with what Bruce Vawter, C.M. calls a "parable in action." That is, Jesus washes the feet of his disciples (Jn 13:4). He performs this lowly task and invites the disciples to do the same. The only way one can be truly happy as a disciple and in the priestly ministry is through humble, loving service.

> You address me as 'Teacher' and 'Lord' and fittingly enough, for that is what I am. But if I washed your feet — I who am Teacher and Lord — then you must wash each other's feet. . . I solemnly assure you, no slave is greater than his master; no messenger outranks the one who sent him. Once you know all these things, blest will you be if you put them into practice. (Jn 13:13-17)

The Apostle Paul was pastor to the Christians at Corinth. They were a very gifted people. They lived in exciting times and new ideas were constantly being discussed. The Corinthians loved to debate. Unfortunately, they also saw their individual gifts in competition with one another. Each believed his or her gift was primary. Naturally, this led to strife and division. The one body of Christ, the faith community, was

being torn apart. Paul, the prudent pastor, is not opposed to
their gifts. Paul, however, challenges them to use their gifts in
a complementary and not competitive manner. The gifts of
each person are to be used for the common good. Above all, the
Corinthians are to "set their hearts on the greater gifts" and be
ambitious for the higher things. It is only through Christian
love that the many gifts of the Spirit come together for the good
of the community as a whole. In the words of Paul: "There are
in the end three things that last: faith, hope, and love, and the
greatest of these is love" (1 Cor 13:13).

The adjustment from seminary to full time parish ministry
as a priest is not easy. There is a tremendous desire to do the
Lord's work as well as fit into the new situation. It is all too easy
for the demon of ambition to corrupt the best of intentions and
the sincerest of priestly zeal. Cecil R. Paul, who has done
extensive work with clergy of various denominations, writes
the following concerning the challenges facing the newly
ordained:

> The task of commencing any occupation is a demanding
> reality; for those called to minister it is as difficult, or
> more so, as for those laymen who initiate themselves in to
> the job market. . . Establishing oneself in the ministry
> both excites and threatens the young adult, for it is
> unpredictable whether his goals and aspirations will be
> realized. Due to the complex functions of the pastoral
> role, the young adult in the ministry is immediately faced
> with more responsibilities and greater pressures. . . Now
> he finds he is expected to be an administrator,
> coordinator, educator, and public relations expert.
> Therefore, it is no wonder that his vision is frequently lost
> in a maze of complexities, as the young minister faces
> task after task while undertaking personal identity crises
> and suffering the loss of much personal need fulfillment.
> (*Passages of a Pastor*, p. 35)

Again, we ought not rush to condemn Father Ken too
quickly. He is a very gifted young man. He may come out of his

present situation having learned a very important lesson, namely, that every gift of the Spirit requires a placing of one's gifts at the disposal of the community. Such a placing-in-trust of a gift calls for the priest to experience a kind of dying to self. Father Karl Rahner, S.J. writes the following concerning gifts:

> A charism always involves suffering. For it is painful to fulfill the task set by the charism, the gift received, and at the same time within the one body to endure the opposition of another's activity which may in certain circumstances be equally justified. One's own gift is always limited, humbled by another's gift. Sometimes it must wait until it can develop, until its *kairos*, its hour, has come and that of another has passed or is fading. This painful fact is to be viewed soberly as an inevitable consequence of there being one Church and many gifts. (*The Spirit in the Church*, p. 68)

If Father Ken is able to move beyond his initial hurt and resentment, his priestly ministry will bear much fruit. If, however, he continues to simply "play the game" and use his present assignment as a means to some other parish, he will not be happy. His chances of leaving the priesthood or simply becoming an embittered, lonely old priest are good. Father Ken's zeal and gifts can easily be used by the demon of ambition for a tragic end. The noted Lutheran pastor, Richard John Neuhaus writes with great insight about the dangers of ambition:

> From ambition we should draw back as from lethal poison. But, it is countered, we should be ambitious for doing good. If the attainment of some position of greater power and influence can increase the good we can do, what could possibly be wrong with that? It is a seductive line of reasoning. It is the reasoning that underlies the corruption of careerism in the ministry, that makes it almost automatic that successful ministers move on to successively larger churches until they are crowned by executive posts, honorary doctorates, and the bishop's

> miter. Whoever ministers in one place with an eye on the next is ministering with a divided heart. (*Freedom for Ministry*, p. 212)

In the final analysis, ambition destroys our ability to love and only drives us on in a frenzy toward greater fame, acclaim, and more titles. When we are driven by ambition, we often use everyone and everything for our own selfish ends. Ambition allows us no peace, for there are always more honors and human respect to be had. Every new assignment is merely a means to some other end which in time becomes a means as well. The process never ends. Our spirits are deeply restless. What may seem to all appearances to be a case of burnout may in reality be the effects of the demon of ambition.

Jesus calls our attention to the angel of love as revealed in the one poor widow. She gave all that she had, not compulsively, or in order to gain attention; but she gave out of an abundant heart. Love magnifies even the smallest of gifts. The angel of love is essential for priestly ministry. The priest is called to love and serve *this* church, *this* parish, and in *this* particular setting. Pastoral love requires reality. We must love the people we serve as they are. If we truly love as Jesus loved, if we truly give generously as this one poor widow gave, then we shall know a peace which the world cannot give or take away. It is the peace which comes from serving in love. Then no parish is too small. No assignment is beneath our dignity. No service is without meaning or effect. For when we open our hearts to the angel of pastoral love, we find Jesus and the one poor widow who "gave from her want, all that she had to live on."

The Demon of Success v. The Angel of Fidelity

The ambulance roared up the ramp of the emergency entrance to the hospital. With great speed and precision, the medical staff rushed the patient inside. The man lying on the stretcher was about forty-five years old. He was suffering severe chest pains and an inability to breathe. The man suffering the heart attack was Father Dave, pastor of a large suburban parish complex. His parish was a model of appropriate liturgical celebrations, educational diversity, social justice ministries, and a general good spirit of Christian fellowship. None of this happened by chance. Dave worked hard.

Father Dave was well liked and respected throughout the diocese. He was a very successful pastor. Father Dave often "trouble-shoots" for the diocese by being assigned to parishes which are in financial or pastoral difficulty. Father Dave was a man who got things done. He took pride in this ability. His schedule was hectic. Sometimes Father Dave worked 16-20 hours a day for weeks on end. He prided himself on seldom taking a day off. He was fond of quoting (and misapplying) the words of Pope John XXIII: "We shall have all eternity in which to rest. For now we must be about the Lord's work." At the present moment, there was some doubt as to whether Father Dave would ever do the Lord's work on earth again!

In order to understand Father Dave (and the many Father Daves in ministry), we need to be aware of three things: his early childhood experiences; the current social climate in which ministry is practiced; and the existential questions facing Father Dave.

Dave's father demanded a great deal from him as a child. He wanted Dave to be successful in whatever he did. And success always meant being number one. This demand of his father to be number one became Dave's driving force throughout his seminary days and continued to be so in his present assignment. Dave carried in his head the tape of his father's expectations for success. His self-image and self-worth were dependent on his ability to be number one — and then surpass that!

The drive for success is not merely internal but also external, that is, our society is one which extols winners and being number one. The "big is best" mentality has found its way into the holy of holies. How often does clergy talk center around assignments and parishes in terms of numbers, size, and money? Too often. Big parishes, flourishing schools, and money on deposit are signs of the successful pastor. Naturally, all of this is reinforced by our society. It is more than a little coincidental that in recent years we have witnessed scandals on Wall Street and in some of the so-called major televangelist ministries. Big money, power, and popularity are very addictive. When the social construction of reality, with its emphasis on bigness, combines with a personality that equates self-worth with success, the result is too often a scandal or a heart attack.

Finally, Father Dave found himself in "the middle course" of life. He had found uncomfortable questions increasingly making their presence felt: Am I truly happy doing what I am doing? Why am I doing the work of a priest? What does all of my priestly ministry mean to me? To others? Have I really been doing the Lord's will or have I just been doing my own thing? Have I really dealt in a mature way with issues of sexuality, marriage, and family? What have I done to prepare for the senior years of my priestly ministry? All of these questions had made Father Dave anxious. He had tried to put them off to some later and more convenient hour. Dave had tried to throw himself into his ministry with even more zeal as a way of dispelling their presence. However, Dave had experienced increasing bouts with depression. He found himself being haunted by the words of Rabbi Harold Kushner — "when all you ever wanted isn't enough." Father Dave had been feeling increasingly restless, doubtful, and inwardly empty. It would not be an exaggeration to say that Dave was experiencing a spiritual crisis; a dark night of the soul.

The demon of success confronted Jesus throughout his ministry. Even before his public ministry, Jesus was tempted to be a superstar by jumping from the temple. Such a spectacular show would certainly have drawn large numbers to Jesus. Yet we know that throughout Jesus' ministry there were many attempts to carry him off and make him king. Jesus rejected all such coronations. In fact, Jesus fled from the crowd on several occasions. Furthermore, Jesus told the disciples to keep his messianic identity a secret and often admonished those whom he cured to tell no one what had happened. Jesus was not interested in the praise of men but only the glory of the Father.

The demon of success was a constant temptation to the disciples of Jesus as well. In the Gospel of Luke, we read that Jesus sent out seventy-two disciples to preach and do the work of the reign of God (Lk 10:17-20). They returned in jubilation at their success. Yet Jesus added a sober corrective to their reaction: he told them that the joy of ministry did not come fundamentally from outward success. Rather, true joy came from having their names inscribed in heaven. The focus was not on the immediate results but in the realization that they were doing the work of the kingdom. For there would come a time when the results would not be so spectacular or sudden. They would sow and another would reap. Their best efforts would bear little apparent fruit. At times they would encounter the hostility of those whom they served. If the focus of their ministry, the reign of God, were lost, then they would soon despair and turn to other things. If, however, they rejoiced in doing the work of the Father, all would be theirs.

The demon of success must be exorcised by the angel of fidelity. The pastoral ministry is an act of faith lived over a lifetime of service. There is so much about the daily life of the priest that seems to be barren, meaningless, futile, and even counter-productive. The world so often ignores the Gospel we preach and the Lord we proclaim. While the world places its surplus in the treasury, we are like the one poor widow contributing our two small copper coins. Yet Jesus calls attention to any contribution when done with love, generosity, focus on the Father, and in a spirit of fidelity. Jesus does not judge the value of our ministry by the immediacy of results or the acclaim of others. What matters is the spirit of fidelity to doing the will of the Father in all things and in all circumstances.

In the Gospel of Mark, the apostles returned and told Jesus of their experiences (Mk 6:30-33). Jesus responded by saying, "Come by yourselves to an out-of-the-way place and rest a little." Pastoral ministry requires times to reflect so as to keep things in perspective and to keep oneself focused on the reign of God. Every priest is in need of inward renewal and rest. The people kept coming after Jesus and the apostles. There were so many genuine needs. Yet Jesus insisted that the apostles recognize *their limits*. The apostles must recognize the need for the gift of grace making up what is lacking in their efforts.

The middle course of life and ministry is a time of reevaluation, renewal, and regaining a focus on the kingdom. For some, the middle years contain loss of vision, serious self-doubting, and a general loss of enthusiasm about ministry. For others, it is a time of resting a little while so as to be renewed for the journey. The difference often comes down to whether one is open to grace and a spiritual renewal. The middle years can be a time for a mature assessment of oneself and one's ministry. Such a mature, grace-filled assessment helps one to further confront the demon of success with the angel of fidelity. Once again, the words of Cecil R. Paul are insightful:

> There are powerful internal and external demands for achievement and advancement throughout the young adult and early middle-life years. A major task becomes focused during these middle years, which involves set- tling some basic questions about his vision, his goals, and for what and to whom he will be accountable. While there are those who come up with either answers of apathy or radical change, others settle for more creative alterna- tives. There is what Erikson means by the power of generativity in the middle years, expressed through care for community and the next generation. No other vocation better prepares a man for this task than does the ministry, since the pastor has been expressing this process throughout his professional life. This gives him a signific- ant advantage in confronting the related personal tasks. The accountability dynamics are shifting from self- imposed and societal norms for success toward the Au- thor of the vision who has also promised to enable his

disciples to fulfill that call. This is why the passage of mid-life becomes a positive pilgrimage in the life of the pastor. The upward focus is primarily on the enabling power of God's love and grace working in all the expressions of the pastor's personal pilgrimage. (*Passages of a Pastor*, p. 76)

The Demon of Remorse v. The Angel of Integrity

"Come grow old along with me, the best is yet to be . . ." is a poetic invitation that many in our society would just as soon decline. For growing old is not an invitation to the best but to the least respected, valued, honored, and sought after in our youth worshiping society. To be old is to be obsolete. To be old is to be removed from public view so as not to remind us of our temporality and mortality. The senior years of ministry are not always the best either. The transition from pastor to retired priest carries a special cost of discipleship.

Father Albert had been a priest for over 40 years. He had served in many parishes and even founded two parishes in the diocese. In recent years, his health had been in decline. However, Father Albert still managed to keep his various pastoral appointments and duties. He was a great storyteller and loved an audience. Father Albert could tell you many stories about the past without dwelling in the past. He was fast approaching the age of retirement from the so-called active ministry. In fact, Father Al would be "retiring" in about two months. A huge parish celebration was being planned. Father Albert fought such things every step of the way — but not too vigorously!

What will Father Albert do now that he is no longer pastoring a parish? Father Al had not simply waited for the "winged chariot of time" but he had actively planned for this "new phase of his priestly ministry." How so? Father Al had requested from his bishop the opportunity to continue serving in some capacity. His bishop, a man of vision, had asked Father Al to work with fourth year theological seminarians as well as young priests with their first assignments. Father Al had kept up with theological trends and his style of pastoral leadership was one of empowering rather than simply giving orders. His pastoral experience was second to none, and the bishop said, "I would be crazy not to accept the generous offer of Father Al."

Father Albert is often the exception rather than the rule. And his bishop is indeed a wise and caring shepherd. Too often, the demon of remorse becomes a "second self" in the senior years of life. The temptation is great to look back in anger, regret, and guilt. As the role, priest, which has been so much a part of one's identity changes, the temptation is to focus on the self and fall victim to self-pity and inactivity. Regrettably, the priest in senior years can simply become bitter and fade away. The senior priest does not draw on his experience and reflections and spirituality as a gift to those who will follow, but he uses these to compare the present with the past. Needless to say, the present is always found wanting and the future is filled with despair. As the roles that have been important to us change or disappear, the self becomes more visible. What we are at our core is revealed. Robert C. Atchley, in *The Social Forces in Later Life*, has written:

> With each withdrawal from a role, the individual becomes increasingly preoccupied with himself or herself. Gradually the individual equilibrium achieved in middle age and oriented toward society is replaced through the process of disengagement by a new equilibrium centered around the individual's inner life in old age. (p. 210)

After speaking with Father Al, one has a profound sense of a man in whom the angel of integrity dwells. The inner life of Father Al reveals the soul of a man who has journeyed in faith and knows he has found the pearl of great price. One of Father Albert's favorite passages from Scripture comes as no surprise. It is the words of Paul to Timothy concerning his ministry which is about to end:

> I for my part am already being poured out like a libation.
> The time of my dissolution is near. I have fought the good
> fight, I have finished the race, I have kept the faith. From
> now on a merited crown awaits me; on that Day the Lord,
> just judge that he is, will award it to me — and not only to
> me, but to all who have looked for his appearing with
> eager longing. (2 Tm 3:6-8)

The dissolution of Paul was not one of bitterness or waste
but one of helping to prepare the future. Paul is sharing with,
and encouraging, Timothy, as well as all who long for Jesus'
appearance, to be men of faith and integrity. Father Albert is
now continuing this Pauline legacy — helping to prepare the
future. His dissolution, the passing on of the ministry to the
next generation, is a kind of dying. Dying with integrity in the
Lord assures us that every dissolution yields a resurrection.

A Concluding Word

The one poor widow extolled by Jesus, the one we used as
our disclosure model for discipleship in the priesthood no
doubt seems strange. There are so many more obvious and well
known models available. This one poor widow is not even
known by name. She is anonymous. Why this one for our
model? She teaches the priest throughout his ministry the cost
of discipleship. She is especially important for today because
she is anonymous, obscure, and often ignored by the crowd
which fixes its attention on the spectacular. This one poor
widow speaks to the priest who often labors in ways unnoticed
and who lays the foundations of faith in ways known only to
God alone. Yet in the midst of priestly obscurity, the abiding
presence of Jesus sustains and takes note of what is done.
Jesus looks beyond the externals and reads the heart.

The one poor widow can teach Father Ken the value of
even small things when done with a generous heart. Ambition
for higher things requires that we learn to be humble servants
and do all that we do out of selfless love for Jesus and those

whom we serve. The widow teaches Father Dave to recognize his limits and even rejoice in them. For it is only when we acknowledge our limits and dependency that God's grace can fill up what is lacking in us. The love of God is unconditional. God especially loves those who give only two coins when it comes from a generous, trusting heart. And finally, this widow can teach Father Albert, and all who are in their senior years of ministry, that serving the Lord continues even when one's resources become quite small. The Lord does not judge our offerings in comparison to others, but he values our service based on our motivation. The poor widow gave all she could. The senior minister can only give what he can out of love. Both offerings are treasured by God.

At this very moment, there are countless priests laboring for the Lord and bringing the gospel to the whole world. Few, if any, will be acclaimed by the crowd which continues to give from its surplus and take note of the "lifestyles of the rich and famous." In those moments when we are tempted to despair and to question our ministry, let us pause and reflect on the life of that one poor widow. Let us remember her action of generous, trusting giving and do likewise. Let us remember the words of Jesus: "I want you to observe that this poor widow contributed more than the others who donated to the treasury. They gave from their surplus wealth, but she gave from her want, all that she had to live on."

CHAPTER FOUR

MARY MAGDALENE:
The Priest and Self-Image

Among the sinful situations we priests encounter most often, high on the list is self-hatred. Examples abound: The married couple who simply cannot believe that they are worthy of enjoying each other's love. The adolescent who hates herself and feels she has no friends. The young rebel without a cause who rejects all authority and social convention so that others will find him as repugnant as he finds himself. The middle-aged executive who continues his workaholic schedule in order to prove to himself and others that he is worthy of respect. The sad condition of the elderly parishioner who is bitter and lives in isolation. He hates what he has made of himself and his life. Only a deeper loneliness, isolation and fear of death await him. In all these situations, we see the destructive forces of self-hatred at work.

Unfortunately, priests and religious are not immune from the poison of self-hatred. At a recent gathering of priests, someone mentioned a mutual friend who had recently left the priesthood. The conversation was not mean or judgmental. One of the priests said, "I could picture myself falling in love, getting married, and enjoying family life. I feel I would be a good husband and father. I am a pretty lovable guy!" This seemingly boastful self-analysis was too much for one priest. He spoke up by saying, "Well, I couldn't picture myself leaving the priesthood for love, marriage, and a family. Be-

sides, I don't know of any woman who would have me." Both
priests spoke the truth in jest. The first priest could see himself
happy in another vocation. He saw himself as lovable. He
could picture himself giving and accepting love in marriage
and family life. The second priest felt such talk was a danger to
one's priestly vocation and a sign of spiritual failure, for to say
that one is lovable is a sign of pride and arrogance. Humility
demands that we be self-effacing and deny our gifts and skills.
We are simply unworthy servants just doing our duty. All the
glory goes to God and not to the narcissistic self.

The attitude of the second priest is as prevalent in the
priesthood as the attitude of the first priest is rare. The real
spiritual failure is found in the attitude of the second priest. It
is easy for some men to "back into" the priesthood as a way of
avoiding intimacy, love, caring, and passing on new life to a
tired world and a wart covered Church who waits for her Lord.
The real spiritual failure is the confusion concerning humility
(truth). True humility is not self-hatred, low self-esteem, and a
self-image which has no room for giving and receiving love.
True humility is an honest acceptance of our gifts and limitations. The humble person is self-aware and is able to give
thanks for gifts and open himself to the grace of God so as to
change what needs changing. Christian humility is the virtue
of truth concerning the self which allows us to respect
ourselves, rejoice in our lovability, and share our gifts with
others. Father Andrew Greeley, in his early writings on the
priesthood, called for the priest to respect himself so as to help
others respect themselves. In his words:

> We ought to realize in theory though we don't understand
> in practice that all creatures of God are likeable, and all
> of us have the potential for charm. Our refusal to respect
> and to acknowledge our worth and attractiveness as hu-
> man beings is in fact an escape — an excuse for with-
> drawing from human relationships and hiding our
> tortured insecure little egos behind the smoke screen of
> false humility.

> Self-respect, at least respect for the possibilities of
> one's self, is absolutely essential for effective relation-
> ships with other human beings. Since the priest is a man
> whose role is primarily relational, he obviously must have
> a great deal of self-respect. (*New Horizons for the Priest-
> hood*, pp. 25-26)

Furthermore, if we do not respect ourselves and value
ourselves as persons, it is hard, if not impossible, to provide
pastoral care to others. For how can we give a gift, the self, that
we find unworthy and inferior? We cannot. If we are to be the
kind of priest people turn to, we must be men who love
ourselves in the proper way. We must be open to the totally
accepting love of God and the love offered to us by others.
Sidney Callahan, writing on the spiritual works of mercy, says,
"The first requirement for counseling the doubtful is to believe
that we matter to one another, we can make a difference. If we
believe we are members of one another, it is worth the effort to
try to connect. We must see each other through" (*With All Our
Heart & Mind*, p. 69). Yet we can only counsel, make a
difference, connect, and see each other through if we see
ourselves as valuable and gifted. We can only matter to others
because we matter to ourselves. We matter to ourselves because we ultimately matter to our loving God.

No doubt the question lingers, "Is not all of this talk of
self-respect, self-love, and self-acceptance just another sign of
our narcissistic age?" While few would doubt that ours is a
"culture of narcissism" (Christopher Lasch), it must be emphasized that proper self-love and authentic self-respect are
not narcissistic. Christian self-love, the kind of love the priest
must experience and share, is a love which is grounded in the
unbounded love of God. Unlike narcissistic love or pride,
which finds value outside the person in terms of money,
success, power, glory, or beauty, Christian love looks within at
the heart and finds the very love of God already present. This
already present love of God proclaims us as good, lovable,
likeable, talented, gifted, and worthy of dignity and respect.

The goodness that we are does not come by way of the goods that we own or achieve. It is a pure gift from the God who knows what we need before we ever ask him. And what we are most in need of, but can never earn because it is freely given, is the total love of God. Self-love from the Christian viewpoint is always theological, that is, self-love is always talk about God's love for us. This divine love empowers us to love ourselves and others.

The sinful dimension of self-hatred is the rejection of God in whose image we are made. When we refuse to love and respect ourselves, we refuse to love the God who gave us life and wants to be with us for all eternity. To reject our lives as a gift from God is to reject God. To see our lives as worthless is to debase the very good creation of God of which we are a part. The sinful dimension of self-hatred is as old as the history of humankind. The book of Genesis tells us that the original sin is fundamentally a sin of rejection of self and of the God in whose image and likeness we are made. The serpent's temptation is to be like God. In other words, it is an invitation to be what we are not. To be human, to be a creature, is an inferior condition in comparison to being like God. The way out of the human condition is to grasp for what is beyond our reach. Unfortunately, the rejection of our human condition leads to alienation and banishment. We find ourselves separated from others, nature, our own self, and, worst of all, from God. When we reject the unique gift of who we are, we experience enormous pain. The inner pain of self-hatred cannot be healed by money, achievements, power, or worldly success. If we lack a mature sense of self-esteem, nothing in our priestly ministry provides us with a sense of joy, for all that we do is inadequate and found wanting. The good sermon is just luck. The effective counselling session was very inadequate and the effects will not last. The interesting class just taught will soon be forgotten by the students. The list is endless. No matter what one does, it is worthless and inadequate. When we fail to esteem the unique gift that each of us is, we fail to praise God and serve those entrusted to our care.

Father James E. Sullivan, in his beautiful book, *Journey to Freedom*, indicates that lack of self-esteem is the major impediment to human freedom and happiness. The lack of self-esteem can be attributed to three major sources: false attitudes, guilt, and the compulsion to prove oneself. Often we find ourselves depressed and filled with feelings of inadequacy despite family, friends, material comfort, or ministerial success. Why is this so? There is present within us unhealthy attitudes which keep us from being truly free and joyful. There is present at work within us sin which keeps us from doing the good we desire. We fight the war within. We find ourselves very much like St. Paul:

> I cannot even understand my own actions. I do not do what I want to do but what I hate. . . My inner self agrees with the law of God, but I see in my body's members another law at war with the law of my mind; this makes me the prisoner of the law of sin in my members. What a wretched man I am! (Rm 7:15, 22, 24)

In addition to false attitudes or the inward effects of sin, we can find ourselves filled with self-hatred because of guilt. The guilt which fills one with self-hatred and loss of self-esteem is the neurotic guilt by which we feel blame or shame without good reason. With neurotic guilt, there is no objective or real basis for my feeling bad about myself. With real moral guilt, I can point to the cause of my feeling bad or depressed. For example, I have lied about a person and thus have severely damaged his or her reputation. It is a sign of moral health that I *do* feel remorse and so I am moved to make reparation for my offense. By contrast, with neurotic guilt, there is simply the guilty feeling or the depression for which I am unable to indicate the reason. A not uncommon experience is one in which I receive some good news. I feel really excited. Things are looking up and I am feeling good about myself. In the midst of my little peak experience, an inner voice or feeling says, "This won't last very long. Or if it does feel good, you do not have a right to be so happy or joyful." Neurotic guilt takes away the joy and grace of life.

Finally, we feel ourselves constantly being judged and under inspection. Such feelings of living in a fish-bowl and constantly having to prove oneself is especially acute with priestly ministry. The priest is a public man, a man of and for the community. He is watched for what he says and does not say. His every action, thought, and presentation of self are held up for analysis. And the standards are quite high, if not at times impossible to achieve. It is very easy to fall short of such standards and expectations. Father does not always have the right answer. Father does get angry, tired, and impatient. Father can feel very inadequate in the face of human suffering, sin, and death. Father can feel very unworthy to be Father when he examines his conscience and realizes how far from the glory of God he is. Simply put: Father can feel little self-esteem because he *is* human!

The inner power of sin, neurotic guilt, and the compulsive need to prove oneself causes enormous pain. Father Sullivan writes about the psychic pain which results from loss of self-esteem:

> No other pain strikes so deeply at my person than this psychic pain of self-hatred. No other pain is so potentially destructive to self-fulfillment and happiness. Lack of self-esteem is the core of almost every other roadblock on my journey to freedom and fulfillment.
>
> It is precisely because psychic pain strikes at my innermost core that it robs me of internal freedom. I want to reach out in love, but I am afraid to do so. Who would want me as a friend? . . . And how can I develop my talents? I'm convinced that I don't have any real talents. . .
>
> The pain that is most difficult, however, and *almost irredeemable*, is the psychic pain of a diminished self-esteem. . . If I were to experience real affirmation and love, it would be a great boost to my self-esteem. But

there's the rub! Because I don't have self-esteem to begin
with, I have a high roadblock which *prevents* me from
experiencing affirmation and love. It's a vicious cycle.
(*Journey to Freedom: The Path to Self-Esteem for the
Priesthood and Religious Life*, pp. 16-17)

The key question arises: who will deliver us from this
terrible slavery and pain? Who is the one who has the power to
heal and restore the brokenness of our lives? Who is able to
show us a love so pure, faithful, and life-giving that we will be
liberated from the prison of self-hatred? Such a love must be
one which is both beyond our abilities to effect and yet, at the
same time, a love which lies deep within our hearts. It must be
a love which has its source in God and a love which is made
visible in our all too human condition. The love we need to
experience so as to be liberated from the destructive forces of
self-hatred is offered to us in the person of Jesus Christ. Jesus
is the blessed answer which assures us that we are loved and
totally accepted by God. It is through communion with Jesus
that we come to experience ourselves as loved and forgiven.
Our hearts are renewed and we are able to love, forgive, and
accept ourselves and others. This is the invitation Jesus extends to each of us: "Come to me, all you who are weary and
find life burdensome, and I will refresh you. Take my yoke
upon your shoulders and learn from me, for I am gentle and
humble of heart. Your souls will find rest, for my yoke is easy
and my burden light" (Mt 11:28-30).
   One such person who had the courage to accept the
invitation of Jesus was Mary Magdalene. Her story (which is
ours as well) has much to teach us about facing ourselves, our
past sins and guilt, the temptation to self-hatred, and the
power of Jesus' love to call forth new life. The story of Mary
Magdalene is not about a fallen woman, but a fellow human
being who is raised to newness of life. Her story gives us all
cause to hope.

A Woman Possessed

In the Gospel of St. Luke, we read, "The Twelve ac-
companied him, and also some women who had been cured of
evil spirits and maladies: Mary called the Magdalene, from
whom seven devils had gone out, Joanna, wife of Herod's
steward Chuza, Susanna, and many others who were assisting
out of their means" (Lk 8:1-2). There is no attempt to cover up
or down-play Mary's past. She was possessed by seven devils.
Yet here is Mary with Jesus and the Twelve, "assisting them
out of their means." Mary's past sins, guilt, and possession are
real. However, Mary has encountered the One who came to
make all things new. Jesus came to announce the good news of
salvation. It is to those such as Mary that the healing, forgiving, and totally accepting love of God is offered. With Jesus,
there is liberation from self-hatred and self-pity. The lure of
the future with its hope of new life is more powerful than the
pull of the past. Mary has met Jesus and she will not be denied
this opportunity of grace for a new beginning.

Mary is not simply with Jesus, but she is actually
ministering to him. And Jesus is wonderfully wise enough to let
her. That's the way it is when one encounters grace and one has
the courage to follow Jesus. One who has been set free from
devils is now *free for* serving and loving others. Mary is not
content to simply count her blessings. She is now sharing her
blessings with Jesus. She is doing her part for the reign of God
by ministering to Jesus and the Twelve after they return from
various travels. No doubt many who knew Mary were as-
tonished at the change. Many were skeptical and refused to
allow for her new way of life. Human opinion and expectations
are of no account. Mary had been set free from her devils. She
would not let human judgments repossess and enslave her. All
that mattered was that she belonged to Jesus. It was Jesus who
had given her the precious gift of self-respect.

The fact that Mary was possessed by seven devils and was
still found ministering to Jesus tells us that Jesus does not
choose the perfect for priestly ministry. Before one is a priest,

one is a human being. One remains a human being after ordination, no matter has much this causes embarrassment. How often do we priests try to hide our humanity and fail to share our struggles, weaknesses, joys, and victories of grace with those whom we serve? Too often. We feel we must present an image of superhuman strength, faith, and virtue. We feel that our congregations demand of us perfection. Our ego-ideal and ego-expectations get out of control. When we fall short of the glory of God, we suffer from neurotic guilt and the psychic pain of low self-esteem and even self-hatred. Parental influence, seminary formation, unrealistic expectations from self, parish, and religious and diocesan authorities can all team up to compound the feelings of inadequacy and unworthiness.

Again we see disclosed to us in the story of Mary Magdalene a life renewed by encountering Jesus. Jesus calls the weak so that grace can make them strong. Jesus announces good news and forgiveness to those most in need and least deserving by the standards of the world. It is because Mary has known the bondage of sin, the suffering of possession, the scorn of the crowd, and the doubts expressed by friends that she is able to minister so effectively. The reality of our own weakness need not be a cause of shame but an opportunity to experience grace and be compassionate toward others. The reality of being a vessel of clay in whom the Spirit is at work is essential for priestly ministry. The writer of the Letter to the Hebrews puts it this way: "Every high priest is taken from among men and made their representative before God, to offer gifts and sacrifices for sins. He is able to deal patiently with erring sinners, for he himself is beset by weakness and so must make sin offerings for himself as well as for the people" (Heb 5:1-3). What a liberating and healthy vision of priesthood! The priest is a man of and from the community. He is human and a sinner like those whom he serves. Yet his sinful humanity is not an excuse for self-hatred, but a great resource in his pastoral ministry.

A Faithful Witness

Mary Magdalene does not merely minister to Jesus' needs after she is liberated from her seven devils; she continues to be a disciple by following Jesus to Golgotha. The testimony concerning Mary is simple and eloquent:

> Many women were present looking on from a distance. They had followed Jesus from Galilee to attend to his needs. Among them were Mary Magdalene, and Mary the mother of James and Joseph, and the mother of Zebedee's sons. (Mt 27:55-6)

> Near the cross of Jesus there stood his mother, his mother's sister, Mary the wife of Clopas, and Mary Magdalene. (Jn 19:25)

And the testimony of Matthew when Jesus is finally laid in the tomb:

> Taking the body, Joseph wrapped it in fresh linen and laid it in his own new tomb which had been hewn from a formation of rock. Then he rolled a huge stone across the entrance of the tomb and went away. But Mary Magdalene and the other Mary remained sitting there, facing the tomb. (Mt 27:59-61)

The beauty of Mary Magdalene from the above quoted passages is her fidelity to the small but significant things that really matter: presence, meeting basic needs, fellowship, waiting at the Cross and sitting at the tomb. These things can seem so small, meaningless, and futile. None of them were going to change the fate of Jesus. He would die and be buried. Once again, Mary would be on her own. Perhaps she would return to her former ways and be repossessed by seven devils worse than the first group. Yet none of this happened. Jesus gave Mary back her self-respect and liberated her to love and to serve. She would not go back to a past life of slavery and self-hatred. Regardless of what little she would do, it would be of value. Why? Because everything she had done was motivated by love for Jesus. What she did had value because Jesus told her and showed her she was of value and was precious to God. Mary was a person of worth and what she did was of worth as well.

The daily pastoral ministry of the priest is one of being called to do the ordinary things extraordinarily well. The priest finds that so much of his day involves such little things as: being present to others, meeting basic needs, keeping company with the hurting, consoling the grieving, accepting those who feel rejected, and simply sitting and waiting. In all of these little, mundane things, the priest must find Jesus. In being faithful to these little things, our priestly commitment is strengthened. It is in the least of our brothers and sisters and in the most routine aspects of priestly ministry that we encounter Jesus. There are no really small and insignificant aspects of ministry when we are genuinely trying to lead others to Jesus.

If we pay careful attention to what is often called the ordinary or everyday aspects of ministry, we find that what is required is the giving of oneself. And that's the rub. We must give ourselves. Yet how can we give a self we find lacking in value and having no worth? How can we be present with others when we believe our personal presence makes no difference because we make no difference? We can't. Self-hatred and feelings of inferiority keep us from giving ourselves to others. Our ministry is devoid of warmth. Ministry becomes the performance of ritual as we hide behind our Roman collar. How tragic all this is when we consider that central to the Christian story is the Incarnation — the Word becoming flesh. Our words, ministry, and priestly presence must take on flesh as *we* continue to make present and visible God's love.

Mary Magdalene had every reason to persist in self-hatred and feelings of unworthiness. She was possessed by seven devils. But such would not be the case. Mary met Jesus and her life began anew. Mary served Jesus as best she could with what she had out of love. She wasn't perfect, far from it. Yet Jesus healed her and allowed her to serve. The priest has much to learn from Mary. No matter what our limitations,

devils, or bondage, Jesus has called us to serve. His call also
empowers and liberates. The priest people turn to is the priest
who respects and loves himself in the proper way. Such a priest
enables others to love and respect themselves.

"I have seen the Lord!"

How fitting for the Risen Lord to have appeared to Mary
on that first Easter morning! The resurrection of Jesus is the
ultimate story of life over death, light over darkness, grace over
sin, and hope over despair. The Easter victory of Jesus over sin
and death is the story of new life and new beginnings. This is
the Mary who was possessed by seven devils. This is the Mary
who had every reason to hate herself and reject every offer of
beginning again. Such is not the case. She ministers to Jesus'
needs and is a faithful witness at the Cross and tomb. Mary
continues to minister to Jesus even after He is laid in the tomb.
She goes to the tomb on that first Easter morning to care for
Jesus' body. Her love for Jesus is stronger than death.

The encounter between Mary and the Risen Jesus on
Easter morning is one of the most stirring and hopeful in
Scripture. Jesus, at first not recognized by Mary, asked her the
essential question for all disciples, "Who is it you are looking
for?" Mary was looking for Jesus. However, she was looking for
a dead Jesus. She was looking for a body that had been taken
away. It was only when Jesus called her by name that Mary
recognized Jesus. This calling by name was a sign of the
intimacy between Jesus and the disciples. The true disciple
hears the voice of Jesus and responds to it. To be called by
name by Jesus and to follow him is the sign of true discipleship. In John's Gospel, we read: "The sheep hear his voice and
he calls his own by name and leads them out" (10:3). When the
Risen Jesus called Mary, she turned toward him and was open
to his voice. Mary opens her heart to the Risen Jesus so as to
receive the gift of faith. The great German biblical scholar
Rudolf Schnackenberg writes the following about this
encounter:

> The recognition takes place as Jesus calls Mary by her name . . . the risen one reveals himself to one who seeks and believes. Jesus knows those who belong to him and calls them by their name; they know his voice and follow him (cf. 10:3f). The risen one is no other than the earthly Jesus; he now encounters Mary in a new way. She turns to him — an outward gesture, which at the same time expresses an opening up of her inner self and a believing openness to the risen Lord. (*The Gospel According to John*, Vol. 3, p. 317)

Not only does Mary encounter the Risen Lord, she is sent by Jesus to announce his resurrection to the disciples. Mary is both a witness to the resurrection and one who is sent to proclaim the resurrection. On the lips of Mary, we hear what *all* disciples must say, namely, "I have seen the Lord." Mary would continue to serve by sharing with the disciples and others the Easter story — Jesus is alive and sits at the right hand of "my Father and your Father, to my God and your God"!

The priest people turn to is one who has seen the Risen Lord and helps others to experience his presence as well. The priest people turn to is one who helps them to hope and turn in faith and openness to Jesus. He enables them to live a new way. Such a priest is not perfect. He must struggle with his own devils and limitations. However, like Mary Magdalene, he has met the Lord and all things are new. Yes, he still struggles with sin, doubts, fears, frustrations, and feelings of emptiness. The priest is still a vessel of clay and all too human. But within the heart of each priest is the continual calling of his name by Jesus. Jesus' call to serve, to be a good shepherd in service of people, is not once and for all but an ongoing invitation which requires of us our continuing, daily acceptance of proclaiming the Risen Lord.

Mary Magdalene as witness and herald of the resurrection may seem like an unlikely choice. Not to the God of endless surprises and unbounded love. Questions of worthiness and virtue all seem a little irrelevant. What is crucial is the power of grace shining through human weakness. The past has been accepted by Jesus and healed. Each priest must struggle with feelings of inadequacy and unworthiness. Each priest falls short of the glory of God and the call of Jesus to follow him. Yet Jesus does not give up on us. Jesus continues to call us by name again and again. The real issue is whether we have the faith and courage to proclaim with Mary, "I have seen the Lord!"

A Concluding Word

A not uncommon question: Do people still respect priests? The research findings of the National Opinion Research Center and the Gallup Poll clearly indicate that priests are respected. The more troubling question goes like this: Do priests respect themselves? Unfortunately, there are too many priests and religious who suffer from low self-esteem, feelings of unworthiness, and self-hatred. These feelings cause terrible pain to the priest and seriously impair the quality of pastoral ministry extended to the faith community. Fortunately, we are not left orphans. Jesus has sent the Holy Spirit to dwell in our hearts. The work of the Spirit is to make all things new and to break the chains of self-hatred and fear. The Holy Spirit is a Spirit of liberation and second chances (seven times seventy chances). The indwelling Spirit helps us to see ourselves as worthwhile, loved, talented, and accepted by our loving Father. Likewise, those whom we serve experience themselves as loved, accepted, worthwhile, and forgiven by God.

All of this may sound like pride and just another sign of our narcissistic culture. Such is not the case. We are simply allowing Jesus to do for us what he did for Mary Magdalene, namely, to set her free to love and to serve. Jesus freed her from her devils and freed her to be the unique person she was. Mary knew she couldn't free herself. Her rebirth was the work of amazing grace. So it is with the priest. He has been called and sustained by amazing grace. In the words of St. Paul:

This treasure we possess in earthen vessels, to make it clear that its surpassing power comes from God and not from us. We are afflicted in every way possible, but we never despair. We are persecuted but never abandoned; we are struck down but never destroyed. Continually we carry about in our bodies the dying of Jesus, so that in our bodies the life of Jesus may also be revealed. While we live we are constantly being delivered to death for Jesus' sake, so that the life of Jesus may be revealed in our mortal flesh. (2 Cor 4:7-11)

SECTION II

Pastoral Ministry

CHAPTER FIVE

MARTHA:
The Priest and Work

In our first section, *The Fundamentals*, we reflected on four aspects of priestly life: faith, mystery, discipleship, and self-image or self-esteem. We used as our disclosure models Abraham, John the Baptizer, the one poor widow, and Mary Magdalene. Abraham provided us with a model of courageous faith in times of transition and new beginnings. Such a faith believes and hopes God will provide while acting as if everything depends on us.

The priest is a man who dwells in mystery and continues the work of John the Baptizer by pointing out the presence of Jesus in the marrow of our everydayness. The priest points to that other dimension beyond this world while also reminding the faith community that the One beyond is also in our midst.

Much of priestly ministry is done in obscurity and is known to God alone. At times, the priest can feel he does not make a difference in the lives of those whom he serves. The example of the one poor widow who gave all she had out of love reminds us that fidelity, and not worldly success or notoriety, is the mark of the true disciple. Nothing done out of love for Jesus is meaningless.

Finally, an essential aspect of pastoral ministry is assuring people that God loves them and that each person is precious in God's eyes. Jesus came to announce the good news of salvation. Sin and self-hatred do not have the final word, but

rather, grace and self-respect. The priest must love and respect himself so as to help others love and respect themselves.
The story of Mary Magdalene is one of meeting Jesus and the
miracle of moving from self-hatred to self-love. Mary reminds
us that the past can be transcended and transformed by forgiving, totally accepting love. This kind of love Jesus proclaims
and makes visible. The priest is called to walk in the way of
that kind of Jesus-love.

In this section, *Pastoral Ministry*, we now turn our attention to the following: work, preaching, liturgy, and pastoral
care. These major aspects of pastoral ministry cannot be
separated from the fundamentals of the priesthood. The
priestly ministry of preaching, celebrating the liturgy, and
caring for those in pain must flow from a priest who is at once a
man of faith; who points to the hidden presence of Jesus in
every situation; who does these ministries out of love and not
self-glory; and who ministers to the community in love because
he loves and respects himself. Before turning our attention to
specific aspects of priestly ministry, we must consider the
overall topic of work as it relates to the priest.

Father Ed: For He's a Busy Good Fellow

Father Ed is an activist. He is not the sixties activist of
picket lines and barricades. He is a more mundane, but no less
serious activist, who is always looking for something to do and
fix or someone to serve. Father Ed finds it difficult to be still.
He is always up and doing for others, even when they don't
want or need help. Father Ed is excellent at anticipating and
manufacturing needs (or problems) so as to be helpful. For
example, at every parish meeting, Father Ed is a constant buzz
of energy, making sure that everyone has coffee, pads, and
pencils, and is generally comfortable. He considers meetings a
waste of time anyway, but if he can help others in small ways,
then all is not lost. Father Ed has boundless energy and is
always willing to help and be involved in people's lives. You
can always count on Father Ed.

To observe Father Ed, one would think he is the model of priestly ministry. Yet on closer inspection, Father Ed's wants become visible and troubling. While Father Ed has the wonderful capacity to meet countless needs, he subtly refuses to acknowledge *his* needs. Father Ed is great at giving, doing, and serving, but he will not allow anyone to minister to him. Father Ed believes he has no needs, and besides, he is a priest called to serve and not be served. Almost every conversation with Father Ed ends with the parishioner saying, "Thank you, Father Ed. You have helped me so much. I don't know what I would have done without you." Father Ed knows how to serve *and* elicit gratitude. He feels good about himself when he is serving and doing for others. His relationships are basically helping relationships in which he (powerful) does for another (powerless or needy). Father Ed finds relationships which do not require his help unsatisfying. He feels empty inside and useless as a priest. He only feels good about himself and his ministry when he meets needs. Between episodes of service, he feels somewhat lost.

As mentioned above, Father Ed is unaware of, or refuses to admit, his own needs. However, Father Ed is quite aware of all that he does for others. In the final analysis, Father Ed is a master manipulator. In the name of selflessness, he is quite selfish and self-serving. He uses others to validate his own existence and ministry. Their needs become his. He serves others, though, not out of love but out of the need to control and receive gratitude. Father Ed is really a man who craves power. Through guilt, Father Ed is able to get others to do what he wants. In subtle ways, he is able to remind others of what he has done for them. While others suffer from feelings of guilt and anger over being manipulated, Father Ed must contend with his own deep resentment when others do not express gratitude, refuse to be controlled, or fail to return favor for favor.

How did Father Ed get this way? Little Eddie was taught early on by his parents to be helpful. Of course, this was all to the good. However, Eddie's parents conditioned their love on his being helpful. Love was earned and self-worth was bought through acts of service to others. In fact, when Eddie came home from school, his mother wanted to know what acts of kindness he had performed that day. At times, Eddie had to make up stories in order to be termed "a good and helpful little boy." Early on, Eddie had to deal with feelings of guilt when he lied and feelings of inadequacy when he failed to serve others.

This distorted view of service and being helpful was compounded in his seminary formation. All the spiritual reading and conferences on the priest as servant of the people were read and heard through the filters of his early childhood experience. If the man is found in the child, then little Eddie the helper became Father Ed the compulsive server of others' needs. Father Ed felt inadequate when he told others he just couldn't help them in a given situation or with a particular request. In order to overcome this guilt, he would double his efforts at being of service. The words of an old song became his refrain, "the difficult I'll do right now, the impossible will take a little while."

Recently, Father Ed has found himself fighting feelings of increased resentment and depression. More and more, he finds himself mentally and physically exhausted. He has become more critical of others; especially what he perceives to be their lack of service as well as appreciation for what he does. In a confrontation with a parish leader, Father Ed was expressing his dissatisfaction with the lack of cooperation and help from others. Finally, when Father Ed had finished, the woman said to him, "Father Ed, part of the problem is that you never allow others to help you. You always say you don't need help. You have everything under control. Why then are you angry when people take you at your word?" Why indeed!

In some ways, Father Ed is every priest. Much of contemporary spirituality and ecclesiology has emphasized the service dimensions of the Christian life, priesthood, and church mission. Too often, the term "service" goes undefined. Service becomes equated with a compulsive, obsessive doing for others. Service means the priest is the "man for others" while too often forgetting about his own real needs. Forgotten in all this service-talk is the example Jesus left us of service. After long and intense days of meeting many needs, Jesus would often seek out a quiet place to pray and rest. Jesus instructed his disciples as well to learn to balance the active and contemplative demands of ministry. Jesus wanted them to avoid an activism which knew no prayer or reflection as well as a contemplation which had nothing to do with true pastoral needs. In the Gospel of Mark, the apostles returned to Jesus and told him of "all that they had done and what they had taught" (Mk 6:30). The crowds continued to follow them, wanting more and more. It would have been so easy for Jesus and the apostles to get caught up in their success. After all, the people were in need and Jesus had been sent to serve. Yet Jesus placed pastoral activism within its proper perspective. He said to the apostles, "Come by yourselves to an out-of-the-way place and rest a little" (Mk 6:31). Jesus was well aware that they could not serve and meet needs without respecting their needs for rest, reflection, and renewal.

The story of the Good Samaritan provides us with another splendid example of healthy service (Lk 10:25-37). The Samaritan came across the man who had fallen in with robbers. The Samaritan risked involvement with another's plight and allowed himself to be moved by pity. He saw that this man needed him and the Samaritan responded. However, the Samaritan did not allow the man in the ditch to be his lifelong project. The Samaritan turned the beaten man over to the innkeeper. The Samaritan continued on his journey where others were waiting and different commitments required his attention. The Samaritan would pay the innkeeper if there were any further expense. He did not break relationship with the man who was in need, but called on others to provide their unique services. The Samaritan could not do it all. He was wise enough to allow others to serve so that he could continue his other responsibilities. The Good Samaritan teaches us that good service is the prudent pastoral practice of calling forth everyone's gifts to be used for the common good. The prudent

pastoral priest knows how to encourage gift-sharing for the
good of the community. In the words of St. Paul:

> There are different gifts but the same Spirit; there are
> different ministries but the same Lord; there are different
> works but the same God who accomplishes all of them in
> everyone. To each person the manifestation of the Spirit
> is given for the common good . . . it is one and the same
> Spirit who produces all these gifts, distributing them to
> each as he wills. (1 Cor 12:4-7, 11)

Authentic Christian service is not only calling forth the
gifts of others, it is the ability to *empower* the one being served
to develop his or her talents and call forth his or her gifts. The
one being served is not to be kept in a state of perpetual
dependency. No one likes to continuously be on the receiving
end of others' good works. This only causes self-hatred, feelings of inadequacy, and resentment towards those who are
constantly helping. The true servant is one who liberates
people to see their own power to effect change and overcome
obstacles. Service is liberation. True Christ-like service is that
which never seeks to foster a manipulative dependency or tries
to control another. There is always a danger that we will come
to need those whom we serve more than they need us. In the
name of selflessness, we can be quite selfish.

Jesus healed others and sent them on to continue their
lives. Jesus did not allow someone to follow him simply because of some healing. Jesus was not controlled by others nor
did he conform to their expectations. In the life of Jesus,
service is liberation. We see this expressed in the Gospel of St.
Luke. The reputation of Jesus spread as he continued to
minister to the needs of the people. The people, naturally,
wanted to keep him and make Jesus their own. Yet Jesus would
have none of it. We read:

> The crowds went in search of him, and when they found
> him they tried to keep him from leaving them. But he said
> to them, "To other towns I must announce the good news

of the reign of God, because that is why I was sent." And
he continued to preach in the synagogues of Judea.

(Lk 4:42-44)

Father Ed is not a bad priest. Far from it. He is a generous
man and a holy priest. He needs to know (and not just intellectually) that it is important to acknowledge his own needs
and limitations and allow others to minister to him. Father Ed
need not do it all but he can be a servant who calls on the gifts
of others for the common good. Above all, Father Ed needs to
find time to be alone with himself and God. Busy work and a
full schedule can be a way of avoiding oneself and God. A day
which has no time for God may be busy but it is not full. It lacks
the completeness which only God can provide. The priest who
fails to be alone with God in prayer is in danger of losing
something which may never be regained. Edwin O'Connor, in
his masterpiece *The Edge of Sadness*, has Father Hugh Kennedy offer the following description of how a priest can lose
himself in the name of being busy in the service of others:

> What he may not see is that he stands in some danger of
> losing himself in the strangely engrossing business of
> simply "being busy"; gradually he may find that he is
> rather uncomfortable when he is not "being busy." And,
> gradually too, he may find fewer and fewer moments in
> which he can absent himself from activity, in which he
> can be alone, can be silent, can be still — in which he
> can reflect and pray . . . the loss of such moments is grave
> and perilous . . . Something within him will have at-
> rophied from disuse; something precious, something vi-
> tal. It will have gone without his knowing it, but one day
> in a great crisis, say, he will reach for it and it will not be
> there. (*The Edge of Sadness*, p. 136. Quotation from
> *Pastoral Presence and the Diocesan Priest*, by Paul T.
> Keyes, p. 75)

The danger is always present that we make our work an
end in itself. Our ministry does not then point to the Lord Jesus

and it is not done out of love for others. Our ministry then becomes self-serving. It becomes our God and is beyond all criticism and correction. Anyone who questions or challenges our work is labeled ungrateful, ignorant, and even sinful. The parish, the ministry, and the projects which consume us can become a way of gaining vicarious immortality. They will be our lasting monuments to ourselves. Self-worship can replace the worship of the living God who alone gives life in abundance. What slips away from us is the deep spiritual truth that any work directed only to the self is idolatry and bound to disappoint. Gifts only become blessings when we share them for the glory of God. Gifts become selfish possessions when they are directed only to the ego.

Busy With All The Details

The predicament of Father Ed is not new. Jesus had to gently but firmly confront Martha about her compulsive attention to details while overlooking the better portion. Yet it must be stressed that Martha was a good woman. She was a person of hospitality and she paid attention to details. After all, the only reason Mary could sit at the Lord's feet and listen to his words was because Martha was busy with the details. When Jesus finished his discourse, no doubt he and Mary wanted to eat. There would have been no meal if both Mary and Martha had sat and listened to Jesus. We need the Marthas of the world (and the Father Eds) so that the basic requirements of life can proceed. Even Jesus did not say that Martha was acting sinfully. Martha was simply losing perspective and running the risk of ruining the good work she had done. Jesus did not condemn Martha. He gently corrected her ministry of hospitality which had become an end in itself.

This little episode in the life of Martha provides us with an example of the functional approach to ministry. Worth and value are earned through doing for others. If I am busy and involved with many things, I am deserving of respect. I can feel good about myself. I feel uneasy and guilty if I am not up and doing. Others value me for what I do and contribute. My personal presence is only significant when I am active through word or deed. To misquote Descartes, "I do, therefore I am." However, two destructive aspects arise which severely impair ministry, namely, a loss of personalism and an increased sense of resentment.

Martha welcomed Jesus to her home in a spirit of true hospitality. However, she soon became consumed with the many details of hospitality. These were important but *not ultimately* important. Hospitality is for persons and not persons for hospitality. The person must always remain the focus of hospitality and ministry. Martha lost sight of Jesus because she centered on the details. She forgot *why* she was *providing* hospitality in the first place, and thus ceased *to be* hospitable. Likewise, it is easy for the priest to become absorbed in the details of ministry. Details are important but not ultimately important. Jesus must be the center of priestly ministry. Jesus-centered ministry is one which touches lives, proclaims good news to those who feel rejected, and incarnates the unbounded love of God. Ministry seeks to touch and change lives. The externals and details are means and never ends. Jesus-centered ministry respects persons because they are children of God and deserving of respect.

Jesus provides us with many examples of placing persons at the center of ministry. In chapter eight of Matthew's Gospel, Jesus healed a leper (Mt 8:1-4). The conventional wisdom of the day required lepers to live apart from the healthy community. However, this leper suddenly appeared and asked Jesus to heal him. What follows is shocking: "Jesus stretched out his hand and touched him and said, 'I will do it. Be cured.' Immediately the man's leprosy disappeared" (Mt 8:3-4). Jesus could have healed the leper with his words. Jesus could have kept a safe distance and not risked involvement. Yet Jesus dared to *touch* the leper. He risked contamination and ritual impurity. Why? Jesus is showing us that true healing requires that we touch people. Authentic ministry challenges all social, religious, and ritual conventions which keep people apart.

Jesus reminds us that God ministers to our human condition by touching, becoming involved, and loving us as we are. God enters our human condition in the person of Jesus. God touches the leprosy of our hearts with the healing grace of his only Son.

Besides a diminished sense of the importance of persons in ministry, a second destructive force is resentment. Eventually, when ministry becomes an end in itself; when we forget to touch people; and we are no longer motivated by Jesus we become bitter at what we perceive to be the laziness, indifference, and ingratitude of others. We feel abused, taken for granted, and unappreciated. Martha tried to draw Jesus into her resentment and wanted him to chide Mary. Martha wanted Jesus to take notice of all she was doing and also take note of all that Mary was *not* doing. No doubt if Jesus and Mary would have offered to help, it would have been rejected as unnecessary. Martha's ministry of hospitality had lost its graciousness. It was now filled with anxiety and conflict. Jesus refused to be drawn into Martha's game. He would not counsel Mary into a busy, compulsive activity. Jesus simply reminded Martha that Mary was also showing an important dimension of hospitality — fellowship with the guest. Martha's destructive behavior would not be allowed to overwhelm Mary's choice of the better portion.

The priest of today can easily identify with Martha. The priest's day is so filled with the many activities and details of ministry. It is easy to be swallowed up in the constant tug and pull of those in need. Personal contact can become impersonal, faceless routine. Resentment can grip any heart and spread its poison to the most generous of spirits. Perhaps what is most serious about Martha, and priests like Father Ed, is the high degree of anxiety. Busyness and working in a compulsive fashion are ways of denying death. We want to avoid our temporality and limitations. One day we will be no more. The world will continue without us. Life goes on. In time we will be forgotten. This is especially painful if there are no children to carry on one's memory or story. Priests find work and the drive to build (the edifice complex) a way of being remembered. This ministry or parish will be a perpetual reminder that one lived, touched lives, and mattered to others. We made a difference and a contribution to that small part of the world which made up our everydayness. Too often, we busy ourselves with many things as a way of denying death. Our very ministry bristles with anxiety and dis-ease. Into such frenzy and denial, Jesus comes with words of peace: "Choose the better portion. Be faithful and dedicated to ministry. However, none of these will save you. Only when you learn to center your heart on me will you know a peace beyond all understanding. Only when all your doing flows from an inner being of love will there be a joy which the world cannot give or take away. Choose my words of life and be at peace, for they shall not be taken from you."

But the idea that choosing the better portion necessarily rules out the choice of an active ministry is ludicrous. The difficulty for priests, and for all Christians, is one of balance. Certainly Martha's work was necessary, and her attention to detail provided comfort for both Jesus and Mary. When Jesus held up Mary as an example of one who chose the better portion, he did not belittle or trivialize the work that Martha had done. Martha's error was one of balance, focus, losing sight of the "big picture" in her obsession with the little details. Martha's opting for activity over contemplation was not, in and of itself, bad. Rather, she made an injudicious choice in busying herself with the trivial in the presence of the Ultimate Reality.

Toward A Spirituality of Work

The clinical experience of Sigmund Freud led him to conclude that love and work were indispensable for human well-being. The healthy person is one who is able to invest himself or herself in a project or relationship outside the self. In other words, to be able to love and to work requires that we be able to forget ourselves and turn outward to the larger world of work and others. Only the mature are able to be so self-forgetful. It takes a great deal of courage to focus our time and talents on something other than what Alexis de Tocqueville

called "the puny self." Such courage and maturity are all the
more important (and too often lacking) in our "culture of
narcissism."

The Christian, too, knows the value of love and work. Yet
the Christian approaches these essential aspects of humanity
from the testimony of Scripture and the experience of the faith
community. From the opening pages of Genesis to the closing
verses of Revelation, we are offered stories of the God whose
work is love and who loves his work. The God whom we
proclaim to be the Lord of history, the Creator of all that is, and
the goal of everything which exists takes delight in his handi-
work. And what is most astounding and breathtaking is the fact
that this God wants *us* to be his partners and fellow workers on
behalf of his very good creation. We are to be his prudent,
caring, and loving stewards who respect the work of the Artist
and thereby show loving respect for him.

The work of God throughout history, as attested to by the
witness of Scripture, is threefold: creation, liberation-salva-
tion, and new creation (re-creation). The book of Genesis tells
us that God's spirit is one of order and creativity, structure and
growth. God overcomes chaos with the power of his creative
word. God takes delight in his creation and, with the creation
of the human person, we are told that "God looked at everything he had made, and he found it very good" (Gn 1:31). Even
God knows the importance of rest and the need to take pleasure
in the work of his hands. God does not compulsively go on to
the next project. Neither does God withdraw from what he has
made. Rather, when "God was finished with the work he had
been doing, he rested on the seventh day from all the work he
had undertaken. So God blessed the seventh day made it holy,
because of it he rested from all the work he had done in
creation" (Gn 2:2-3).

The work of creation begun by God must continue. Who
will take up this vocation to continue the creative work of God?
It is to the human being, man and woman, that the creative
advance is entrusted. The human being is made in the image

and likeness of God and filled with the very life breath of the Creator (Gn 1:27, 2:7). God calls the human being to care for and revere the good earth. Specifically, God calls the human person "to fill the earth and subdue it. Have dominion . . ." (Gn 1:28). This dominion is not one of control and exploitation, but a dominion which calls us "to cultivate and care for it" (Gn 2:15). The human person is called to continue the creative work of God. No task, when joined to God's work of creative love through service, is valueless. All the works of our hands give dignity to the human person when done out of praise for God and the common good of the human family. The human person realizes a deep part of his or her nature through work. In the words of Pope John Paul II, in his encyclical, "On Human Work" (*Laborem Exercens*):

> Man is made to be in the visible universe an image and likeness of God himself and he is placed in it in order to subdue the earth. From the beginning, therefore, he is called to work. Work is one of the characteristics that distinguishes man from the rest of creatures, whose activity for sustaining their lives cannot be called work. Only man is capable of work, and only man works, at the same time by work occupying his existence on earth.
>
> Thus, work bears a particular mark of man and of humanity, the mark of a person operating within a community of persons. This mark decides its interior characteristics; in a sense it constitutes its very nature. ("On Human Work," *The Pope Speaks*, Vol. 26, No. 4, 1981, p. 289)

Tragically, the very good creation of God is spoiled by human sin evidenced as egoism, pride, and rebellion against the loving will of the Creator. Work is not left unaffected by the reality of sin. Humankind rejected the high vocation of being God's steward and loving caretaker of the good earth. Rather, human will became arrogant and prideful. Such will-to-power now brings a curse instead of a blessing. In Genesis, we read:

Cursed be the ground because of you!
　　In toil shall you eat its yield
　　all the days of your life.
Thorns and thistles shall it
bring forth to you,
　　as you eat of the plants of the field.
By the sweat of your face
shall you get bread to eat,
　　Until you return to the ground,
　　from which you were taken;
For you are dirt,
　　and to dirt you shall return. (Gn 3:17-19)

A consequence of sin is the alienation of humankind from nature. The cooperative venture of man within nature has been destroyed. It will only be by toil and sweat that the basic necessities of life will be obtained. There is now a fallen, alienating, and exploiting dimension to work. The creative aspects of work must also take into account the mundane and routine. Work is no longer simply a participation in the creative work of God. Work becomes a necessity for staying alive. Work becomes the means by which we gain some measure of security. However, work also becomes a source of power, of domination over others and nature. It provides us with the illusion that we are self-sufficient. Because of sin, the work of God now becomes that of liberation and salvation. God's loving attention turns from creation to history.

God does not abandon his creation but further commits himself to what his creative word has brought into existence. God's love is not only creative but also salvific. The good creation has been wounded by human sin. Nature and humankind are in need of healing and God's healing love will be offered. The Lord God chooses for himself a people, the Israelites, and calls them to be his instrument in history bearing the message of salvation. Israel is a sign to all the nations of the might and justice of Yahweh. Israel's special mission is to be a sacrament, a revelation, of the mighty creative and liberating acts of God. The God who spoke creation into existence and liberated the Hebrews from bondage in Egypt is the same God who calls all peoples to be saved. The earth and all that is in it belongs to the Lord. The words of the Psalmist beautifully capture the connection between creation, liberation, and the role of Israel in salvation history:

> Shout joyfully to God, all you on earth,
>   sing praise to the glory of his name;
>   proclaim his glorious praise.
> Say to God, "How tremendous are your deeds!
>   for your great strength your enemies
>   fawn upon you.
> Let all on earth worship and
> sing praise to you,
>   sing praise to your name!"
> Come and see the works of God,
>   his tremendous deeds among men.
> He has changed the sea into dry land;
>   through the river they passed on foot;
>   therefore let us rejoice in him . . .
> Bless our God, you peoples;
>   loudly sound his praise;
> He has given life to our souls,
> and has not let our feet slip. (Ps 66:1-4, 5-7, 9)

The salvific love of God reaches its ultimate expression and is made visible in the person of Jesus of Nazareth. God's work of salvation is entrusted in a decisive way to Jesus. Jesus comes to do the will of the Father who sent him. The work that Jesus is sent to do is to make known the Father's name which is Love and to liberate humankind from its ultimate enemies, sin and death. The will of the Father, the work Jesus is sent to accomplish, does not come at a cheap price. Jesus must accept his baptism of fire and drink the cup of his passion and death. It is on the Cross that the glory of God is revealed. The very heart of God is made known as suffering, enduring love. Through the death of Jesus on the Cross, sin is denied ultimate victory and death will not have the last word.

The Jesus who died on the Cross is also the Jesus who is risen and lives at the right hand of the Father. The creative, salvific work of God invites us to hope. The Cross of Good Friday passes into the Empty Tomb and the proclamation, "He is risen!" The God who creates and saves is also the Lord of the new creation. God did not abandon his creation with the fall of humankind. Likewise, Jesus does not leave the community of faith orphaned as he returns to the Father. Jesus sends the Paraclete, the Holy Spirit, who abides within the heart of each disciple, and the community as a whole. Until the Lord returns in the fullness of glory, the Church, by the power of the Spirit, is given the mission to help renew the face of the earth. The old order has passed away and all is made new in Christ. The Church, through the Spirit, continues to proclaim the good news of salvation. Because of Jesus' victory, we have the hope of forgiveness of sin, reconciliation, and being born anew.

The Church as the community of hope proclaims the message of the new creation. Each person who opens his or her heart to the Spirit is born again. The work of the Spirit is the work of the new creation. In the words of St. Paul:

> This means that if anyone is in Christ, he is a new creation. The old order has passed away; now all is new! All this has been done by God, who has reconciled us to himself through Christ and has given us the ministry of reconciliation. (2 Cor 5:17-18)

The message of reconciliation and the hope of a new creation is entrusted to the Church. In the midst of sin, death, cynicism, and pain, the Church proclaims, "now all is new!" Certainly this is a hope and a vision based on the promises of the One who is ever faithful. Paul continues his message to the Corinthians by reminding them (and us) that they are "ambassadors for Christ, God as it were appealing through us" (2 Cor 5:20). Such a vision of the new creation with its ministry of reconciliation and hope has tough going in today's rationalistic, pragmatic, and cynical world. Yet the message and ministry of reconciliation and the hope of a new creation are ours. In the boldest possible terms, we proclaim the vision of John on Patmos:

> Then I saw new heavens and a new earth. The former heavens and the former earth had passed away, and the sea was no longer. I also saw a new Jerusalem, the holy city, coming down out of heaven from God, beautiful as a bride prepared to meet her husband. I heard a loud voice from the throne cry out: "This is God's dwelling among men. He shall dwell with them and they shall be his people and he shall be their God who is always with them. He shall wipe every tear from their eyes, and there shall be no more death or mourning, crying out or pain, for the former world has passed away. Rv 21:1-4)

The concept of the spirituality of work expressed above is Trinitarian: creation, salvation, and reconciliation, with its hope of a new creation. This spirituality of work is relevant for a spirituality of priestly ministry. The work of the priest is not simply spiritual, but it must be grounded in, and strengthened by, a spirituality. The priest, as leader of the community of faith, is called to be the disclosure model of God's creative, salvific, and reconciling work. The priest is called not only to reveal this Trinitarian work of love but also to call forth from and empower others to use their gifts for the common good in Christ.

The priest reminds those whom he serves of the dignity of every person and the dignity of *all* work as it relates to the creative advance of God in history. Each person is given a special work to do and a unique way of continuing God's creative work begun in Genesis. All work, from the great advances in science to the most ordinary tasks of daily life, have great value as part of God's evolving plan. Above all, the priest reminds each person that he or she is always superior to and more valued than the work produced. The worth of a person cannot be reduced to one's ability to produce or consume. Pope John Paul II, in a homily delivered to 130,000 workers in South Korea, put it this way:

The Son of God became man and worked with human hands. *Work*, then has a dignity of its own in *God's plan for creation.* . .

So we know, not only by reason alone but through Revelation, that by his work man shares in the Creator's work. He continues it and, in a sense, perfects it by his own work. . .

Jesus himself gave particular emphasis to this truth: That through His work man shares in the activity of the Creator. . . From Jesus' own teaching we can see that *man who works is much more important than the product of his work.* Human work comes from man; it is intended to benefit man, to promote his God-given dignity. ("Human Work," *The Pope Speaks*, Vol. 29, No. 3, 1984, pp. 225-26, emphasis in the original)

The priest dwells within the community of faith as God's man of healing love and the grace of total acceptance. The priest ministers this healing and accepting love in a special way through the Sacraments of Reconciliation, Eucharist, and Anointing of the Sick. The priest makes visible by his words and actions the unbounded love of God. The priest people turn to is one who lures people with a vision of the God who is madly in love with us. The priest people turn to is one who offers them the good news of salvation. All who are lost, hurt, confused, sick, in need of compassion, and filled with fear and guilt are offered the words of new life. Each priest must again and again follow Jesus' example and open the scroll where it is written:

The Spirit of the Lord is upon me;
    therefore he has anointed me.
He has sent me to bring glad tidings
to the poor,
    to proclaim liberty to captives,
Recovery of sight to the blind
    and release to prisoners,
To announce a year of favor from the Lord. (Lk 4:18-19)

The priest is God's man of hope. He proclaims the new creation. The priest continually proclaims the hope of a new beginning and the possibility of starting again. Sin and death, the ultimate enemies, will not have the final word. The Really Real has won the ultimate victory in Jesus. Life is stronger than death; darkness is overcome by an invincible Light; hope and not despair is at the center of the human condition; and sin has been conquered by the abundance of grace. The God of surprises is at work calling us to ever greater heights of love, hope, and adventure. We are a pilgrim people who go forth in hope and are bound together in the trust of a loving God who told us "to fear not." The priest people turn to, and the priest who leads the community of faith, is one who lures others to the God who is Absolute Future and the God who dwells in our midst. The God in whom we hope is at work even now!

The exciting, demanding, adventurous but never boring, work of the priest is that of continuing the creative, salvific, and renewing-reconciling work of God. The priest must be a man of vision and hope. He is a man of confidence in the Spirit and engenders confidence in others. The priest does not feel that he has to do everything himself. He has the ability to call forth what is best in others for the common good. "Burnout" can often result from the priest trying to do everything himself. There is always another project to be started and not enough time to finish the many details of the present project. Too often, we don't allow ourselves the time to rest and see that our ministry is good. We don't extend to ourselves the delight which God permitted himself after creation. Yet if we are to participate in God's creative work, we must also allow ourselves the sense of inner satisfaction which comes from work. Any authentic spirituality of work must allow for, and in fact encourage, quiet time, prayer, study, reflection, and a good sense of inner wholeness. The priest people turn to is one who has integrated such time and disciplines within his life and helps the community to do likewise.

A spirituality of work must always be grounded in the reality of grace. All that we have, are, and hope to be is pure gift from our loving God. The old arguments over grace and works establish a false alternative. We don't choose either

grace or works. Both are present. It is God's amazing grace
which provides us with the talents, resources, and skills for all
that we do and build as a society. All of our ministries and
projects flow from grace. Simply put, grace empowers,
grounds, and directs our work and our good work is a response
to the gift of grace. In the end, we come gratefully to realize the
truth of St. Paul's words:

> It is not ourselves we preach but Christ Jesus as Lord, and
> ourselves as your servants for Jesus' sake . . . to make it
> clear that its surpassing power comes from God and not
> from us . . . We do not lose heart, because our inner being
> is renewed each day . . . We do not fix our gaze on what is
> seen but on what is unseen. What is seen is transitory;
> what is unseen lasts forever. (2 Cor 4:5, 7, 16, 18)

A Concluding Word on Grace

What we moderns (priests included) try to avoid is the
reality of the giftedness of all that is. The fact that there is
something rather than nothing invites us to the deeper realization that this something has been given as pure gift. My
existence is not of my own making or choosing. I am here
because of a power beyond myself. I owe my very being to the
Being which makes all being possible. Such talk is too often
dismissed as metaphysical or theological babble. Straight talk
calls for us to gain control of our world and make something of
ourselves. The reality principle of the contemporary mind is
one which tells us that we are our "own-most." The human
project is to acquire, gain power, and have an impact on the
world. At the center of our doing is the ego driving us relent-
lessly to the goals and prizes of this world whose glory passes
away. In the end, we are left empty and disappointed.

In spite of all our compulsive activity, frenzied ministry,
and anxiety over the many things of daily life, we simply can't
shake the deep down feeling of being *called* by a power greater
than ourselves. We are aware, however dimly, of the wonder of
creation and the sheer miracle of our existence. Regardless of

what we have been told, we feel grasped by a sense of wonder and awe. We grasp, or rather we are grasped by, a rumor of angels which signals that the Ultimate Reality cares about us. Even more, this Ultimate Being has revealed itself in Jesus and desires that we respond in love. We do not need to earn the gift of life or the grace of this unbounded love. Life and love are not bestowed through our well-earned efforts, but as a pure gift from a loving God. Rabbi Abraham Heschel has put it this way:

> The soul is endowed with a sense of indebtedness, and wonder, awe and fear unlock that sense of indebtedness. . .
>
> In spite of our pride, in spite of our acquisitiveness, we are driven by an awareness that something is asked of us; that we are asked to wonder, to revere, to think and to live in a way that is compatible with the grandeur and mystery of living. . . The more deeply we listen, the more we become stripped of the arrogance and callousness which alone would enable us to refuse. . .
>
> The awareness of being asked is easily repressed, for it is an echo of the intimation that is small and still. It will not, however, remain forever subdued. The day comes when the still small intimation becomes "like the wind and storm, fulfilling His word." (See *Man Is Not Alone* and *God in Search of Man*)

Rabbi Heschel has put his finger on our struggle as well as our hope: the need to listen more deeply. Martha could not listen because she was too busy with the many details of hospitality. The priest often allows himself little time for prayer, reflection, study, and simply being alone with the alone. The many details of ministry consume our day as we are pulled in a hundred different directions. All the appointments, meetings, and functions are important. But they are not ultimately important. What is ultimately important is the One who calls us by name. We can only hear his voice if we follow the example of Mary and choose the better portion. We don't turn our back on our daily commitments. Rather, we experience our ministry as a way of loving God and others. We do not need to prove our worth or show God that we are deserving. By the mere fact that we exist, and we are called to do God's work on earth, a deep sense of gratitude fills our hearts. "There are moments," writes Rabbi Heschel, "in which there is a lifting of the veil at the horizon of the known, opening a vision of what is eternal in time."

Within the horizon of our everydayness, with all its banality and profaneness, there are moments of grace and signals of transcendence. In the midst of a sermon, a confession, a Sunday afternoon baptism, the simple answering of the telephone, a wave of grace and divine acceptance floods our being. In the midst of what can so easily be predictable and standard, we see the world and what we are doing with fresh eyes and a renewed heart. When we feel that the world is too much with us and we can go no farther, the words of Israel's great prophet lift us up on eagle's wings:

> Comfort, give comfort to my people,
>> says your God.
> Speak tenderly to Jerusalem,
> and proclaim to her
>> that her service is at an end,
>> her guilt expiated . . .
>
> Go up onto a high mountain,
>> Zion, herald of glad tidings;
> Cry out at the top of your voice,
>> Jerusalem, herald of good news!
>
> Like a shepherd he feeds his flock;
>> in his arms he gathers the lambs,
> Carrying them in his bosom,
>> and leading the ewes with care. (Is 40:1-2, 9, 11)

The God in whose name we minister is not the God of compulsive work and anxious attempts to win salvation. Our God is one of comfort and good news. The God in whose name we work in love is the God who desires to draw us to himself. The priest people turn to is one who learns how to listen to the Lord and can help them do the same.

CHAPTER SIX

PAUL:
The Priest as Preacher

The Second Vatican Council's *Decree on the Ministry and Life of Priests* accords a primary place to preaching and the ministry of the word of God. We read:

> The People of God are joined together primarily by the word of the living God. And rightfully, they expect this from their priests. Since no one can be saved who does not first believe, priests, as co-workers with their bishops, have the primary duty of proclaiming the Gospel of God to all. In this way, they fulfill the command of the Lord: "Going therefore into the whole world preach the Gospel to every creature" (Mark 16:15), and they establish and build up the People of God. (#4)

The Decree goes on to take note that "priestly preaching is often very difficult in the circumstances of the modern world." To preach the Gospel in the modern context requires that the word of God illuminate and provide meaning to the human condition. The light of the Gospel's truth must be gently but confidently brought to bear on the problems and possibilities of the human heart and human family. Abstract, disembodied preaching of theology will only serve to hinder the living word of God. The priest is called and commissioned not merely to fill the air with words, but he is to help "the word become flesh." To preach is to give visible, fleshy testimony to what one is inviting others to believe, hope, and love. One of the great preachers of our time, Father Walter J. Burghardt, S.J., expresses this need to incarnate the word as follows:

> A word is real; a word is sacred; a word is powerful; a word is . . . I.
>
> Ultimately, *I am* the word, the word that is heard. And — I say it fearfully — it is not a clever rhetorician the people need, but a holy homilist. Holy in what sense? Because aware that I am only *a* word, not *the* word; if God does not speak through me, I am "a noisy gong, a clanging cymbal" (1 Cor 13:1). Because my homily is a prayer: in preparation and pulpit, I stand before God in praise of Him, not of my own rhetorical perfection. Because aware of my own weakness: I too need the word I preach, I too need forgiveness, I too am vulnerable, I am a *wounded* healer. Because, like my healers, I too ceaseless murmur: "I believe, Lord, help my unbelief." Because I am in love: with the things of God, with the people of God, with God Himself. Because the hungers of God's family are my hungers: when they bleed, I weep. Unless some of this breaks through, the word may indeed be proclaimed, but it will hardly be heard. The word is . . . I. (*Tell the Next Generation*, pp. 6, 16)

Yet for all the importance given to the priestly ministry of preaching by the Second Vatican Council and the eloquence of such preachers as Father Burghardt, honesty compels us to admit that the general quality of the Sunday sermon is poor. Father Andrew M. Greeley and his associates at the National Opinion Research Center (NORC), through extensive surveys and interviews with the Catholic laity, are forced to conclude:

> . . . the strongest correlate of church attendance and Catholic identification for both the young people and for the general Catholic population were not issues of sex, birth control, abortion and the ordination of women. Rather, the strongest predictor of Catholic behavior and identification was the quality of the Sunday sermon

preached in the respondent's parish church. Unfortunately for both the clergy and laity, only a fifth of the Catholic adults . . . and a tenth of the young adults . . . thought that the quality of the Sunday sermon which they might hear in their parish church was "excellent." That which is most important among priestly activities (at least insofar as it relates to the religious behavior of the laity) is also that which priests seem to do, at least in the judgment of their laity, most poorly. (*American Catholics Since the Council*, pp. 112-113)

Furthermore, Catholics are, contrary to popular opinion and media elites, coming back to the Catholic Church. Catholics are returning and providing Church leadership with a grace moment (*kairos*) to learn why they are returning, how we can minister to those returning, and how we can enhance the process of returning home in the future. This will call for a great deal of pastoral prudence and sensitivity. Church leadership will have to listen and ponder all three things in its collective heart. But one thing is for sure: priests are very important in the lives of those who return. And secondly, the empirical evidence indicates that the Sunday sermon was the crucial thing the priest did well. A good sermon moved the drifting and the drifted away Catholic to give it one more try or to finally return to the community of one's religious beginnings. Again we turn to Father Greeley and his sister, Dr. Mary Durkin:

> . . . priests have a powerful positive influence which can draw people into the church. In our study of young adults, we discovered that those young people who describe themselves as closer to the church than they were five years ago were five times as likely as those who were still at the fringes of the church to say that they had a close personal relationship with a priest. Moreover, they were six times as likely . . . to say that the sermons that they heard were excellent. For young people in their thirties, at any rate, the influence of the priest/confidant and of **the priest who was an excellent preacher as a factor in**

leading to the return to the church is very powerful indeed. (*A Church to Come Home to*, pp. 39, 67)

To Sow The Word

Preaching the word of God has never been easy. Jesus, in his parable of the seed (Mt 13:1-23), highlighted the major obstacles to sowing the word of God. First, there is the word that falls on the footpath and is easily snatched away by the devil. There is a lack of understanding on the part of the one who hears the word. This lack of understanding is not an intellectual deficiency, but a failure to integrate the word of God into one's heart and everyday life. If the word of God simply remains an intellectual exercise or an exercise in academics, then the word is easily lost by crafty arguments and idle speculations. The word of God remains on the surface and cannot sustain one in the face of the many rival explanations. The one who hears in such a manner usually falls victim to skepticism or disillusionment which yields a harvest of cynicism.

Secondly, there is the word that is heard and accepted with great joy and enthusiasm. However, there is a lack of depth and commitment to the word. When opposition and trials come, the person feels cheated. The word is received one-dimensionally, that is, in such a way that the Cross is negated. The person is willing to follow Jesus and serve the Kingdom as long as there is no real suffering or dying to self. Unfortunately, when the forces of darkness gather, the person falters.

Thirdly, a person can hear the word of God, but his heart is too filled with the anxieties and worries of everyday life. The word of God is blocked off by the many concerns of self and the need to obtain worldly security through material possessions. The word of God becomes one word among many words promising happiness, peace, and freedom. In time, however, the promises of the world leave one empty. The abundance of material possessions, the acquisition of power, and the acclaim of others provide us with a yield of bitterness and disappointment.

Finally, there is the open, receptive heart which hears the word of God and takes it in. Such a heart is searching for more than intellectual understanding or academic information. There is a depth of commitment to the word of God which is willing to accept opposition from the world. The heart of such a person centers himself or herself on the promises of God's love. Within such a heart, the daily concerns of life are real but they do not cause a level of anxiety which drives one to seek security in worldly honors, power, or material possessions. A heart which is open to the word is an abundant heart. It experiences a harvest of mature joy, inner peace, and a richness which the world cannot provide.

Jesus' parable of the seed is addressed to those who hear the word of God. The sower of the seed bears responsibility as well for the harvest. After all, it was the sower who tossed the seed on the footpath, on the rocks, and among the thorns. The heart of the hearer can be open and well-disposed to receive God's word but the preacher may not exercise the proper care for sowing the word of the Lord. For a fruitful harvest, there must be a covenant between the preacher and the hearer of the word. The well prepared heart of the hearer requires the preacher to be clear about the message, the manner, and the moment.

The Message

The Apostle Paul, in his first letter to the Corinthians, provides the fundamental message for all preaching:

> As for myself, brothers, when I came to you I did not come proclaiming God's testimony with any particular eloquence or "wisdom." No, I determined that while I was with you I would speak of nothing but Jesus Christ and him crucified. When I came among you it was in weakness and fear, and with much trepidation. My message and my preaching had none of the persuasive force of "wise" argumentation, but the convincing power of the Spirit. As a consequence, your faith rests not on the wisdom of man but on the power of God. (1 Cor 2:1-5)

Paul was not anti-intellectual. After all, faith does seek
understanding and we are to be ready to provide a reason for
our hope. Paul preached not from human knowledge but from
the very wisdom of God made visible in Jesus. The message for
every preacher is the person of Jesus Christ. While not reject-
ing eloquence, philosophy, and rhetorical skills, Paul is aware
of how easily these can become a source of human pride. We
are in danger of preaching ourselves and not Jesus Christ and
him crucified. The Jesus preached is not an abstract idea but
the very living Son of God and Lord of our lives. The Jesus
proclaimed is one who lights up our life; inspires our days;
carries us through trials; provides rest at the end of our day;
and is the one, true hope of glory. The message of the preacher
is the living person of Jesus whom he has met and wants to
share with others. The message about Jesus rings true because
it comes from one who has met Jesus. The preacher's heart is
aflame with Jesus and he inflames the hearts of the faith
community.

In proclaiming Jesus, we proclaim a crucified and risen
Lord. This is a scandal and offense to the world. The temptation is always present to remove this scandal so that the
message and the messenger will be more readily received. The
temptation in our media conscious age is to package the
message of the Crucified God so no one will be offended or
turned off. Yet if no one is turned off, neither is anyone turned
on to the person of Jesus and the Kingdom of God. Simply put,
there is something offensive, troubling and challenging about
Jesus. The crucified and risen Lord is the source of our
authority. Without the Jesus of Good Friday and the Christ of
Easter Sunday, we are still in our sin and we are the most
pitiable of men (1 Cor 15:19).

The priest is called by God on behalf of the community to
lead them to Christ. At the heart of this call and the center of
this service is the preaching of Jesus as Lord. All forms of
ministry return again and again to the person of Jesus. The
priest is the ambassador of Christ and represents Christ to the
world. It is in preaching Christ and him crucified that the

priest does his priesthood and serves the community. In the words of Father Karl Rahner, S.J.:

> He [the priest] is the envoy, the representative of Christ and the Father, the steward of the mysteries of God (1 Cor 4:1); he is the fellow-worker of God (1 Cor 3:9). It is said of the apostles, the first priests, that they are Christ's friends (Jn 15:15), that they bear witness to Christ (Ac 1:8), that in a particularly impressive way they are the heralds, the preachers of the word of God (Rm 15:16). Always and everywhere among all nations and at all times, they preach *metanoia*, the advent of the Kingdom of God. They preach the good news, but Christ's mandate, as his envoy (Ep 3:8). Their task is described as the ministry of the word. (*The Priesthood*, pp. 105-106)

The Manner

Once again, we turn to the words of the Apostle Paul: "When I came among you it was in weakness and fear, and with much trepidation" (1 Cor 2:3). The manner of preaching is an essential part of the message. The manner involves more than good posture, clear outlines, eye contact, and even scholarly preparation (though none of these should be minimized). The manner of preaching calls for the preacher to look inward and prepare his heart to listen, pray, and ponder before he dares to be God's man in the pulpit. The preacher must feel the awesome weight of his call to proclaim the word of the Lord. The preacher must inwardly prepare himself to be open to the Spirit who speaks to and through his spirit.

The great preacher Paul preached Christ crucified not in a spirit of arrogance and self-righteousness, but "in weakness and fear, and with much trepidation." The message of Christ is mediated through the poor, limited, and sinful flesh of the priest. The preacher must always be the first to hear the word and be open to its call to repentance and a decision for Jesus and the Kingdom. The priest who fails to live under the proclaimed word will find that, in the end, he is disqualified.

The priest who ignores his own sinfulness and need for forgiveness may win many souls for Christ, build churches, and gain renown as a pastor (for grace does not depend on the worthiness of the minister), but suffer the loss of his own soul. If the physician is called by Jesus to heal himself, so much more is the preacher called to prayerfully ponder the word he proclaims.

The priest who is able to accept his own sinful limitations is able to touch the minds and hearts of the community. Such a priest stands before the community as a man who is able to be compassionate, understanding, and challenging, while offering a vision of hope and new beginnings. The community sees, with the eye of faith, God's herald who is also adept at listening to the message. The words of such a preacher contain the attractiveness and power of one who lives the message. The preacher can speak about sin and grace, despair and hope, death and life, sadness and joy because all of these are present and at work in him. The preacher does not proclaim himself, but offers his life as testimony of what God can do through grace. St. Paul, writing to the Galatians, offered his own life story as an example of God's generosity:

> You have heard, I know, the story of my former way of life in Judaism. You know that I went to extremes in persecuting the church of God and tried to destroy it . . .
> But the time came when he who had set me apart before I was born and called by his favor chose to reveal his Son to me that I might spread among the Gentiles the good tidings concerning him. (Gal 1:13, 15-16)

The Moment

Pulpit time is holy time and transcends the bounds of Rolex time. There is no time more precious than when the word of the Lord is proclaimed, preached, and received. It is a time (*kairos*) when the community is addressed by the living God and called to a decision. Within the particularity of each person's situation (and the word of God is always addressed in a particular way to an individual heart), the word of God comes

as a two-edged sword. Each person finds himself or herself
addressed and called to make a decision for or against the
Kingdom. The word as proclaimed and preached never leaves
one indifferent or unchanged. Even when one ignores the word
or is moved to boredom by a too familiar passage or deficient
sermon, one is summoned by God. To ignore or pretend indifference is itself a decision. The time of preaching is a time of grace
and a time when our hearts are revealed by our responses.

The preacher must always be aware that his time in the
pulpit ultimately belongs to God and his grace. While grace
favors the well-prepared mind, the preacher must never forget
that it is God's word which is being proclaimed. It is God's word
of grace which alone can cut through the countless other words
which fill the heart and cause distraction. Only the word of the
Lord has the power to rouse us out of our sinfulness, compla-
cency, and boredom. God's word of grace comes to us with an
urgency which demands a response. There is no later and more
convenient hour to consider the message. In the words of St.
Paul: "We who live by day must be alert, putting on faith and
love as a breastplate and the hope of salvation as a helmet" (1 Th
5:8). The word of the Lord is not one word among other words
but *the* Word which makes all other words meaningful. The
word of the Lord serves as the horizon against which all human
words are judged. The word of the Lord is the word of grace
which awakes us to acceptance and total love.

The message, the manner, and the moment can be neatly
divided on paper. These three blend together to form one
reality. This one reality of God's grace always runs the risk of
being understood intellectually, yet lacking a flesh and blood
believability. The message, the manner, and the moment must
be found at work in the preacher. And they must be found in the
same way in which we find them in the Preacher from Galilee.

To Preach As Jesus Did

All three aspects of God's saving word — message, manner, and moment — are found at work in the person of Jesus.

The central theme of Jesus' preaching is this: "This is the time of fulfillment. The reign of God is at hand! Reform your lives and believe in the gospel!" (Mk 1:15). With these brief words, Jesus announced the message of the decisive action by God against sin and for humankind. The active rule of God is about to become visible in a way not imagined and with a grace beyond human measure. The year of the Lord's favor is at work and made visible in the person of Jesus. Jesus is both the one who preaches the Kingdom and embodies the Kingdom itself. God is now actively showing his mighty works of love in Jesus. How do we know this to be so? Jesus himself responded this way:

> Go back and report to John what you hear and see: the blind recover their sight, cripples walk, lepers are cured, the deaf hear, dead men are raised to life, and the poor have the good news preached to them. (Mt 11:4-5)

The active rule of God's liberating love is visible in Jesus who forgives sins, heals the sick, expels demons, and has table-fellowship with the wretched of the earth. Jesus did not merely preach words but his words are given the eloquence and power which comes from a life that gives flesh to the preached word. Jesus touched the sick as he called them to healing. Jesus went to the house of sinners for a meal and celebrated their return to the Father. Jesus did not tell the lost to return home, but he actively sought them out and indicated that all of heaven was rejoicing. Jesus did not tell the sick to shape up or ship out, but he loved those who needed the healing love of the Divine Physician. What is the Kingdom? How do we know it is among us and within us? Simple. Just look to the person of Jesus.

The message of the Kingdom calls for a reforming of one's life. This conversion, or *metanoia*, does not result from fear of being crushed in the hands of an angry God. Rather, the call to conversion is extended by a loving God through Jesus. Jesus did not come to crush people under the weight of a heavy law or the burden of a greater guilt. Jesus came preaching a gospel, a good news, which offers rest to the weary, the heavy laden, and those who are cut deep by the yoke of external religion. Jesus was continually moved to compassion because of the daily burdens of the people. Jesus is the Good Shepherd who lay down his life so that the ultimate enemy, sin, can be conquered. Jesus entered into the crucible of the human condition so as to be one in love with us. It is by drinking the chalice given by the Father that we are healed. In the words from Isaiah:

> Yet it was our infirmities that he bore,
> our sufferings that he endured,
> While we thought of him as stricken,
> as one smitten by God and afflicted.
> But he was pierced for our offenses,
> crushed for our sins,
> Upon him was the chastisement
> that makes us whole,
> by his stripes we were healed. (Is 53:4-5)

The manner and the message are one in Jesus, namely, both proclaim a time of new life and healing love. Jesus did not offer a word of grace without making that grace visible. Jesus did not merely talk about forgiveness, but he extends forgiveness and fellowship to those who are in need. The motivation for repentance is the offer of a splendid hope and an unbelievable opportunity to live a new way. If we reject Jesus' offer, it is because we don't want nor believe in good news. If one fails to preach in the manner and with the message of Jesus, then one becomes, in the words of St. Paul, "a noisy gong, a clanging cymbal."

The central theme or message of Jesus is the reign of God. And it is at hand. The kingly reign of God is taking place this very moment. There is an urgency that requires of the hearer a decision. There can be no delays. Even the most pressing of worldly obligations and family considerations can stand in the way of following Jesus and the Kingdom. Jesus told the parable of a man who gave a dinner. When everything was ready, the guests began to excuse themselves: one had to survey some newly acquired land; another bought some oxen which needed to be tested; a third guest had just gotten married which required him to be elsewhere; a final guest had to bury his father. None of these obligations were of sufficient weight to take precedence over the invitation to the banquet (Lk 14:12-23). So it is with the invitation to the heavenly banquet in the Kingdom of God. Such an invitation is extended to all peoples. Only the foolish refuse to come and find other concerns more pressing.

The appropriate response to Jesus' invitation to the Kingdom is one of total joy and the immediate following of Jesus. One becomes divested of all earthly entanglements so as to be free for a complete response to Jesus. Several of Jesus' parables highlight the ultimate importance of the Kingdom. Every other possession, commitment, and treasure pales in comparison. The following passage from the Gospel of Matthew indicates the great joy and decisive manner present when one is open to the Kingdom:

> The reign of God is like a buried treasure which a man found in a field. He hid it again, and rejoicing at his find went and sold all he had and bought that field. Or again, the kingdom of heaven is like a merchant's search for fine pearls. When he found one really valuable pearl, he went back and put up for sale all that he had and bought it. (Mt 13:44-46)

No doubt the man did not expect to find a treasure. He was surprised by the reality of a pure gift (grace). He went away thrilled at the thought of his good fortune. All of his possessions together could not equal the treasure hidden in the field or the pearl of great price. There was no time to waste or play it safe. Someone else might have found the treasure and jumped his claim. An equally shrewd buyer might have come along and spotted the pearl. To delay is to miss out on an opportunity which may never come again. The man in the field and in the marketplace came to realize that what was once so valuable pales in comparison to what has been found. The only thing that can ruin this opportunity is timidity. The merchant was not forced to buy the pearl. Neither will Jesus force anyone to accept the Kingdom. A free response is crucial. Now is the time.

To preach as Jesus did is to proclaim the present and future reign of God as the pearl of great price and the treasure hidden in the field of our everyday lives. All that we hold dear and of great importance runs a poor second when compared to what is being offered to us. The priest who preaches as Jesus preached is one who offers a message in a manner which inspires, invites, challenges, and lures one to live in a new way. We no longer need live in fear and look for security in the things of this world. We have been liberated for the Kingdom which empowers us to love God, self, and neighbor. The Kingdom of God invites us to hope and look through the present moment in order to see what is awaiting those who love God. The invitation to the Kingdom is offered here and now. Our response of acceptance must be here and now as well. The testimony of Paul must become that of the preacher and parishioner as well:

> But those things I used to consider gain I have now reappraised as loss in the light of Christ. I have come to rate all as loss in the light of the surpassing knowledge of my Lord Jesus Christ. For his sake I have forfeited everything; I have accounted all else rubbish so that Christ may be my wealth and I may be in him, not having any justice of my own based on observance of the law. The justice I possess is that which comes through faith in Christ. (Ph 3:7-9)

Pastoral Preaching: A Pauline Perspective

An essential pastoral ministry of the Church and the priest is preaching. The pastoral Church is the community which heralds the Lordship of Jesus Christ. The great preacher and pastor of the early Church, Paul of Tarsus, teaches us that pastoral preaching involves three interrelated elements: the power of grace working through a wounded healer; the need for moral excellence; and the reality of opposition to the preaching of the Gospel. A brief word about each is in order.

1. *"I thank Christ Jesus our Lord, who strengthened me. . . I was once a blasphemer, a persecutor, a man filled with arrogance . . . but I have been treated mercifully . . . that I might become an example to those who would later have faith in him and gain everlasting life" (2 Tm 1:12-17).*

   The pastoral preacher is a *wounded* healer. The preacher begins with the reality of *his* own sinful condition. Every preacher falls short of the glory of God and must be ever mindful of, and thankful for, God's work of grace. Such a priest who preaches from his wounded yet graced human nature is a priest people turn to because such a priest turns to them in love and humility. We cannot deny our past sins and rejections of God. Our sins are before us. Yet even more before our eyes is the abundance of grace. The preacher as wounded healer becomes a flesh and blood example of what God's love can do. The preacher who has been treated mercifully will be moved to treat *other* sinners with compassion. Those who are fearful and imprisoned by past sin and guilt will be encouraged to turn to the Lord. Why? Because those who are fearful will see in their pastor a word of grace preached by one who has received such a word himself. What the preacher has been given he now joyfully shares in return.

2. *"The grace of God has appeared, offering salvation to all men. It trains us to reject godless ways and worldly desires, and live temperately, justly, and devoutly in this age as we await our blessed hope, the appearing of the glory of the great God and our Savior Christ Jesus" (Tt 2:11-13).*

   The reality of our wounded condition is not an invitation to more laxity. The preacher struggles with his own sinfulness, all the while doing his best to inspire others to live a life worthy of their calling. The preacher must be a man of virtue who challenges others to follow the way into Jesus. God's grace is given so the leaders of the community will offer disclosure models of true joy and peace as the fruits of the Holy Spirit. The virtues of the pastoral preacher include integrity, piety, faith, love, steadfastness, and a gentle spirit (1 Tm 6:11). The temptation is always present to say that the word preached does not depend on my personal holiness. God's word of grace is independent of personal holiness by the priest. True enough. But this does not mean personal holiness and priestly integrity are of no consequence. We are a community of faith in which more is required than the *objective* administration of the sacraments and the preaching of an *objective* word. The existential, subjective integrity of the preacher is crucial. The objective word preached and the sacrament celebrated call both priest and community to holy conversion. In the words of Father Karl Rahner, S.J.:

> The priesthood of the church is completely the priesthood of holy men and not holders of office for whose meaning and importance this personal holiness is a matter of indifference . . . the merely institutional priest of the *opus operatum*, who does not fill this with the whole force of his personality, thus sustaining what he does, preaches, ministers and so on, is not the person he ought to be . . . how understandable it is therefore when the Western priest wants and is also urged by the church to be more than a mere "massing priest," only taking care of the continuation of objective cult and objective administration of the sacraments in the church. (*The Priesthood*, pp. 111, 112, 113)

3. *"Remember that Jesus Christ, a descendant of David, was raised from the dead. This is the gospel I preach; in preaching it I suffer as a criminal, even to the point of being thrown into chains — but there is no chaining the word of God!"* (2 Tm 2:8-9).

Opposition to the Gospel has been and will always be with us until the Lord Jesus comes in glory. Jesus was not spared this hostility and neither will those who preach the Gospel in his name: "If you find that the world hates you, know that it has hated me before you. If you belonged to the world, it would love you as its own; the reason it hates you is that you do not belong to the world" (Jn 15:18-19). The hatred of the world was turned against Paul. He suffered loss of worldly reputation, imprisonment, beatings, and countless hardships for the sake of the Gospel. The world does not want to hear good news. The world stands in opposition to anything which challenges the trinity of greed, lust, and power. Yet what we preach is Jesus crucified and risen. We preach the good news and the hope of glory offered to us from the unbounded love of God.

The priest people turn to for a word of comfort, inspiration, and challenge is the priest who preaches the Gospel in the best of times and the worst of times. He does so because he knows that all time is in God's loving hands. The priest who dares preach the Gospel and climb into the pulpit is a preacher who is:

> afflicted in every way possible, but not crushed; full of doubts, but never given to despair; persecuted but never abandoned; struck down but never destroyed; continually carrying the dying of Jesus, so that the life of Jesus may also be revealed. (2 Cor 4:8-10)

CHAPTER SEVEN

HEBREWS:
The Priest and Liturgical Celebration

In Chapter Two, I advanced the notion that the priest, like John the Baptizer, is a man called to dwell in mystery. The priest is called to proclaim the God who is totally Other, yet near at hand. The priest points to those signals of transcendence and rumors of angels which speak of that other dimension active in the marrow of everydayness. The priest invites the community of faith to look beyond the bread they eat and the cup they share; to look beyond the visible and the ordinary; to see in the dying of this old world the signs of the new creation begun in Christ.

I also indicated that the term "mystery" was highly problematic in the modern context with its scientific and technological social construction of reality. The major reality policemen, those who define what is true, beautiful, and good, tell us that only the measurable, quantifiable, and empirical deserve the label "truth." Everything which falls outside of the method of science (or better yet, the dogma of scientism) is subjective, private, and meaningless when it comes to speaking about the really real. Of course, those within the holy of holies have done their part to call the whole notion of mystery into ill repute. The term "mystery" was too often and too easily applied to everything which defied a clear and distinct explanation. Also much that was labelled as mystery was presented in such a way that there was little or no contact between heaven and earth.

Hence, we were left with this mystery which is unapproachable and even indifferent to our plight.

The problematic concerning mystery is also present when it comes to considering liturgy. Once again, we are confronted with obstacles on a cultural and religious level. The cultural climate for the celebration of liturgy is one that is unfriendly and highly antagonistic to things liturgical. And secondly, the priest, as the man who is expected to be the model of liturgical celebration, has often failed at this crucial pastoral, ecclesial task. The priest is called to be the celebrant of God's mysteries. Yet we frequently fall short at being celebrants. Before we advance a vision of the priest as celebrant of "the people's business" with God, we need to explore briefly the cultural and priestly obstacles to liturgical celebration.

Cultural Obstacles To Liturgy

Father M. Francis Mannion, in his brilliant article, "Liturgy and the Present Crisis of Culture," advances the following thesis:

> I will suggest, accordingly, that the fundamental reason why liturgy has lost much of its cultural and social power is related to the absorption into post-conciliar American Catholicism of profoundly negative dynamics operative in modern secular culture. I will argue that the appropriation of these dynamics has generated conceptions of liturgy that are exceedingly destructive and disorienting of the social and cultural generativity of liturgy. (*Worship*, 1988, p. 102)

In order to support his thesis that modern secular culture has proved destructive and disorienting to liturgy, Father Mannion identifies three major cultural movements: the subjectification of reality, the intimization of society, and the politicization of culture. Each of these have worked in negative ways on liturgy. A brief word about each is in order.

1. *The Subjectification of Reality.* The primary reality of the American social, political, and economic contexts is the

individual. America, what the noted historian Henry Steele Commager calls the "empire of reason," has prized the Enlightenment notion of the individual (isolated, unattached, free *from*, calculatingly rational, and self-interested in individual rights and economic gain at the expense of others), often at the expense of institutions, tradition, group loyalty, and the common good. The individual is the sole determinant of what is true, beautiful, and good. Private taste and the doing of one's own thing are more than slogans and characteristics of our current passing parade. They capture a fundamental approach to life. They bespeak a character which becomes inwardly fixed and seldom ventures beyond what Alexis de Tocqueville called "the puny self."

The consequences of such individualism have been well documented in recent times. Philip Slater (*The Pursuit of Loneliness*) and Christopher Lasch (*The Culture of Narcissism*) propose the theory that ours is a culture which fosters loneliness and narcissism. Our uniqueness and self-absorption blind us to our common humanity and the ability to share common experiences. We experience a great deal of loneliness as we withdraw deeper and deeper into the shadowy cave of our own making.

Robert Bellah (*Habits of the Heart* and *Habits of the Heart Reader*) and Philip Rieff (*The Triumph of the Therapeutic*) highlight the sociological and psychological consequences of the rush to the private domain of the inward. Meaning, truth, and destiny are no longer found in shared social traditions (religious, political, family) but in one's ability to eke out whatever narrative and meaning one can in order to make sense of daily life. The individual is happy just to survive and feels fortunate if indeed he has "a nice day." The areas of religion and morality have not escaped what Bellah calls "ontological individualism." Alastair MacIntyre (*After Virtue* and *Whose Justice? Which Rationality?*) and George Lindbeck (*The Nature of Doctrine*) powerfully trace the historical development of subjectivism and its effects on morality and doctrine. For MacIntyre, the problem lies with the victory of the Enlightenment Project over the Aristotelian-Thomistic world view. This victory gave birth to the highly privatized, isolated individual who makes moral decisions on the basis of will and feelings (Nietzsche and G.E. Moore). There is no objective morality. The predominant moral system is emotivism. Statements about right and wrong are nothing more than statements about one's feelings, preferences, or attitudes. Morality lacks the status of objective truth.

Doctrine fares no better than morality. Beginning in the eighteenth century, Lindbeck contends, there was an historical "turn to the subject." This modern subjectivism finds its way into a mode of religious reflection termed "experiential-expressive." That is, the individual encounters God in the depths of one's heart. Only later may one be moved to join a community or church. What is crucial and significant is the inner experience which is highly private.

The subjectification of reality profoundly affects liturgy. God is encountered and celebrated within the heart. Public worship, a community of faith, shared experiences, and historical traditions are no longer the mediating realities to the sacred. Since God is encountered within, there is no need for liturgy to function as a "go between." The individual alone with himself can "make contact" with the inward God. Hence, liturgy, if it is to be entered into at all, is of value as long as it meets the highly private needs of the individual. Liturgy must become tailored to the inwardness of each heart. In effect, litur*gies* replace the structured, formal mode of the community's liturgy. Liturgy is reduced to my needs and wants. If a liturgy does not meet these needs, it is defective. The liturgy must conform to the reality of the community's celebration. The imperial self, with its highly privatized worship, replaces the rite and celebration of the historical community. Father Mannion writes: ". . . because of the tendency to withdraw into individual subjectivity as the foundational source of meaning and value, the liturgy is shorn of its traditional, sacramental formality and reconceived and practiced as therapy" (p. 107).

2. *The Intimization of Society.* The phenomenon of

subjectification extends itself in terms of intimization, that is, "the process by which social complexity is eschewed in favor of a model of human co-existence that puts ultimate value on bonds of intimacy, personal closeness, and radical familiarity" (p. 108). Human encounters are of value only if they yield intimate relationships which bring individuals closer together. Personality is no longer the gift of the community in terms of social role and integration of the self within the larger context of public or civic life. Personality comes through one-on-one relationships which are characterized by an intense degree of warmth, sharing, and self-revelation. Richard Sennett, in his classic book, *The Fall of Public Man*, masterfully analyzes the replacement of public life (custom, manners, etiquette, shared roles and expected patterns of role-specified behavior) with the "ideology of intimacy." The whole sphere of public and civic life loses its moral powers to control and legitimate the behavior of the citizenry. Institutional life becomes merely functional and utilitarian. The moral glue and commitment which forms and holds a people together as a people is eroded. The secular or public liturgy of a society is abandoned. Shared codes, beliefs, and values are lost and replaced by individuals who experience close encounters of the most tenuous kind.

The effects of intimization on liturgy are complex and profound. Suffice it to say that many believers want from their church a community which provides opportunities for sharing, personal encounters, caring relationships, and an inward feeling of joy which comes from reaching out and touching someone. Big churches and complex structures are looked upon with disdain in favor of the small, intimate praying community where everyone knows your name. One of the most important services provided by such intimate communities is teaching the skills of relating. Good liturgies and good celebrants are those which help the participants grow in intimacy and togetherness. However, such service and approaches to liturgy come at a price. Namely, "in the process of intimization, liturgical rites and symbols lose the scale and complexity capable of engaging the Christian assembly with society, tradition, and history" (p. 113). The effects of intimization are felt within the Church as its official liturgy "is shorn of broader cosmic symbolism and consequently loses the traditional ethos of grandeur, glory, and majesty. In effect, the journey into intimate community is a journey out of the public world" (p. 113).

The intimization within society reduces the transforming power of the liturgy to the heart and one-on-one encounters. The much needed social transformation of society is often ignored. Liturgy meets the needs of intimate groups and not the larger concerns of the outside world. Sinful social structures are not challenged and called to repentance and conversion.

3. *The Politicization of Culture.* The final cultural dynamic which serves to obstruct and disorient liturgy is the politicization of culture. By this, Father Mannion means "the collapse of the multi-modal processes and codes of culture into the single process of political activity" (pp. 113-114). Mannion draws on the much discussed book by Richard Neuhaus, *The Naked Public Square.* The Neuhaus thesis goes something like this: religious and moral values have been assigned to the inward, the subjective, and the highly private. The public arena of life is naked or devoid of any transcendental reality or value which serves to critique the social construction of reality. Society does not tolerate a vacuum. Into the void of public life rides the political. All relationships within a society are now understood exclusively in terms of politics. This process of politicization evidences itself in "the growing litigiousness of the American people." Secondly, there is a general abandonment of symbolic structures of culture (norms, etiquette, civic cult) which provide civil and humane ways for individuals and groups to interact. Finally, there is a general loss of a sense of the sacred and the transcendent. There is no moral authority beyond the politically mighty who sit on their thrones. Moral authority is replaced by naked power.

As with the rise of subjectification and intimization, the politicization of culture has affected liturgy. While the Church must be concerned about sinful social structures and stand in solidarity with the wretched of the earth, great prudence must be exercised so as not to be coopted by any one political party or ideology. The danger is always present that the Church and the preaching of the Gospel will be too clearly aligned with a given political program. The Church ceases to be prophetic and stops calling all earthly power to bend in humble adoration before the Lordship of Jesus Christ. The Church's liturgy must avoid being manipulated by either the political right or left. The liturgy must not be used to inflame passions of violence and hatred. Reconciliation, and not political revolution, is the goal of liturgy. When the liturgy is misused to keep the mighty on their thrones or to promote rage, the Lordship of Jesus Christ is replaced by the demonic powers of this eon.

These cultural obstacles to liturgy are indeed formidable. Yet this is by no means the whole story. In addition to obstacles erected by culture, there are powerful obstacles to liturgy which are to be found within the Church and the priest, specifically, the priest's diminished sense of the importance of liturgy; the inability of priests to be celebrants; and the poor self-image of the priest which manifests itself in liturgical celebration. A brief word about each is order.

1. *Diminished Sense of Liturgy.* One of the important by-products of the Second Vatican Council was the development of an enriched sense of ministry as it relates to *all* the baptized. Unfortunately, this was viewed as being gained at the expense of ordained priestly ministry. Deacons, sisters, religious, and lay people were serving in various ministerial capacities in the parish. In the absence of a clearly articulated sense of general ministry and ordained ministry, priests were often left feeling that there was less and less for them to do. Their role and function within the Church was shrinking as the role and ministry of others was on the rise. Liturgy, specifically the celebration of the Eucharist and Reconciliation, was the last ghetto for the priest to take his stand. Liturgy (Eucharist and Penance) was the final refuge which provided the priest with a sense of identity, uniqueness, and power.

If liturgy is seen as nothing more than a haven of meaning

and identity in the midst of a changing Church, then liturgy's intrinsic beauty, its power to inspire, and its absolute necessity for the community of faith is lost. The priest is reduced to nothing more than a "sacramental man" or a "mass-saying machine." Liturgy, by association, is also diminished. In addition, the liturgy becomes the special preserve of the priest. Lay involvement can be viewed as intrusive and a further grab for power. This is most unfortunate for priest and parish. Lay people want their priests to be celebrants of the liturgy and they value the liturgy in itself. Rather than being an island for priests to gather, the liturgy is still "the people's business with God." In the most comprehensive study of the Catholic Church since Vatican II, Joseph Gremillion and Jim Castelli write:

> . . . in less than a generation, the new liturgy has become both the ideal and the standard in American parishes. American Catholics have accepted and endorsed the new liturgy and they take it seriously. They are less likely than before the Council to participate out of obligation alone and far more likely to participate because they want to. And they want to because they find meaning in the Mass and feel a part of it. (*The Emerging Parish*, p. 140)

2. *Lack of Priestly Celebration.* The Eucharist begins with the priest calling the faith community together for liturgical, celebrating prayer. The priest says, "As we begin to *celebrate* the sacred mysteries of our faith. . ." and we know that much of our so-called celebrating is "the noise of solemn assemblies" (Peter L. Berger). We priests are often not very good at celebration. We have come to believe that life and liturgy are somber business. The presence of smiling faces, humor, personal engagement, and playfulness are sure signs of the Sacred Liturgy being contaminated by enthusiasts. Mixed with our Catholic baptismal waters is cultural Calvinism and the work-ethic which looks with suspicion on celebration and play. We priests must often fight our natural dispositions,

training, and culture in order to celebrate. But celebrate we must.

Why? While doing our best to avoid the culture of intimization spoken of earlier, we *must* celebrate because Jesus told us that our heavenly Father celebrates and loves to give banquets when the lost sheep is found, the misplaced coin shows up, and the prodigal son finally comes to his senses. If God's will is to be done on earth as it is in heaven, then we must be concerned with celebrating the unbounded love of God. The priest must carry out the hilarious mission of calling the most unlikely folk to the Lord's table. The ever widening circle of compatibility, which is the Lord's table, is made up of saints and sinners; scientists and poets; virgins and the married; the elderly and the merest of babes; conservatives and liberals; priests, bishops, popes, and even an atheist or two. The list is endless since Jesus desires to draw *all* to himself. One thing is clear: you must have a good sense of humor to show up. If the truth be told, the table of the Lord at the Sunday Eucharist requires a good sense of humor as well.

3. *Poor Priestly Self-Image.*   In order to celebrate and *risk* liturgy, the priest must be graced with a good self-image. He cannot hate himself or give in to destructive doubts about the importance of ordained priestly ministry for the Church. Only those who are secure in their personal and priestly identity can dare stand before the community as God's man. Just think about it: a human being, sinful and finite, proclaims the Gospel and calls the community to hear and share good news. If the heart of humor is incongruity, then few things rival liturgy as the laughing heart of the cosmos. It is not the laugh of the cynic but the loving, gentle laughter of the God who loves us without limit.

In Chapter Four, we examined the self-image of the priest. Unfortunately, priests experience serious doubts about the worth of what they do and the contribution they make in the lives of those they serve. The priest who does not value himself as God's precious gift, and who seriously doubts the importance of his priesthood for the community, will simply not be a man who can celebrate. He will be too somber, self-absorbed, and despairing of having anything to offer or proclaim. He will be unable to preside over a meal with the community of Jesus' friends. Such a priest will be filled with self-doubt and self-hatred. There is no playfulness or celebration. The liturgy will be put on "auto-pilot." The word will be read, the sermon preached, the hosts distributed. The letter of the liturgy will be followed but the Spirit, who alone gives life, will have taken flight. And everyone will promptly go off and forget what they heard, did, and celebrated.

The barriers of culture and the above-mentioned limitations of those called to preside at the people's celebration of God's love continue to make it tough going for things liturgical. Tough, but not impossible. We need to continually remind ourselves of the beauty and power of the liturgy. We need to recover a sense of the sacred in order to celebrate worthily. We need to befriend our biblical stories and models of celebration. Above all, we need priests who are able to *be* celebrants of what God has done, is doing, and will do in the future. The real renewal of liturgy comes when we rediscover our Catholic imagination, that is the analogical imagination (Father David Tracy). Poor sermons and dull liturgies are directly related to a failure of imagination. The Catholic story contains a rich heritage of liturgical celebration. The priest people turn to is one who can help them to celebrate the unbounded love of God made visible in the death and resurrection of Jesus. Such a priest is a disciple of the kingdom of heaven "who brings out from his storeroom things both new and old" (Mt 13:52). It is to that abundant storeroom that we now turn.

All is Grace: A Biblical View

The two stories of creation presented in the book of Genesis (chs. 1-2) both affirm a central reality, namely, all that is has its origin and destiny in God. The spirit of God hovers over the waters of chaos and the formless, deep dark void that was earth. From that primal stuff, God's creative word is present establishing order and bringing forth life. It is the active word of God that adorns the creation and the very breath of God which brings forth human life. From the creation of the smallest seed, to the might acts of separating the waters from dry land, to the awesome creation of the human being, the spirit of God is at work. And this spirit is grace. All reality is filled with the grandeur of God and bespeaks his wonders. Everything that lives, moves and has being carries the potential for revealing the unbounded love of God. Even the most destructive and seemingly banal occasions can speak of God's wondrous power to heal and recreate. All that is belongs to God and carries within itself a hymn for his praise. The realization that all is grace moves the Psalmist to proclaim:

> The heavens declare the glory of God,
> the vault of heaven proclaims his handiwork;
> day discourses of it to day,
> night to night hands on the knowledge. (Ps 19:1-2)

In another moment of graceful awareness, the Psalmist lifts his heart in cosmic praise of all the Lord has done:

> Alleluia!
>
> Let heaven praise Yahweh;
> praise him, heavenly heights,
> praise him, all his angels,
> praise him, all his armies!
>
> Praise him, sun and moon,
> praise him, shining stars,
> praise him, highest heavens,
> and waters above the heavens!
>
> Let them all praise the name of Yahweh . . . (Ps 148:1-5)

Not only does creation speak of the wonders of God, but so does human history. Yahweh is involved in the ongoing story of his people (Israel) and he cares about the story's outcome. Yahweh has made himself known to them and en-

tered into a lasting covenant. They will be his people and they
are to love and worship him exclusively. God's grace and love
are revealed in the very process of selection. God chooses
Abraham and Sarah to bear Isaac and begin the story again of
God's life-giving, creative ways. Yahweh comes again and
again through the judges, prophets, and the holy men and
women of Israel to speak a word of comfort, challenge, and
renewal. From Abraham to Moses; from Ruth to Samuel; and
from Isaiah to the martyred mother and her seven sons (2 M
7:1-42); all of these are instruments of God's intervention in
the history of his people.

In addition to his involvement through special individuals, Yahweh also reveals his loving will through various historical events. The exodus experience revealed God's liberating
power on behalf of his people. The establishment of the covenant at Sinai marked Israel as Yahweh's special people and
required of them fidelity. When Israel broke the covenant by
worshiping other gods, placing their confidence in military
might and political alliances, or failing at the demands of
social justice, Yahweh punished his people. Israel's defeats as
well as her prosperity reflected the extent to which she kept the
word of the Lord. The historical experiences of slavery, flight,
possession of a promised land, exile, and restoration spoke of
Israel's special mission as a sacrament, a revelation, of God's
holy will. Again, the words of the Psalmist capture the
sovereignty of Yahweh as the Lord of history:

> Why do the nations rage
>   and the peoples utter folly?
> The kings of the earth rise up,
>   and the princes conspire together
>   against the Lord and against his
>   anointed. . .
> And now, O kings, give heed;
>   take warning, you rulers of the earth.
> Serve the Lord with fear,
> and rejoice before him;

> with trembling pay homage to him;
> Lest he be angry and you perish
> from the way,
>> when his anger blazes suddenly.
> Happy are all who take refuge in him! (Ps 2:1-2, 10-11)

From the perspective of the Bible, creation and history are anything but value neutral and separated from God. Creation declares the wondrous activity of God and history unveils the drama between the Lord and humankind. One can look at a distant star as well as a small flower near at hand and experience the beauty and goodness of God. History is not the mere rise and fall of great nations. History is the stage on which God encounters the human family and demands a response. Time is not purely mathematical or secular, but fundamentally sacred. All of time and creation are in the hands of a loving, active God. Simply put: all is grace.

As beautiful as the testimony of creation is and as powerful as the will of Yahweh in history can be, the grace of God would become even more visible. The pure grace and unbounded love of God would become visible in the person of Jesus. The Word of grace became our poor flesh "and made his dwelling among us, and we have seen his glory: the glory of an only Son coming from the Father, filled with enduring love" (Jn 1:14). It is to this Word of grace, this Word of love following upon love, that we now turn. Jesus invites us to *risk* celebrating the good news of salvation.

Jesus: That Your Joy May Be Complete

Jesus is the master storyteller. And a constant theme carried in his stories (parables) is joy. In the Gospel of Matthew, Jesus compared the reign of God to buried treasure which a man found in a field. He sold everything he had in order to buy the land. Filled with great joy at his good fortune (grace), he knew that what had been revealed to him was worth much more than he possessed or ever had hoped to possess (Mt

13:44). Also, the kingdom of heaven is like a merchant's search for a fine pearl. Once again, he could not believe his good fortune (grace). He also sold everything in order to take advantage of what was being offered. Both the landowner and the crafty merchant were "surprised by joy" at the opportunities waiting to be received. The God who is proclaimed by Jesus is the God of surprises. In the midst of our everyday routines, God's grace is at work, ready to offer us opportunities to find the hidden treasure and the valuable pearl. We must risk selling everything we hold dear in order to take advantage of that which is beyond price. Only those who are willing to take such a risk and are open to grace can know the joy of the reign of God.

Other parables of Jesus call for basic trust in the God whose grace takes meager beginnings and produces abundant yields. Again, in the Gospel of Matthew, Jesus told the parables of the mustard seed and the yeast (Mt 13:31-33). The mustard seed is the smallest of all the seeds; however, it grows into the biggest shrub and provides shelter for the birds of the air. Likewise, the kingdom of heaven is compared to yeast which a woman mixed with flour until it was leavened throughout. Jesus is calling for all who have ears to hear to understand that even in the smallest of things, and in ways unseen to the natural eye, our loving God is at work. In the midst of what may seem to be insignificant results, God's grace will supply what is lacking so as to bring forth a great work of service for others. In the midst of what may seem to be God's absence, he is at work mixing his invisible grace with our visible efforts. What is required is basic trust that God will be faithful to his promises. Jesus invites us to risk being joyful, and with good reason, because such a risk is grounded in the God who never forgets his own. Commenting on these parables of Jesus, Father John Shea, in his excellent book, *The Challenge of Jesus*, writes:

> Preaching the Kingdom was not as easy as it seemed in the first flush of enthusiasm. Success was neither quick enough nor sure enough. Jesus' response to these doubts

is to live in hope and not discouragement. The mustard seed is the smallest of all seeds yet one day it is a magnificent bush. The leaven is tiny but it permeates and raises the entire mass of dough. To the modern mind, this might suggest the process of growth but Jesus' point is contrast. He stresses the miracle of difference between an insignificant beginning and a glorious end. This Great Assurance that God will see His purposes through is the source of Jesus' freedom. This does not mean that Jesus knows the future but only that he trusts it. His confidence is not the crystal ball variety but the conviction that the God who is coming to be in him is faithful to his promises. (pp. 94-95)

The invitation to risk joy and celebrate extends beyond being surprised by grace and the basic trust that God is the fellow Companion whose love sustains our every moment of existence. Jesus invites us to celebrate and be joyful because we are forgiven of our sins and accepted unconditionally by our loving Father. In the fifteenth chapter of St. Luke's Gospel, Jesus told three stories (parables) about the mercy of God and the joy of reconciliation. These stories were told to a mixed audience of tax collectors and sinners on one side and the Pharisees and scribes on the other. The self-righteous fold were complaining that Jesus associated with all the wrong types. Rather than become indignant or self-righteous himself, Jesus offered his audience three stories and invited them to hear what they hear.

Jesus told them (and tells us as well) that God is like an imprudent shepherd, a compulsive woman, and a heartbroken father. God is like a shepherd who leaves ninety-nine sheep and goes in search of the one lost in the wilderness. God is like a compulsive woman who loses a small coin and cleans out the whole house until she finds it. And God is like a brokenhearted father who loses an impetuous son and longs each day for his return. At the level of pure rationality, none of this makes sense. Why go after the one who is lost? After all, the ninety-nine may run away as well. No doubt the compulsive woman

spent more on fuel for the lamp and lost a great deal of time
over such a minor thing. Wouldn't her energies be more
economically and profitably spent doing other things? And
finally, shouldn't our heartbroken father simply forget this
ungrateful son? Life will teach this boy how good he had it. In
time, he will return home and then dad can lower the verbal
boom, "I told you so!"

Yet Jesus does not buy into our notions of prudence,
rationality, proper fatherly behavior, and even images of God.
Jesus tells us the shepherd, the woman, and the father all have
one thing in common — the absolute ability to REJOICE and
CELEBRATE! The shepherd placed the lost sheep on his
shoulders and threw a party. The woman called together her
friends and neighbors to rejoice with her. And the brokenhearted father killed the fatted calf and invited everyone to a
huge banquet of celebration. Jesus shocks us to the very core of
our religious sensibilities when he says that all this rejoicing,
celebrating, and partying is just what God does when we turn
from sin, get found, and make our way home. Jesus' stories of
God are anything but sedate, controlled, and austere. They tell
us of a God who is madly in love with us and wants us to
respond to his love. Our God loves to celebrate. Most especially, God loves to throw a party when the lost are found, those
in the wilderness return to the community, and the dead are
brought back to life.

All this talk of joy, celebration, and banquets may be
nothing more than pure escape from facing what Camus called
the only real philosophical question — death. How does all of
this talk about grace, hope, and trust confront, in his words,
"that cruel mathematics which claims our condition"?

No doubt the modern mind finds such talk infantile
(Freud), an act of bad faith (Sartre), and unauthentic (Heidegger). Such talk is a refusal to face the temporality of our
condition and the existential truth that one day we will be no
more. Out of nature we have come, and nature is ready to
receive us. Both the coming forth and the returning as well as
all points in between are taken note of with grand indifference

to our sufferings and our hopes. This stoic creed is given powerful expression by Jacques Monod:

> Man must at last finally awake from his millenarian dream; and in doing so, awake to his total solitude, his fundamental isolation. Now does he at last realize that, like a Gypsy, he lives on the boundary of an alien world. A world that is deaf to his music, just as indifferent to his hopes as it is to his suffering or his crimes. (*Chance and Necessity*, pp. 172-173)

Yet beneath this seemingly heroic proclamation of humankind come of age, the riddle of human existence goes unsolved: Why the striving? Why the loving, hoping and caring? If, as Loren Eiseley, in his autobiography, *All the Strange Hours: The Excavation of a Life*, says, "there is nothing to explain the world . . . Nothing to explain the necessity of life, nothing to explain the hunger of the elements to become life, nothing to explain why the solid realm of rock and soil and mineral should diversify itself into beauty, terror, and uncertainty," then why is there also present in our hearts Camus' "invincible summer"? In the midst of perpetual perishing, we look and cannot but hope for Someone to preserve and cherish all that is true, beautiful, and good. Far from being an escape, the invitation to hope and trust and rejoice calls for the courage to proclaim the scandal and the hope that has been entrusted to us: "He suffered, died, and was buried" and in the next breath, "On the third day he rose again . . . ascended into heaven . . . and is seated at the right hand of the Father."

The ultimate reason for our hope of glory and the essential cause for rejoicing is found in Jesus who came so that we might have life in abundance. The real enemies of the human condition, sin and death, have been confronted and overcome through the death and resurrection of Jesus. The message of Easter is clear: life is stronger than death; the Light shines in the darkness and is not overcome; grace, not sin, is the stronger reality; and hope carries the day in the face of despair.

Each Christian, and every new generation, must walk the road of Emmaus. The lively discussion must continue about Jesus of Nazareth. There is a fork in the road. One way leads to despair and disillusionment. The other path is travelled only by those who have the courage to hope and celebrate. Those who choose this road less travelled continue to implore Jesus to stay with them. Their hearts burn inside and they proclaim to the world, "The Lord has been raised! It is true!" (Lk 24:34).

The message of Easter did not come by way of cheap grace. The Messiah had to suffer and be rejected by all the respectable folk. The great victory of Easter comes at the dear price of Good Friday. Jesus reminded the disciples (and us as well) in that sharing of the meal before the Ascension that they are to be his witnesses and preach the good news to all the world (Lk 24:46-47). In order to be faithful to this commission, the community must return again and again to the Lord's table, and must continually remind itself that it proclaims a crucified and risen Lord. And through his ultimate act of loving sacrifice, the new and eternal covenant was established. We are celebrating the new covenant written on our hearts. It is to that sacrifice of love that we now turn our attention.

Letter to the Hebrews: Covenant of Sacrificial Love

Much of recent Eucharistic theology and spirituality have tended to downplay the sacrificial aspects of the Mass. Greater emphasis has been placed on the Eucharist's other dimensions as a sign of our ultimate unity and the centering prayer of the faith community. Creative and significant theologies and spiritualities have been developed through relating the Eucharist to the demands of social justice. Also the Eucharist, grounded in the theology of hope, is the eschatological sign of the Lord's second coming when every tear will be wiped away and we shall see him as he is (Rv 21:1-4). All of these developments have made significant contributions to the faith-life of the Church. However, there are important insights which endure when discussing the Eucharist as sacrifice. Far from being morbid, the sacrificial aspects of the Eucharist give us cause for joy, celebration, and hope. The Letter to the Hebrews highlights three aspects of Christ's sacrifice which deserve mention.

1. The sacrifice of Jesus on the Cross is a sacrifice of *liberation* and *salvation*. Through the death of Jesus, we are freed from the lasting power of sin and death. This liberation *from* death and sin through the death of the One who was sinless brings about reconciliation with God. "Jesus saves" is no mere slogan, but the fundamental truth of grace which guides the Christian vision. We have been reunited with God and offered the hope of glory. St. Paul, writing to the Romans, captures the connection between Jesus' death, the forgiveness of sin, and the joy of reconciliation:

> We were still helpless when at the appointed moment Christ died for sinful men. . . Having died to make us righteous, is it likely that he would now fail to save us from God's anger? When we were reconciled to God by the death of his Son, we were still enemies; now that we have been reconciled, surely we may count on being saved by the life of his Son? Not merely because we have been reconciled but because we are filled with joyful trust in God, through our Lord Jesus Christ, through whom we have already gained our reconciliation. (Rm 5:6, 9-11)

The sacrifice of Jesus on the Cross is the perfect sacrifice which completes and surpasses the offerings of the old covenant. This new covenant of grace destroys the power of sin and brings salvation to God's people:

> The blood of goats and bulls and the ashes of a heifer are sprinkled on those who have incurred defilement and they restore the holiness of their outward lives; how much more effectively the blood of Christ, who offered himself as the perfect sacrifice to God through the eternal Spirit, can purify our inner self from dead actions so that we do our service to the living God. He brings a new covenant,

as the mediator, only so that the people who were called
to an eternal inheritance may actually receive what was
promised: his death took place to cancel the sins that
infringed the earlier covenant. (Heb 9:13-16)

The sacrifice of Jesus on the Cross is a supremely priestly
act by which he not only offers the perfect sacrifice but he *is* the
perfect sacrifice; sinless and freely laying down his life.
Through the priestly death of Jesus, we are freed from sin and
reconciled to God. Noted French biblical scholar, André
Feuillet, in his masterly work, *The Priesthood of Christ and His
Ministers*, writes:

Above all, it is while on earth that Christ sheds his blood
and thereby purges men of their sins. Purgation from sins
is an essentially priestly act, and Jesus does it by reason
of the priesthood he has possessed since he came into the
world; his very coming was motivated by the intention to
substitute the offering of his own body for the sacrifices of
the Old Testament. (p. 111)

2. The sacrifice of Jesus is a sacrifice of *love*. In the
Gospel of John, Jesus told his disciples, "A man can have no
greater love than to lay down his life for his friends" (Jn 15:13).
The sacrifice of Jesus is motivated by pure, selfless, love.
Jesus is the priest who offers the perfect sacrifice to the Father.
What must not be overlooked is Jesus' unbounded love for us.
Jesus is the Suffering Servant who stands in our place and
takes our sins upon himself. Jesus fulfills the words of Isaiah:

And yet ours were the sufferings he bore,
ours the sorrows he carried.
But we, we thought of him as someone punished,
struck by God, and brought low.
Yet he was pierced through for our faults,
crushed for our sins.
On him lies a punishment that
brings us peace,
and through his wounds we are healed. (Is 53:4-5)

The priesthood of Jesus is one of compassionate love which reaches its climax on the Cross. It is there that the suffering heart of God is revealed as pure love. Jesus on the Cross reveals that God is not an angry, judgmental deity looking for vengeance. The God of Abraham, Isaac, Jacob, and Jesus (and ours as well) is a Lover who, out of compassion for his people, sends his only begotten Son. It is this compassionate priesthood of Jesus which unfolds throughout his ministry and culminates on Golgotha. The Letter to the Hebrews captures the compassionate priesthood of Jesus in this way:

> Since in Jesus, the Son of God, we have the supreme high priest who has gone through to the highest heaven, we must never let go of the faith that we have professed. For it is not as if we had a high priest who was incapable of feeling our weaknesses with us; but we have one who has been tempted in every way that we are, though he is without sin. Let us be confident, then, in approaching the throne of grace, that we shall have mercy from him and find grace when we are in need of help. (Heb 4:14-16)

The priesthood of Jesus in its sacrificial dimensions is characterized by compassion, grace, and mediation. Jesus became our poor flesh so that we might be elevated to the very glory of God. Jesus stands ready to help us in our need and be our advocate before the Father. In other words, the sacrifice of Jesus continues down through the ages of history. This brings us to our third aspect for reflection.

3. The sacrifice of Jesus is *eternal*. The prophet Jeremiah spoke of that new covenant planted deep within the human heart (Jr 31:31-34). This new covenant replaces the imperfect one characterized by animal sacrifice and levitical worship. The once and for all sacrifice of Jesus atones for all sins. There is no need for a further sacrifice:

> All the priests stand at their duties every day, offering over and over again the same sacrifices which are quite

incapable of taking sins away. He, on the other hand, has
offered one single sacrifice for sins, and then taken his
place for ever, at the right hand of God, where he is now
waiting until his enemies are made into a footstool for
him. By virtue of that one single offering, he has achieved
the eternal perfection of all whom he is sanctifying . . .
When all sins have been forgiven, there can be no more
sin offerings. (Heb 10:11-14, 18)

Why is this sacrificial self-offering by Jesus so unique
and effective? Jesus is the incarnate Son of God (Heb 1:1-4).
The Son is superior to the angels and to all of the great men and
women of the old covenant. It is the Son who brought all things
into existence and it is this very same Son of God who, out of
compassionate love, will be lifted up on the Cross so that
humankind may be reconciled to its God (Heb. 1:5-14). The
very act of being lifted up and freely offering himself out of love
heals the world and moves the human heart to rejoice with hope
of new life.

From what has been said, we can conclude that the
sacrificial aspects of Jesus' priesthood and crucifixion are
anything but morbid or fixated with death. The death of Jesus
brings forth new life and liberates humankind from sin so as to
truly love God. The sacrifice of Jesus is a lasting one. We
always have before the throne of grace a Priest who pleads our
cause and who compassionately understands our all too human
condition. Above all, the loving sacrifice of Jesus allows us to
hope and live each day with confidence, not the arrogant
confidence of egoism, but the confident gratitude that, in
Jesus, all has been made new.

Throughout this section on the Bible and celebrating the
wonders of God's love, we have been guided by a single angle
of vision, namely, that *all is grace*. From creation to history;
from the parables of Jesus to his death and resurrection; we
have been surprised by grace and awed by its omnipresence
and its ability to transform. The Catholic imagination (which
Father David Tracy calls the "analogical imagination") shares
this biblical vision that all is grace. The Catholic imagination

has a keen sense of the rumors of angels (even those that do an Irish jig on the heads of pins) and the signals of grace. To such a grace-filled imagination we now turn.

The Catholic - Analogical Imagination

The late noted English writer C.P. Snow advanced the thesis that the modern period has given rise to two cultures — the culture of science and the culture of the humanities. And never shall the two cultures meet. The culture of science is characterized by calculating, utilitarian reason in search of the most efficient means of achieving human ends. The scientific culture is in possession of a method which prides itself on clear and distinct ideas. The method of science bestows the coveted label "reality" on those entities which can be measured and quantified. Things religious and artistic are highly suspect. For these dwell in the realm of the highly private, subjective and deeply personal. The truth claims of religions and the humanities are nothing more than expressions of one's inner preferences and attitudes. They carry no objective reality and hence, have no serious claim to truth. The natural world is simply dead stuff out there waiting for human reason to impose order.

By contrast, there is the culture of the humanities. This is the culture which claims the poetic, the imaginative, and the mystical. The humanities place a great deal of emphasis on human creativity and freedom. Truth is existential and subjective. There is a truth which cannot be captured by the method of science. There is more to reason than the instrumental intellect which focuses only on the surface qualities because they can be measured and classified. The humanistic culture takes seriously human values. Those who dwell in the humanist culture have great respect for imagination. Human imagination does not confront nature and impose an order resulting from reason. Rather, imagination creatively awaits nature's revelation. The imagination searches for deeper meanings and looks for the ways in which reality connects and forms part of a unified whole.

We are in desperate need of reconciling these two cultures. Science without imagination and the poetic loses its soul and vision. The humanities without a respect for the empirical can often degenerate into a destructive frenzy. What we are in need of is a vision of the whole person. We need a vision which joins together the instrumental intellect with the creative imagination. The two cultures are reconciled in the Catholic imagination. Such a reconciliation not only benefits society at large, but benefits every bit as much the community of faith. A rationalistic religion without the imaginative and metaphysical is mere straw. A religion without respect for reason easily falls victim to fanaticism and solipsism.

The Catholic imagination is analogical and metaphorical. (See Father David Tracy's brilliant book, *The Analogical Imagination*. Also Fathers John Shea, John Navarro, S.J., and Andrew M. Greeley have used the analogical, metaphysical, and narrative in very fruitful ways. A number of Protestants, most notably Stanley Hauerwas and Sally MacFarlie, have used the metaphorical and narrative as well.) Such an imagination rejects the narrow approach to reality in favor of the both/and. The analogical imagination constantly tries to see how various aspects of reality connect, fit together, enrich one another, and speak of fundamental things. The analogical imagination is always trying to integrate things that, at first blush, seem antagonistic. The analogical imagination uses metaphorical language in discussing the rich texture of reality. Anything which can be used to help further our understanding is made a member of the family.

Examples of the Catholic imagination at work abound: many of the pagan feasts were taken over by Catholic Christianity. The Roman pagan spring fertility rite of water and fire became part of the elaborate Catholic baptismal ritual. The celebration of Easter draws much from the Jewish Passover, Roman fertility rites, and the Anglo-Saxon worship of the spring goddess Easterne. The celebration of Christmas contains many elements drawn from the northern European mid-winter solstice symbolized by the Tannenbaum, an evergreen tree extending to the heavens so that the new life of spring would come forth. St. Augustine drew on the insights of Plato and Greek philosophy. St. Thomas Aquinas baptized Aristotle. These great saints and scholars didn't incorporate Plato and Aristotle uncritically. However, they, and the Catholic imagination, are not afraid to be open to new ideas. The Catholic Church, in its more creative moments, had the courage and insight to see the valuable contributions of others' experience and learning. The Catholic imagination holds on to its core beliefs, values, and ritual all the while looking for new ways to proclaim that "Beauty ever old and ever new."

The Catholic imagination rejects the religious version of C.P. Snow's two cultures. That is, the Catholic imagination desires to express religious truths in imaginative as well as propositional language. *Both* imagination (what St. Thomas called the agent intellect) *and* the reflective intellect are required if we are to engage in fruitful God-talk and celebration. Our religious insights began with the experience of God's self-revelation. We are constantly looking for, and being surprised by, grace. We then take these experiences and reflect on them. We take our reflections and turn them into propositions. These propositions undergo changes as new experiences and reflections take place. Under the guidance of the creative, dancing, Holy Spirit, the Catholic imagination creatively plays with the buzz and boom of the world. We hang on to our symbols, stories, metaphors, and propositions so that we can go along for the adventurous ride of the Spirit.

When all is said and done, the Catholic imagination is courageous, joyful, and hopeful. It dares to incorporate and learn from nature, history, and other religions, cultures, and philosophies. The analogical imagination is wise enough to know that God cannot be contained in any one of our systems, symbols, or philosophies. The dancing God who became one like us in Jesus simply refuses confinement to any one culture or historical movement. Our God keeps luring us forward and inviting us to celebrate the great adventure of his love. The Catholic imagination is filled with hope. And why not? The

Word became flesh and lived among us. It was the same Word which spoke everything into existence and proclaimed it to be "very good." The Word that became flesh died for us out of love and rose for us that we might have eternal life. In discussing the hopeful dimension of the Catholic imagination, Father Andrew Greeley writes:

> In the tremendous optimism of their experience of the risen Jesus, Catholic Christians had already decided that everything that was good, true, and beautiful was "naturally" Christian. In the years after Constantine Catholic Christianity generalized from the tentative compromise that the Hebrew prophets had made with pagan rituals: If everything good and true and beautiful was Christian, they would baptize and make Christian anything that looked like it was good and true and beautiful in pagan ceremony and custom. . .
>
> It must not be forgotten that the compromise was attempted because early Catholicism was permeated with optimism generated by its faith in the Incarnation and Resurrection of Jesus. If Jesus became man, if Jesus took on human flesh, if Jesus was part of the material things of this world, then everything is sanctified, everything is Christian, everything's a sacrament, everything will tell us something about God.
>
> (The above passage is from *A Catholic Theology of Popular Culture*, by Father Andrew M. Greeley, to be published by Thomas More Press.)

Talk about reasons to celebrate and rejoice!

Implications For Priestly Ministry

The twin visions of the Bible (all is grace) and the Catholic imagination (both/and) join forces to provide the priest and the faith community with powerful resources for celebration. The implications for priestly ministry and the faith-life of the Church can only be outlined. However, once again, we see the exciting, adventurous play of the Holy Spirit. The question is whether we have the courage to play along.

1. Greater emphasis should be given in seminary formation and theological education to the faculty of the creative intellect or imagination. Seminarians should be encouraged to read Shakespeare, Blake, and Browning as well as Rahner, John Paul II, and Raymond Brown. Homiletical training involves more than good technique and physical presence (although I would certainly not want to minimize these). The homilist-in-training needs to be skilled in the use of narrative, symbol, and metaphor. He needs to be able to make the necessary existential and analogical connections between the faith we proclaim and the lived experience of those to whom he is preaching and serving.

2. The priest as religious leader of the community must be a man of vision; a man at home with the creative imagination; and a man who is able to direct (not force) the community to experience God's loving presence in all things. The priest, schooled in the Catholic imagination and knowing that all is grace, is able to help illuminate moments of wonder, doubt, suffering, death, new life, and reconciliation. The priest lives in reverent appreciation of the world and he is respectful of the experience in others. Nothing human is foreign to him because nothing human is foreign to the Word made flesh.

3. The priest who is a man of the Catholic imagination helps his community of faith to experience the many dimensions of God's love. God is not only Father but also contains the compassionate, nurturing, protecting, and tender love of a Mother for her children. The priest imaginatively offers new models and stories of God which help mature the religious imagination of the community.

4. The priest of the analogical imagination will preach, teach, and lead in ways which invite, lure, guide, and show by example what God has in store for all who love him. Preaching and teaching that draws on story, symbol, and metaphor will excite the imagination and challenge the hearer to explore his or her own experience and encounters with God. Leadership

will not be the giving of orders but rather the calling forth of each person's gifts for the common good. All people have received from God's goodness and all can make a contribution to the community.

5. Finally, the priest of the Catholic imagination and biblical vision is a priest others turn to for celebration, rejoicing, and, above all, hope. Such a priest is able to enable others to come in touch with their own signals of transcendence, rumors of angels, and encounters with the grace that abounds. Such a priest opens eyes and hearts to the Liturgy and the celebration which continues after we are sent forth in peace to love and serve God and neighbor. Everyday life can be short, cruel, and brutish. Life breaks us all and death will have its say. Yet the priest people turn to is one who offers hope and encourages the community to keep on keeping on. Why? Simple: Jesus told us to do so. He gave us his peace and asked that we not let our hearts be troubled or afraid. Jesus is with the Father, and dwelling within each of us is the Paraclete. How can we help but celebrate?

CHAPTER EIGHT

TIMOTHY/TITUS:
The Priest and Pastoral Care

Throughout this section we have centered our reflections on the major work or ministerial areas of priestly life, namely, preaching and liturgical celebration. We grounded these reflections within the larger horizon of a spirituality of work. Such a spirituality of work offered a vision in which the priest (and all the people of God) continue the creative, redeeming, and sanctifying work of God. Work or ministry is not simply understood one-dimensionally as production and consumption. Ministry must always be experienced within the larger context of God's Kingdom and the needs of the historical faith community one serves. Above all, the work of the priest, his mission and ministry, finds its deepest expression in the death and resurrection of Jesus Christ. Noted Jesuit theologian René Latourelle writes:

> Work has not only a theological meaning but a *paschal meaning* as well. Inasmuch as work involves toil and affliction it is a sharing in the sacrifice of the cross and in the transformation effected by the resurrection. This bread and wine, the fruits of man's toil down the centuries, are the matter for the total consecration of man and the universe: they signify the passage into life via the cross. When freely offered, man's work makes him the priest and interpreter of creation; he acts as such not

through an external gesture or a superadded intention,
but by recognizing that he is a savior and consecrator of a
created world that has been given to him by God for the
sake of his own salvation and his own consecration. (*Man
and His Problems in the Light of Jesus Christ*, p. 274)

The temptation is ever present that our reflections on
priestly ministry will take flight from this world and seek the
safety and unreality of Plato's world of Ideas or Eternal Forms.
We can easily fall into the trap of spiritualism by which we
reject the creation, human history, and the needs of that
individual who stands before us. We can seek a security in
ideals as a way of avoiding the ambiguity, complexity, and
fallenness of human heart and history. Our talks about
ministry, preaching, and liturgy can fail to take note that Jesus
grew tired, discouraged, hungry, frustrated, angry, and disappointed. Hence, there is the constant need for the priest to
return again and again to his humanity and the humanness he
shares with Jesus and the community. It is that shared humanity, a deep abiding respect and love for that humanity, which
allows all of his ministry to reflect the ministry of Jesus.

The work of the priest, his preaching, teaching, celebrating, and healing, must be ever one with the Incarnation. The
Logos, the Word who was God and who brought all things into
existence, "became flesh and made his dwelling among us,
and we have seen his glory: The glory of an only Son coming
from the Father, filled with enduring love" (Jn 1:14). The
Word of God who is love becomes visible, tangible in a human
being — Jesus. The Word does not remain disembodied,
offering a love that is notional and devoid of fleshly, real
presence. Rather, the Word becomes our poor flesh and gives
physical expression to love. The Word must always seek to be
enfleshed again and again. Jesus indicated to his disciples the
night before he died that they must remain in the world as the
tangible, historical presence of God's love. In the words of
Jesus, "I entrusted to them the message you entrusted to me,
and they received it. They have known that in truth I came from

you, they have believed it was you who sent me" (Jn 17:8).
Jesus goes on to pray for all the disciples down through the ages
who must continue to proclaim the Word made flesh: "I pray
also for those who will believe in me through their word, that all
may be one as you, Father, are in me, and I in you; I pray that
they may be one in us, that the world may believe that you sent
me" (Jn 17:20-21).

The Incarnation, the Word made flesh, is the perpetual
reminder to all in priestly ministry that preaching, liturgy, and
service *must touch people*. There is no authentic preaching,
celebrating, and service without the cost of self-investment.
The preached word must become flesh in the priest and in the
heart of the hearer. The liturgy must connect with the ongoing
faith-life of the community and not be something merely forced
from outside. Service must follow the example of Jesus by
risking to touch even the lepers who live among us (and within
us if we are to be *wounded healers*). Incarnational priestly
existence is one that not only preaches but listens; takes
seriously the questions of the community before offering answers; and learns as well as teaches. Incarnational ministry is
one that respects the dignity of each person and takes seriously
the experience of the laity. Incarnational ministry is collaborative, that is, a shared ministry of all God's people making
visible the love of God. The collaborative dimensions of
ministry were given eloquent attention by the Second Vatican
Council:

> For the Christian vocation by its very nature is also a
> vocation to the apostolate. No part of the structure of a
> living body is merely passive but has a share in the
> functions as well as life of the body: so, too, in the body of
> Christ, which is the Church. . . (*Decree on the Apostolate
> of the Laity*, #2)

The incarnational dimensions of priestly ministry must
find their way into the Church as a whole. Not only is the
individual parish priest called to enflesh God's love and

preach the kingdom, but, also, the Church in its formal structures and ministries. The Catholic Christian Church is that community of faith which makes visible through time the unbounded love of God. Entrusted to the Church is the Gospel which addresses men and women in every age and culture with the message of salvation and the hope of new life. The timeless good news of Jesus Christ is always timely news which is offered to the world as the Church prudently reads the signs of the times. The Catholic Church is a pastoral Church. It is a Church which is open to the burdens, joys, sufferings, and hopes of the world. Of special concern to the pastoral Church is the cry of the poor and the needs of the oppressed. The pastoral Church stands in solidarity with the wretched of the earth because it is among such as these that Jesus is to be found. The opening words of the *Pastoral Constitution on the Church in the Modern World* sets the tone for the Church and its mission:

> The joys and the hopes, the griefs and the anxieties of the men of this age, especially those who are poor or in any way afflicted, these are the joys and hopes, the griefs and anxieties of the followers of Christ. Indeed, nothing genuinely human fails to raise an echo in their hearts. For theirs is a community composed of men. United in Christ, they are led by the Holy Spirit in their journey to the Kingdom of their Father and they have welcomed the news of salvation which is meant for every man. That is why this community realizes it is truly linked with mankind and its history by the deepest of bonds. (#1)

The world has turned over many times since these words were first promulgated by Pope Paul VI on December 7, 1965. The tremendous advances in technology and the awesome military power at our disposal make it all the more imperative that the Church hear the cries of the poor, the boasting of the arrogant, and call to conversion and faith all men and women of good will. The Third World, with its poverty and human suffering, as well as the First World, with its abundance of things yet deficiency of love and meaning, are in need of the pastoral Church proclaiming the Gospel. It is to the poor that the Church proclaims the Gospel and the year of the Lord's favor. It is to the rich that the Church proclaims the Lordship of Jesus and awakens the sense of our common humanity. We are to be our brothers' brother; sisters' sister; and the good neighbor who cares for those near at hand as well as those in distant lands. As we began our reflections on the priest and his ministry of providing pastoral care, we must define the meaning of such a ministry. Hence, by pastoral care, I mean *a ministry (a service) extended to meet fundamental human needs (corporeal and spiritual) in the name of Christ and as witness to the here and not yet Kingdom of God.* This ministry (service) is always done within and for the Church. Pastoral care is extended to the individual as well as to the whole world.

A crucial question arises at this point: what is the uniqueness of the priest as a pastoral minister? What does the priest have to offer which distinguishes his caring for those who hurt and hope from others who counsel? The uniqueness of priestly pastoral ministry is founded in our biblical witness and the Catholic tradition. We offer as our special gift to the world our biblical faith which proclaims that God is intimately involved with us; all is grace; and God became our poor flesh in Jesus, along with our Catholic tradition (see the previous discussion on the analogical imagination in Chapter Seven) with its "both/ and" approach to theology, which seeks to blend the many ways of speaking about the one true God. The pastoral priest brings the stories of God's unbounded love to the life-story of those who are in need of care. The pastoral priest looks to uncover the many ways in which God's grace is revealed in the everydayness of existence. The Church as a community is able to hear the deepest longings of the human heart and address a word of comfort, challenge, and hope to the human family as a whole. Anton T. Boisen describes this pastoral uniqueness beautifully:

> The priest or minister at his best brings to the task of helping the distressed in mind certain insights. He is

versed in the utterances of the great and noble of the race,
has traced the adventures of the human spirit both individually and collectively in its quest of the more
abundant life. He understands the deep longings of the
human heart and the significance of the constructive
forces which are manifest alike in the religious conversion experience and in acute mental illness. He recognizes the fundamental need of love, and the dark despair
of guilt and estrangement from those we love, and the
meaning of forgiveness through faith in the Love that
rules the universe and in whose eyes no one is con-
demned who is in the process of becoming better. In such
insights lies the important contribution of the competent
minister of religion rather than in any particular technique. (*The Exploration of the Inner World*, p. 285)

The priest people turn to is one who is able to listen with
the heart and speak from the creative imaginative of the
wondrous love of God. The priest people turn to is one who
ministers in the name of the Incarnate Word; hence, his
priestly ministry is incarnational. The Church as a whole, the
community setting for all priestly ministry, is a pastoral
Church reaching out to the whole world with the message of
salvation. If incarnational ministry and pastoral mission are to
have real meaning, we must turn to the ministry of Jesus and
the pastoral counsel of St. Paul.

The Incarnational Ministry of Jesus

The central preaching of Jesus is that the Kingdom of God
is at hand (Mk 1:15). And this preaching becomes visible in
the person of Jesus and the lives of those who believe. The
Kingdom, as well as its effects, become grounded in persons.
Throughout the preaching, teaching, and healing ministry of
Jesus, we see the primacy of persons. The incarnational
ministry of Jesus is a *continuation* of his own Incarnation. The
word continues to be addressed to persons so that it may
become enfleshed again and again. The Gospels provide us

with a narrative of Jesus which shows his great love and respect for persons. This loving respect is evidenced in three ways: conviction, truth, and freedom.

1. *Jesus is a man of conviction.* Jesus has something to say and challenges all who have ears to hear to listen and let their hearts understand. In fact, Jesus comes to announce the greatest news of all time:

> When the book of the prophet Isaiah was handed to him, he unrolled the scroll and found the passage where it was written:
> "The spirit of the Lord is upon me;
> therefore he has anointed me.
> He has sent me to bring glad tidings to the poor,
> to proclaim liberty to captives,
> Recovery of sight to the blind
> and release to prisoners,
> To announce a year of favor
> from the Lord." (Lk 4:17-19)

However, the message and the messenger were not always well received. The mighty and those with a vested interest in the *status quo* rejected Jesus as a blasphemer and a political insurrectionist. The smug and self-righteous were sure that Jesus' call to repentance and conversion was not meant for them. The fearful and insecure found Jesus threatening with all of his talk about change and renewal. The words in the Prologue of the Fourth Gospel were true enough: "To his own he came, yet his own did not accept him" (Jn 1:11).

Jesus did not become vindictive or give in to James and John, who wanted to call down thunder from heaven in order to punish those who refused to believe. Jesus continued to proclaim the Gospel and work within the limits of the situation and the barriers erected by human sin. The passage just quoted goes on to say, "Any who did accept him he empowered to become children of God" (Jn 1:12). Those who did accept him were the poor, the lowly, those forgotten and rejected. They saw in Jesus a man of conviction who was not interested in convicting or judging them. They experienced a man who, unlike their own teachers, spoke with an authority which went beyond mere human wisdom. Those who accepted Jesus found themselves accepted by Unbounded Love in a total, non-judgmental way. For the first time, someone told them of God's love for them and challenged them to respond to that love. Jesus' conviction about the Father's love was more than words in the abstract. The message of loving acceptance became visible with Jesus allowing a penitent woman to anoint him with perfume and cleanse his feet with the tears she wept over her sins (Lk 7:36-50). Jesus dared to invite himself to the home of Zacchaeus, the tax collector, for a meal. Why? Because this is what God's love is about: seeking out the lost and healing the sick. The murmuring of the self-righteous would not deter Jesus from announcing and making visible the year of the Lord's favor.

2. *Jesus speaks the truth in love.* While Jesus never compromises the Gospel, he also never uses the truth to punish, coerce, or "scare straight" those whom he encounters. The truth of the Gospel contains an attractiveness and beauty which has the power to stir the imagination, quicken the heart, and excite the mind to see and live in new ways. It is because Jesus is so convinced that God is love that he is able to invite all to trust and let go of their idols. It is because Jesus speaks that truth with love that others are able to risk and hope that the grain of the cosmos runs in the direction of life, love, and reconciliation.

A powerful example of Jesus speaking the truth in love is contained in the Fourth Gospel (Jn 8:1-11). A woman caught in adultery was brought before Jesus for his opinion as to what should be done. The law of Moses was clear: she should be stoned. The Pharisees were not interested in the law or in that woman. They were simply using her to trap Jesus. The truth was being used as a weapon to discredit Jesus. Of course, all of this was done in the name of virtue and a litany of *shoulds.* Jesus would have no part of this. His silence and figurative writing on the ground indicates that Jesus would not play the game of judge, for he came to judge and condemn no one (Jn

3:17). Jesus ignored their trap by setting one of his own, namely, that the person who was without sin should be the first to enact the sentence of the Law. If Jesus had said the woman should be set free, he would have been putting himself above Moses. If he had said she should be stoned, Jesus would have been contradicting his own message of mercy. The Pharisees then found themselves on the horns of a similar dilemma. If they were to begin to stone the woman, they would place themselves on a par with God — sinless. If they were to refrain, they would indicate their own sinfulness and the need for divine mercy to all. They would illustrate their need of the very mercy which they were not willing to extend to the woman. One by one, they left. Jesus was then alone with the woman.

Jesus asked the woman if there was anyone left to condemn her. The answer was no. Only this woman and Jesus remained. She did not experience Jesus as a condemning presence, but a challenging and merciful presence. Jesus clearly indicated that he was not there to condemn. However, the mercy of God carries with it the challenge to live in a new way, for Jesus told her to go and avoid this sin. Jesus did not try to excuse her behavior, nor did he give her a long lecture. He simply stated that the mercy of God contains the grace to liberate one from sin. The forgiven sinner must face the truth offered in love. Rudolf Schnackenburg, in his magnificent three volume commentary on John's Gospel, writes the following on the pericope of the adulteress:

> Thus the story of the adulteress affirms the central theme of Jesus' message: God desires to exercise mercy and to accomplish it in the person of Jesus . . . the acquittal itself lays an obligation upon the woman: God's mercy has been granted to her that she may avoid sin in the future . . . Jesus does not only receive repentant sinners but seeks them out . . . The point is not the condemnation of sin but the calling of sinners: not a doctrine but an event. Jesus accepts sinners in God's name; his will is not to judge but to save. (*The Gospel According to St. John*, Vol. 2, pp. 168-169)

3. *Jesus respects the freedom of all persons.* Jesus' strong
convictions and his proclamation of the truth of the Gospel do
not ignore human freedom and the dignity of each person.
Jesus respects freedom and leaves each person with the necessary room for making a decision. Each person must take
responsibility for his actions and accept the consequences of
his decisions. Love demands freedom. Truth will set us free.
But we must decide to live that truth freely and without
coercion. Jesus forces no one to follow him. Those who hear the
message of the Kingdom must decide if they can live with good
news and give up the idols of money, power, and pleasure. If
not, they are free to be in relationship with Jesus no longer.
Jesus does not tailor his message to please the crowd. And
neither does Jesus call down God's wrath on those who find him
a stumbling-block.

Once again, the Fourth Gospel supplies us with an excellent example of Jesus' respect for human freedom. Jesus declares that he is "the living bread come down from heaven."
Furthermore, all who eat his flesh and drink his blood will have
eternal life. The reaction of the crowd is understandable: "How
can he give us his flesh to eat?" Their puzzlement turned to
outright rejection of Jesus: "From this time on, many of his
disciples broke away and would not remain in his company any
longer" (Jn 6:51-52, 66).

With so many of Jesus' disciples leaving, it would have
been natural for Jesus to condemn them as weak or sinful; to
change or qualify his message; or in haste remove the Twelve
so that their confidence would not be shaken. Jesus did none of
these. In fact, Jesus turned to the Twelve and placed the issue
squarely before them: "Do you want to leave me too?" Simon
Peter spoke for the Twelve: "Lord, to whom shall we go? You
have the words of eternal life. We have come to believe; we are
convinced that you are God's holy one" (Jn 6:67-69). The
Twelve could not be excused from making the decision
whether to remain with Jesus or leave him as others had done.
Jesus loved them and respected them too much to shield them
from the decision. Commitment to Jesus does not come by way

of force or fear. Jesus freely and lovingly offers himself as the food of eternal life. We can only respond in like manner — freely and lovingly.

Professor Schnackenburg reminds us of a critical reality concerning the Twelve:

> The Twelve are set apart from the disciple whose faith fails. They are exposed to the same attack [the words of Jesus are a hard saying and they caused murmuring among the Jews], but at the moment of decision they remain loyal. They know, as Simon Peter's confession makes clear, that they are bound to the person of Jesus, and accept his words, even when they cannot understand them, as words of the revealer which bring eternal life (67-69). The exemplary behavior of Jesus' closest companions becomes an appeal to the later community. (*The Gospel According to St. John*, p. 69)

We are that "later community," asked to follow the example of our ancestors in faith. That is, we are to remain loyal to Jesus as the world "murmurs" against him and for its lords of money, power, and pleasure. We are invited to keep company with Jesus even when we do not fully understand him or find him troubling. Jesus continues to ask his question, "Do you want to leave me, too?" Jesus continues to wait for our *free* response. Pray that we have the faith and courage to make Simon Peter's words our own: "Lord, to whom shall we go? You have the words of eternal life. We have come to believe; we are convinced that you are God's holy one."

The incarnational ministry of Jesus is an historical ministry. That is, the good news of salvation must continue in history. The departing words of Jesus as he returns to the Father indicate this historical and evangelical mission:

> "You will receive power when the Holy Spirit comes down on you; then you are to be my witnesses in Jerusalem, throughout Judea and Samaria, yes, even to the ends of the earth." No sooner had he said this than he

was lifted up before their eyes in a cloud which took him
from their sight. (Acts 1:8-9)

The Pastoral Letters

Under the guidance of the Holy Spirit, the "little flock"
matured in faith and courage. No one played a larger role than
the Apostle Paul. Of special interest to us are the Pastoral
Letters (1 and 2 Timothy and Titus). The Church was growing
in new and exciting ways. Growth always brings new
challenges and problems. It was no different with the early
Church; it is no different today. The incarnational ministry of
Jesus must be extended to the whole world. Such a ministry is
thoroughly pastoral. That is, it meets the needs of the human
family by preaching the Gospel and teaching the truths of the
faith. The Pastoral Letters call to our attention three major
concerns: the character of the bishop, presbyter, and deacon
must be above reproach; the purity of the Church's doctrines
must be safeguarded; and finally, the Gospel must be preached
without compromise. All three of these, character, doctrine,
and preaching, are profoundly pastoral. They are at the heart
of the Church and central to its mission to the world.

1. *The leader of the faith-community must be above reproach.* All of our preaching and teaching is mediated through
the leader of the community. We may preach and teach with
great eloquence and power, yet obstruct, and be a stumbling
block to, the faith. Too often we want our sermons and
doctrines without personal involvement. We want our
strictures so good that we do not have to be personally holy
(T.S. Eliot). St. Paul spends a great deal of time in the
Pastorals delineating the qualities of character required for the
religious leader. Preaching and teaching are pastoral
ministries which can easily be damaged by a leader lacking in
moral character and spiritual maturity.

Those who aspire to the noble task of bishop must be men
who are irreproachable, temperate, self-disciplined, hospitable, gentle, modest, and generally live a life worthy of their

calling so that others will want to follow their example (1 Tm
3:1-7). The qualities required of a presbyter are no less demanding. He, too, must be irreproachable, a lover of goodness, steady, just, holy, and self-disciplined (Tt 1:5-6).
Deacons are to be tested before they can assume the important
ministry of service. Christian service requires more than
merely helping others. The deacons must be "serious,
straightforward, and truthful. They may not overindulge in
drink or give in to greed. They must hold fast to the divinely
revealed faith with a clear conscience" (1 Tm 3:8-9).

No doubt some may object to this Pauline listing of
qualities as leaving too little room for grace and the mystery of
a vocation. These qualities or virtues can be acquired by
human effort and lead to what Paul most feared: boasting in
one's strength rather than in one's weakness. Yet such is not
the case, for grace builds on nature and lifts up this lowly
condition of ours. It is only through the indwelling of the Holy
Spirit that the bishop, priest, and deacon is able to bear such
fruits of the Spirit. The Holy Spirit works through our limitations and sinfulness so as to make us both strong in the Lord
and compassionate when dealing with others. The moral and
spiritual qualities of the religious leader are not forced down
upon the person. Rather, the Spirit calls forth and matures
those gifts which are already present through Baptism. The
Spirit develops the spiritual and moral qualities of the leader
so that others will see God's grace shining through human
weakness.

In his excellent little book, *Ministry*, Father Richard P.
McBrien asks the question, "What qualities do ministers
need?" Among the qualities needed, such as basic human
wholeness, the theological and cardinal virtues, as well as
various acquired skills and sensitivities to the modern com-
plexities of life, Father McBrien highlights one which is crucial for the Catholic ministry in general and the ordained
priestly ministry in particular: a positive sense of the Church.
In Father McBrien's words:

Ministers and candidates for ministry at whatever level
can not be fundamentally in doubt about the necessity
and purpose of the Church. All ministry is in the service
of the Church. It has no other purpose than to serve the
People of God and to advance the mission they have
received from Christ. Ministers and ministerial candidates must also have a practical understanding of and
commitment to the gospel consistent with ecclesial faith,
or faith in the Church. (*Ministry: A Theological, Pastoral
Handbook*, p. 65)

As Father McBrien goes on to indicate, this sense of the
Church does not mean that one cannot enter into debate and
disagreement. The Church is not frozen in time but a Pilgrim
People on the way to the New Jerusalem. There is always a gap,
because of sin, between the Church as it *is*, and the future
Kingdom which is here but *not yet*. This gap is only closed by
love; God's love for us and our responding in love to Love.
Debates and lively discussions are signs of vitality and commitment. We care about the Church enough to get involved, to
think, and feel passionately. This is all to the good. Yet we
must never forget that what unites us is infinitely more important than what divides us. And what unites us is the love of
Christ. A positive sense of the Church always requires that we
respect and love one another (Jn 13:35).
    2. *The leader of the faith-community must be committed
to teaching sound doctrine.* Times of expansion are always
times of the unexpected, the novel, and the threatening. When
we reach out to share with others and try to influence them, a
similar occurrence comes our way. They want to share and
influence us. The dilemma is always to *both* share what is
distinctive while remaining open to the insights of the other.
Such a balancing act is never easy. Lurking near at hand is the
temptation to rigidity and intolerance or the temptation to lose
one's uniqueness in trying to be all to all. The reconciling work
of the Holy Spirit is especially needed when the Church throws
open its windows to the world. An intemperate amount of new

wine and one becomes drunk. Yet even a temperate amount of new wine in old skins may burst the seams, and all would be lost. Pastoral prudence is essential.

St. Paul in the Pastoral Letters places a great deal of importance on remaining faithful to the teaching of sound doctrine (1 Tm 1:3-7; 4:1-16; 6:3-10, 20-21; 2 Tm 2:14-26; Tt 1:10-14; 3:4-8). The community was then in a very fragile and vulnerable stage. Purity of doctrine must be a high priority so that false teachers and fables will not lead the faithful into infidelity. Part of the leader's pastoral ministry is to safeguard the true Gospel and see to it that the good news of our salvation is correctly taught and preached. The safeguarding of the Gospel and related beliefs is important for the community of faith as well as the community of humankind. It is the true Gospel of Jesus Christ which must be preached and taught to all the world. It is only *this* Gospel which has the power to save and reconcile humankind to its one Lord and Savior. Fidelity to the good news about Jesus is not an issue of academic or intellectual purity, but one of utmost truth. The truth about Jesus must be proclaimed so that the story of salvation may continue until he comes again.

However, we know that the truth about Jesus is an *ongoing* story throughout history. Each generation writes its own paragraph in response to Jesus' question, "Who do you say I am?" (Mt 16:15). No one person, community, or historical period has the final word concerning the Word made flesh. Each generation stands on the shoulders of those who have gone before. We lovingly and gratefully receive from the past so as to understand our present and hope in our future. We pass on to those yet to be the precious, living faith that has been *loaned* to us. We pass it on knowing how incomplete, lacking, and myopic our efforts are. We can risk passing it on because we believe and hope that the Spirit will make up what is lacking through the commitment of the next generation. And so it goes.

There are bound to be disagreements, debates, and even dissent in the community of faith. At first blush, this can be seen as dangerous, threatening to the faith, a sign of decay. While not wanting to dismiss the reality of dissent without love, we must not and should not ignore the other possibility: that of hope and new life. The changing of forms and even the elimination of some structures need not be a signal of the end, but rather, the mark of a new beginning. Jesus asked us to learn a lesson from the grain of wheat. In the dying, there is a rising. Endings contain the possibilities of new beginnings. Nature is replete with passages from death to new life. Jesuit David Toolan captures the glorious ambiguity and creativity of existence without which life would be boring and rigidly determined:

> Turbulence breaks down old forms; it is a sign of death heralding new beginnings. In the pure, noiseless realm of mathematics, then, physicists may play as they like with the clear and distinct idea of time-symmetrical equations. It is an idealist's game, a dematerialization of reason that mistakenly eliminates the demon of noise in the effort to achieve perfect control and perfect communication. Could the effort succeed, we now know, nature's polyphony and our discourse about it would be reduced to the sound of a monotone saying nothing at all. Fortunately for the subatomic world and what's come of it, galaxies and the carnival of animals we live among, things are messy, riddled with a large ambiguity factor. Formless, buzzing chaos sneaks into the structural order and keeps formations open. (*Facing West from California's Shores*, p. 245)

Nature abhors "the sound of a monotone" and refuses to be locked in our neat categories and the "pure, noiseless realm of mathematics." The Church of Jesus Christ in the power of the Spirit dislikes the sound of a monotone no less. The Church is the loving Body of Christ. There is an abundance of gifts and a polyphony of voices. At times gifts will clash and voices will conflict. Yet all this can be signs of the creative advance of the Holy Spirit. Fidelity to sound doctrine does not mean the unthinking, non-reflective repetition of past formulae. We are challenged to make our God-talk our "ownmost." The tradition (those fundamental, core aspects of creed, code, and cult) of the past is always the living faith of the dead and never the dead faith of the living. It is during those times when "people will not tolerate sound doctrine, but follow their own desires" (2 Tm 4:3) and times when people follow the letter and form of religion but neglect "justice and love of God" (Lk 11:42), that the religious leader needs the wisdom in the Spirit for creative fidelity.

3. *The leader of the faith-community preaches the Gospel with courage.* The preaching ministry is more than correct technique and effective packaging. Preaching is that crucial pastoral ministry of the Church as a whole in which is proclaimed the news that "Jesus Christ, a descendant of David, was raised from the dead" (2 Tm 2:8). The substance of the message takes priority over the form in which it appears and the technique by which it is presented. The preaching ministry cannot be effective and Spirit-filled if it deviates from the central reality of the good news:

> God has saved us and has called us to a holy life, not because of any merit of ours but according to his own design — the grace held out to us in Christ Jesus before the world began but now made manifest through the appearance of our Savior. He has robbed death of its power and has brought life and immortality into clear light through the gospel. (2 Tm 1:9-10)

The pastoral preaching ministry of the Church must be one which confronts as well as comforts the world with the Lordship of Jesus. There can be no compromise of the Gospel in order to win the favor of the world. The ultimate authority and power to preach comes from Jesus Christ through the indwelling power of the Spirit to the glory of the Father. Preaching, if it is to be pastoral, must speak to the heart of the world and hear its pains and hopes. Yet such speaking and hearing in no way means that the Gospel must be tailored to fit the audience for better ratings in order to secure a more favorable response. To preach the Gospel is to call the world to conform to God's will. The preacher of the Gospel must never conform to any age and its pantheon of gods. In the words of Lutheran pastor Richard John Neuhaus:

> Preaching that applies for a license from unbelievers is no preaching at all. It elevates nothing. It reduces the gospel of Christ to simply another viewpoint that may or may not be "interesting" or "helpful." The preacher who cannot say with Paul, "I am entrusted with a commission," is, at best, in a perilous situation. We are entrusted with a commission from Christ and from the community that has accepted the commission of Christ. Sometimes, when the commissioning voice of Christ seems faint, we must dare to preach because the community calls us to preach. But finally, while they cannot be equated, the voice of Christ and the voice of his Church can not be separated. Such is the promise that our Lord has made to those who follow him. Somewhere within the Body of Christ the will of Christ is articulated. There are different voices and we must choose; we can never be sure that we have chosen rightly, but ultimately our obedience is rendered to him who surely will judge all things rightly. That is the source of our freedom and of our joy in the ministry of preaching. (*Freedom for Ministry*, pp. 147-148)

To preach the Gospel in spirit and truth requires courage. The principalities and powers of this world and age do not relinquish control easily. Preaching the Gospel calls forth the opposition of the world and demands that the preacher be willing to endure hardships for its sake. Preaching requires the support of the community and a willingness to be used by the Spirit. The opposition incurred by preaching is complex. There is the opposition from political authorities who seek to repress any truth spoken to their power. There is the opposition from less overtly oppressive structures such as the advertisement industry which tries to assure us that we can buy happiness. There is the opposition from the secular media which presents films and programs in such a way as to render the Gospel irrelevant. And there is the opposition which is present in the rectory and parish church in the form of boredom and a familiarity which breeds contempt. The word of God faces the difficult task of being heard and treasured in a heart which is deluged with so many other words and hardened by "having heard it all before."

At times the preacher can become discouraged and lose the passion for proclaiming the Gospel. The congregation may not be moved by our attempts at preaching the good news. The readings may not inspire us as they once did. We may no longer burn inside with the zeal for preaching. We may find ourselves with a growing intolerance for sound doctrines and a willingness to pander to those who want novelty. We are tempted to tickle ears. It is in such a real situation that the words of Paul find application:

> In the presence of God and of Christ Jesus, who is coming to judge the living and the dead, and by his appearing and his kingly power, I charge you to preach the word, to stay with the task whether convenient or inconvenient — correcting, reproving, appealing — constantly teaching and never losing patience . . . be steady and self-possessed; put up with hardship, perform your work as an evangelist, fulfill your ministry. (2 Tm 4:1-2, 5)

The incarnational ministry of Jesus and the pastoral ministry of the Church are not frozen in the first century or locked into the pages of Scripture. Such a ministry and mission are alive and must animate the community of faith down through history. There will be stops and starts; advances and set-backs; division and unity. In other words, the Church is on a pilgrimage with all the humanness and ambiguity involved. However, the pilgrimage of the Church, while historical, is also one that is grounded and guided in the promises of Jesus and the guidance of the Holy Spirit. We do not wander about as a people who have lost our way. We have ever before our eyes the goal — life on high in Christ Jesus. The incarnational and pastoral dimensions of ministry and mission were at the very center of the Second Vatican Council. It is to that vision of Church and ministry that we now turn our attention.

The Second Vatican Council

The vision of Pope John XXIII is beautifully contained in the magnificent *Pastoral Constitution on the Church in the Modern World*. The vision of the Church and its relationship to the world is breathtaking. The Church is not to be understood as scolding and condemning the world. Rather, the Church is a servant in the name of the One who came in our midst as a servant. The Church is called to be open to the hopes and anguish of the world so as to minister the good news of Jesus Christ. In the words of the Document:

> . . . the church has always had the duty of scrutinizing the signs of the times and of interpreting them in the light of the gospel. Thus, in language intelligible to each generation, she can respond to the perennial questions which men ask about this present life and the life to come, and about the relationship of the one to the other. We must therefore recognize and understand the world in which we live, its expectations, its longings, and its often dramatic characteristics. (#4)

Tremendous advances in human learning have greatly increased humankind's power and control over the earth and over one another. This power can be put to the service of the human family or it can be misused as a means to exploit nature and dehumanize members of the one family of God. The Church cannot remain silent or indifferent in the face of such problems and possibilities. The Church must proclaim the Lordship of Jesus Christ and do so in such a way that she also acknowledges *her* need for repentance and conversion. The Church is never above the word she proclaims. In fact, that word only becomes more visible and believable as others are able to see its effects in the life of the Church. The need to revere the good earth and respect the dignity of all persons is not simply an issue for society. The Church must take the lead in providing models and examples of what it means to be wise stewards of the earth and loving brothers and sisters to one another.

The Church, while pastorally attuned to the voice of the world, must always be ready to minister to the needs of the individual. The heart of the human person is in need of the good news of salvation. The mystery of what it means to be human can only be authentically understood in light of the Person of Jesus Christ:

> The truth is that only in the mystery of the incarnate Word does the mystery of man take on light. For Adam, the first man, was a figure of Him who was to come, namely, Christ the Lord. Christ, the final Adam, by the revelation of the mystery of the Father and His love, fully reveals man to man himself and makes his supreme calling clear. It is not surprising, then, that in Him all the aforementioned truths find their root and attain their crown. . .
>
> Such is the mystery of man, and it is a great one, as seen by believers in the light of Christian revelation. Through Christ and in Christ, the riddles of sorrow and death grow meaningful. Apart from His gospel, they overwhelm us. Christ has risen; destroyed death by His death. He has lavished life upon us so that, as sons in the Son, we can cry out in the Spirit: Abba, Father! (*Pastoral Constitution on the Church in the Modern World*, #22)

What the Church must proclaim in and out of season is the innate dignity of the human person. The human person is not to be respected based on economic production, symbols of status, or the ability to get things done. Human dignity is not subject to political authorities or the latest survey on who is to be respected and who is not. The value of the human person cannot be quantified or fit into the Madison Avenue categories of consumer tastes. The dignity and worth of the human person

comes from beyond the "movers and shakers" of this world.
The value of each extends beyond the lifestyle of the rich and
famous. Each person is to be respected because each human
being is made in the image and likeness of God. This innate
dignity is not assigned to mankind by mankind, but instead
should be recognized, reverenced, respected, and celebrated
as a pure gift from our loving God. Without respect for the
dignity of the human person, there is a general breakdown in
social life. Exploitation, violence, injustice, war, and an overall condition of all against all result when human dignity is
ignored. It is only when we truly see with faith and love the
dignity of each person that we have the hope of peace. It is only
when we respect all members of the human community as
brothers and sisters in Christ that we come to have a security
which no military might can establish and no bomb destroy.
When we see each other in the light of Christ, we shall then
know that Light which gives life in abundance. We shall then
experience that Light which shines in the darkness and is not
overcome.

The vision and hope of the Second Vatican Council was
for a Church and a priest people would turn to for the good news
of Jesus Christ. Such a priest and Church would be found in the
midst of the world as servant and herald. The incarnational
ministry of Jesus as well as the pastoral mission of the Church
come together in leading people to know Christ. The priest and
the Church must continue the ministry of washing feet and
touching the untouchable; inviting the wayward to return to the
Lord's table; seeking out the lost and celebrating when they are
found; and providing a living, though imperfect, witness that
Jesus lives. Eugene C. Kennedy, in one of his early books,
captures the incarnational and pastoral dimension of Church
life:

> The world needs a Church which is not interested in
> domination and power but in the service of mankind. This
> is the essence of the Church which Christ founded. This
> is all the more urgent as the twenty-first century draws

near and the specter of an all-embracing technology causes thoughtful men to pause and reflect on the threat to human values which this will occasion. The world needs a Church whose concern is man, a Church which speaks intelligibly about the possibilities of man when he understands his meaning in relationship to his Creator and to his fellow men. Mankind needs the kind of counsel that only Christ's Church can provide. This counsel consists in the dialogue between mankind and the Church whose human servants present themselves at all points of need, to reason and reflect with it in the light of the Gospels. (*Comfort My People*, pp. 201-202)

A Concluding Word: To Hear and To Touch

The priest people turn to and the Church people belong to is both incarnational and pastoral. The priest and the Church are blessed with the vocation and mission to hear the anguish and the hopes of the individual and the world. In order to hear, we must dare to draw near and stand in solidarity with the troubled heart as well as the broken history of humankind. We cannot hear from a distance, for often those who are most in need have no voice or have had their voice silenced by pain or oppression. While the world holds that history is written by winners, the Christian story teaches that history is written and won by victims. Jesus Christ is the supreme victim who is lifted up in solidarity with all who suffer and die abandoned. Jesus is one with all who are relegated to the edges of society and rendered invisible. Jesus offers hope to the lonely sinner as well as good news to the whole world. The Church hears the cries of the poor and lifts up its voice on behalf of the dignity of all persons. The Church hears the pretensions to absolute power by the lords of this world and age and calls them to repentance in the name of the one Lord and Savior, Jesus Christ. The Church does not accomplish this mission by coercion or guilt, but through love in the spirit of He who is Love.

In listening to the concerns and dreams of the world, we must not forget the individual; for our God hears the cries of the lowly and even the whispers of a single child. The priest's everyday demands can be so crowded with the complex as well as the simple, the dramatic as well as the mundane, the structural as well as the personal, the public and the deeply private. Never to be lost is the value of the individual person. All that the priest does and the parish provides must be directed towards leading others to see Jesus. The priest must risk touching the lives of those whom he serves. It is not the touch of control, manipulation, domination, or a compulsive grip which keeps people in line. The priest who touches the imagination, binds up wounds, and offers hope is the priest who hears and dares to be involved in the complexity of human existence.

The priest people turn to is one who dares to enter the lives of others with the good news of Jesus Christ and the good news that *this* priest understands. It is not an arrogant understanding but an empathetic meeting of two human beings who share victory and defeat; moments of grace and sin; and dare to tell each other their fears and hopes. People experience in such a priest a connection and a feeling that they are being taken seriously and are being offered the hope of a new beginning. The priest who follows Jesus is a man of conviction; he speaks the truth in love, and respects people enough to trust them with their freedom. The priest who follows Jesus and leads others to Jesus is a priest who serves by empowering others to recognize their own gifts. The priest who serves always seeks the liberation of persons whereby Christ makes them free.

These reflections on the pastoral dimensions conclude with the powerful words of the outstanding Christian pastor and counselor Howard Clinebell:

> When people touched Jesus' life, they experienced in him the healing power that comes from openness to oneself, others, nature, and God. They encountered a person whose life was a deep channel through which the

source of all healing and growth — the loving spirit of God — flowed freely and fully.

When people touch my life or yours, what do they sense? The noisy static of our harried times, perhaps? As instruments for deepening and enlivening relationships, pastoral care and counseling can help bring continuing renewal to us as ministers and to persons in the church and in the community! Such renewal comes as a refreshing rain to a parched land. (*Basic Types of Pastoral Care and Counseling*, pp. 15-16)

Toward a Priestly Spirituality

CHAPTER NINE

MARY:
The Priest and Holiness

In this final section of reflections, we examine the challenging task of advancing a priestly spirituality. Each word in the task before us must be clarified. I will be suggesting *a* priestly spirituality. What follows should in no way be taken to mean there is only one spirituality to which all priests must conform. Like Joseph's coat and the gifts of the Spirit, there are many colors and a rich diversity of gifts. Taken together, the colors provide one with a beautiful coat and the Church with a talented community working for the common good in the Spirit. There are many roads which lead to the one true God made visible in Jesus. What follows is simply *a* spirituality which will require the reader to be selective. The reader is invited to incorporate what is helpful and lay aside what is lacking. Hopefully, the careful reader will even be moved to supply what is deficient.

What follows is a *priestly* spirituality. Through the sacrament of Baptism, all the people of God are called to be priests and live a holy life. Each Christian, through Baptism, becomes a member of a royal people chosen by God to be his instrument in history. In addition to this priesthood of all believers, there is the ordained ministry of the priest. This is the priestly ministry of those called by God to preach the Gospel, celebrate the Eucharist, and help form a community of faith which acknowledges Jesus as Lord. The *priestly spirituality* advanced

will be one which centers on the needs of the ordained priest
who is called by God from the community for the community.
Such a *priestly* spirituality is not at odds with the spirituality of
the other Catholic Christians. The emphasis and orientation
are different. The needs reflect the concerns of those who are
called to ordained priestly leadership. Yet the *priestly* spirituality advanced will be distorted if it is isolated from the rest of
the community of faith.

Finally, I want to present a priestly *spirituality*. The
approach I have in mind is grounded in the biblical view that
all is grace and in the Catholic analogical imagination which
tries to find creative ways of relating various aspects of reality
into a whole. Simply put, an authentic spirituality is one which
takes seriously nature, history, and human experience as
sacramental. Each of these contain the real possibility of
revealing the saving, healing, unbounded love of God. There is
no area of human existence and no aspect of reality which is
isolated from God's grace. At any time, we may find ourselves
surprised by grace. The priestly *spirituality* propounded does
not seek a retreat into the heavens, but is one which embraces
all of the ambiguity, complexity, and glory of God's good
creation and our gifted existence. The priestly *spirituality*
offered is one which rejoices in all that is truly human. The
glory of God is the human person fully alive!

The concluding section of these reflections will examine
four major areas which will contribute to our priestly spirituality. In this initial reflection, we shall explore the priestly call to
holiness by turning to Mary as the disclosure model for such a
priestly spirituality. Next we will focus our attention on the
priest as spiritual leader of the faith community. Simon-Peter
will serve as our disclosure model. The third major area of
priestly spirituality will be the importance of women in the life
of the priest. It will be my contention that the quality and depth
of priestly ministry and spirituality is greatly enhanced if the
priest is blessed with women friends. The Gospel of Luke
provides us with a number of important episodes in the life of
Jesus for which women played a significant role. We will

examine these episodes and their relevance for a priestly spirituality. Finally, our reflections will conclude with a reflection on Jesus as Priest, High Priest, and the Priest to turn to. In the end, we all must turn to Jesus as the Way, the Truth, and the Life. No matter how much the Church changes and the role of the priest is transformed, there remains the Person of Jesus.

Before we turn our attention to Mary as the disclosure model for a priestly spirituality, a brief word needs to be offered about Mary and her place with the Catholic story and the Christian tradition. Of special concern are the following: Mary as the one who reveals key aspects about God; Mary as revelatory of authentic human existence; and finally, a word about the importance of Mary in our post-Vatican II age.

It Was Mary

Without a doubt, Mary, through her person, story, and symbol, has exerted a powerful influence on the religious imagination of Western Christianity. This influence is especially pronounced in the areas of art and popular piety. Father Andrew M. Greeley highlights the influence of Mary this way:

> Virtually every major painter from the fifth to the sixteenth century painted at least one Madonna. Great cathedrals sprang up all over Europe and still stand. Poets sing her praises, including such improbable characters as Petrarch, Boccaccio, Francois Villon, Shelley, Byron, Rilke. Football teams enter battle in her name. It will be a long time before a football team named after Atlas is number one. On the basis of history, if nothing else, in any competition between Heilbroner's Atlas and Henry Adams' Virgin of Chartres, there isn't much doubt who would win. (*The Mary Myth*, p. 10)

Not only in the areas of art and architecture has Mary made a difference, but also in the hearts of "the little ones." Mary occupies a special place in the faith-life of countless

Christians who cannot resist singing her praises. To be sure, there have been abuses: devotion to Mary has, at times, lacked good taste as well as sound theology; the impression could be easily given that Mary was being worshiped as a goddess; and the piety that surrounded the cult of Mary has led to a quietism and withdrawal from the concerns of social justice. Without denying any of these, we must say that the fault lies not with Mary but with us. Mary would be the first to indicate that she is only a handmaid and servant of the Lord. Honorifics, titles, and official dogmatic pronouncements are not what Mary is about; nor are they what she was after. Mary is the lowly one of God in whom the Word became visible. She never desired to be confused with, or to replace, the Lord who looked down upon her in her lowliness. If and when we find certain aspects of Mariology offensive, know that Mary has found it so before us.

Yet with all of the abuses, exaggerations, and bad taste associated with the cult of Mary, she endures; and Mary has even made a comeback in our Church come of age. Why? Catholic Christians (and, if the truth be told, more and more of our Protestant brothers and sisters are turning to Mary and finding her as fascinating and attractive as we Catholics) know at some deep level that Mary is simply too valuable to let go of. Try as we might, we are hopefully hung up on Mary and we won't let go. At the level where the Holy Spirit speaks to our spirit, individually and collectively, we realize that Mary reveals some powerful truths about God. Namely, Mary reveals to us the womanly aspects of God. Mary reveals to us the passionate, unconditional, life-giving, life-supporting, tender, challenging, non-judgmental, and, above all, hopeful love of God. We see revealed in Mary a real human being who invites us to trust, believe, live, and hope in the God of surprises who makes all things new. Mary tells us that we can risk being given to this God who is faithful to his promises and brings forth new life in the most unlikely of circumstances. Just when all seems barren and when we come to believe that the laws of biology determine our lives, in comes the Holy Spirit with the dance of grace. Sarah will have Isaac:

Elizabeth's reproach is removed with the leaping John in the womb; and Mary will be overshadowed by the Holy Spirit and provide a human face for God. We would be foolish to give up Mary. We would be crazy to give up the God she helps us to experience!

Mary, through her person, story, and symbol, has something profound to reveal about the human condition. When we speak about what God has done for and through Mary, we are also speaking about what God has done for the human family. The Word is to be made flesh in our lives daily. We are to bear and give birth to Jesus in our own personal stables, for we, too, know the pain of rejection since the world still finds no room for the Savior. Our hearts are daily pierced as we journey to Jerusalem and stand beneath the Cross and keep vigil. But the dawn comes on Easter, with its promise of resurrection, and we are there as well. Like Mary, we find ourselves at times locked behind the closed door of fear. Yet we still open our hearts to the rush of the Spirit and it inflames our hearts as on that first Pentecost. We hope one day to be received into heaven and find Mary waiting along with her Son and our Brother. What God has done for Mary, God wants to do for us in our lowliness. Mary reminds us that the way to true freedom and hope lies along the path of faith in the God who does great things for us.

An unfortunate impression was left in the days following the Second Vatican Council that Mary was no longer a "significant other" in the Church or in the life of the Catholic Christian. In the rush to relevancy (in many instances, silliness) and the desire to prove we had come of age, divestment from the old Church was called for. Traditional forms of piety and worship (the cult of the saints, angels and demons, candles and rosaries, novenas and private devotions) were seen as stumbling blocks to renewal. Churches were not build upward but now took on a decidedly horizontal flavor in order to emphasize the immensity of God and the need for fellowship. Even the Eucharist had to undergo a significant theological change. More and more its emphasis had to be on its connection with what was going on in the streets and in front of the barricades. Liturgy became "relevant and meaningful" to the extent it emphasized our common humanity and the need to be "socially concerned." Liturgy and various popular devotions (of which those to Mary seemed a decided stumbling block) were often seen as hindrances to the social justice dimensions of Church mission and Gospel ministry. Lost in all of this frenzy were the words of the Council itself:

> Mary was involved in the mysteries of Christ. As the most holy Mother of God, she after her Son, exalted by divine grace above all angels and men. Hence the Church appropriately honors her with special reverence. Indeed, from most ancient times the Blessed Virgin has been venerated under the title of "God-bearer." In all perils and needs, the faithful have fled prayerfully to her protection. (*Dogmatic Constitution on the Church*, #66)

These words of praise for Mary are balanced by a prudent call to honor her in light of the unsurpassed goodness of God. Again, the words of the Council:

> The Church has endorsed many forms of piety toward the Mother of God, provided that they were within the limits of sound and orthodox doctrine. These forms have varied according to the circumstances of time and place and have reflected the diversity of native characteristics and temperament among the faithful. While Christ's Mother is honored, these devotions cause her Son to be rightly known, loved, and glorified, and all His commands observed. . . .
> Let the faithful remember moreover that true devotion consists neither in fruitless and passing emotion, nor in a certain vain credulity. Rather, it proceeds from true faith, by which we are led to know the excellence of the Mother of God, and are moved to a filial love toward our mother and to the imitation of her virtues. (*Dogmatic Constitution on the Church*, #66, 67)

The Council went on to address a special word to theologians and preachers, exhorting them to "carefully and equally avoid the falsity of exaggeration on the one hand, and the excess of narrow-mindedness on the other." Catholic theologians and preachers (Protestants, as well) have been more and more lending their time and talent to developing a prudent, sound Mariology. The importance of Mary in the life of the Church's social justice mission is but one area of fruitful development (see Harvey Cox's *Religion in the Secular City*, Leonard Boff's *The Maternal Face of God*, and my *Mary: Model of Justice* from Alba House). Other theologians have sought to relate Mary to such issues as God-talk, ecclesiology, ethics, spirituality, and the role of women in Church and society. Such creative and fruitful theologizing should enhance the quality of preaching and deepen one's relationship with Jesus Christ.

With these all too brief preliminary considerations in mind, we now turn our attention to Mary in the life of the priest. To be specific, we want to draw close to Mary as a disclosure model for the development of a priestly spirituality. In what follows, we shall examine five specific areas of Mary' s life as they relate to the life of the priest. From these five specific areas, namely, Annunciation, Visitation, Intercession on behalf of others, Disciple at the foot of the Cross, and Messenger of Hope, a priestly spirituality will be advanced. This relationship between the life of Mary and the life of the priest is constitutive of Christian existence and a priestly spirituality. The turn to Mary seems to guide us into a deeper turn to Jesus. The priest who comes to Jesus through Mary is the kind of priest people turn to. Father Karl Rahner, S.J. writes:

> God's salvation and his salvation-history are completely personalist. Salvation-history is carried on not by things, but by persons, by their freedom, their decision, and thus our relationship to the church is given shape in our relationship to Mary . . . She is not merely a private individual who has made good in her private life: she is an irremovable and necessary factor in God's plan of this salvation-history. We are therefore sustained by what she

did . . . Therefore devotion to Mary, built into and
included within the wholeness of Christian life, is something essential for the Christian and particularly for the
priest; something for which we can and should seek God's
grace, in order really to possess, cherish and maintain
this living personal relationship to Mary the mother of the
Lord and thus our mother also. (*The Priesthood*, pp. 263,
264)

It is to the Mary of the Annunciation that we now focus our
attention and begin the never-ending process of developing a
priestly spirituality.

The Annunciation: Openness to the Word

The Gospel of Luke contains the announcement of the
birth of Jesus (Lk 1:26-38). The angel Gabriel announced to
Mary that she was highly favored, blessed, and would conceive
a child who would be called "Son of the Most High." Her son
would inaugurate the eternal reign of God. Naturally, Mary
was "deeply troubled" by the angel's words, and she wanted to
know how she could conceive and give birth since she was a
virgin. The angel indicated that this child would be born of the
Holy Spirit. Even Elizabeth, in her old age, would be blessed
with a child. There are no limits to the grace of God. The scene
closes with Mary declaring that she is the "servant of the
Lord." God's will, however humanly incomprehensible, would
be realized in Mary. Mary freely opened herself to the mystery
of God's unbounded love.

This beautiful and simple story reveals the soul of Mary.
She is a person of basic trust and deep faith. Mary is not
stripped of her humanity by Luke. Rather, Luke presents us
with a Mary with whom we can identify. She is "deeply
troubled" and filled with many questions. Mary wants to know
how all of this is to be accomplished. She has a faith which
seeks understanding. Her questioning is not a sign of disre-
spect, but an indication that Mary's belief seeks greater
knowledge about God. Yet there are always limits to what we

humans can comprehend. There comes a time when our being "deeply troubled" must give way to basic trust. Even though we do not know the whole of what is being asked of us by God, we surrender into the incomprehensible mystery of his love. This is not an irrational leap into an unknown abyss, but a hopeful walking into the arms of the God who goes before us. There comes a time when God's word addresses the individual with all of its ambiguity and challenge. God waits for a response. God waits for free responses like Mary's "I am the servant of the Lord. Let it be done to me as you say."

The call to follow Jesus and serve the People of God as a priest is part of God's unbounded love and the mystery of grace. While few of us are visited by Gabriel, we all have our own angels, signals of transcendence, and secondary causes (St. Thomas). Each priest is able to point to some witness or messenger (priest, nun, mother, relative, friend) who helped us to first seriously consider following Jesus as a priest. At first blush, we, too, were often "deeply troubled" at the thought of a religious vocation. How can this be, since we are not perfect, we fight with our sister and parents, and we go on dates? Often we found ourselves more like Jacob wrestling with the angel than Mary quietly inquiring as to how all this was to take place. Yet in time, we came to accept without fully understanding (Do we ever fully understand this gift of a vocation?) the working of the Holy Spirit in us. We realize that nothing is impossible with God. Into our ordinary lives, God comes and challenges us to be open to the Spirit. The grace which offers a vocation is the same grace which allows us to say with Mary, "I am the servant of the Lord. Let it be done to me as you say."

The announcement of Jesus' birth to Mary and the call to serve as a priest requires three things: trust, discernment, and surrender. Mary had to trust that the angel's message was true and was meant for her. What was being offered confounded human reason. What was being offered was God's impossible dream working through human limitations. The same holds true for the priest. The vocation to the priesthood is never earned but offered as pure gift. This call to serve is not a right but a privilege. The priestly vocation begins with God, is fostered by others, sustained by others, and brought to completion through the grace of him who first called us. Trust is essential throughout the life of the priest.

The call to Mary required discernment. Mary was moved to ask the angel what his message meant. From seminary to parish and beyond, the priest must ask in prayer what God requires of him. We must be prudent in testing the spirits and courageous in acting on God's word. Discernment requires a life dedicated to *receiving* spiritual direction. The Holy Spirit brought forth new life in Mary and a spirit of understanding which allowed her to be a servant of the Lord. That same Spirit is at work in the priest, who is challenged to let God's Word take root and be born in him. The Holy Spirit is at work in the life of the priest, empowering him to be a servant of the Lord for all God's people. Discernment is not endless introspection, but the prudent balance between prayerful listening and purposeful action.

Finally, Mary surrenders to the will of God and the Word who will become flesh in her. Mary's surrender is not a fatalistic giving up, but a loving handing over of her life to the One who is Life and Light. The Annunciation at first finds Mary "deeply troubled," but, at the end, we find Mary experiencing that peace which comes to all those who surrender to the will of God. Each priest must live a life of daily surrender to the will of God. Only by such a surrender, such a handing over, do we come to know the peace of Christ. This is not a peace of passivity, but a peace within the tension of daily life. We are not always sure that we are making the right decisions, doing the most loving things, or following the will of God. We must simply hand the decision over to the Lord. Again, this is not a surrender of despair, but a willingness to place the final outcome in the loving providence of God.

Prayer for Openness to God's Word

O Lord our God, pour forth your grace into
    our hearts and prepare us daily to receive

and be renewed by grace.
You have blessed us with the call to serve
    you as priests.
Help us to lead a life worthy of our calling.
Help us to trust in your Word when doubts
    assail us;
help us to discern your will when confusion
    clouds our thoughts and will;
and help us to surrender to your loving will
    when we are tempted to pride.
Lord, aid us in following the example of Mary
    so that your will may be done in us
    and we may be your faithful servants.

The Visitation: The Woman for Others

Mary is not self-important. After the angel Gabriel announced that she would be the mother of Jesus, we might
expect Mary to have gathered her friends and relatives for a
party. After all, Mary had been chosen by God to be the mother
of "the Son of the Most High." We might expect Mary to have
used this announcement for her advantage. She would want to
be served and honored by others. Mary's special status and
vocation were signs of privilege and she would let others know
that she was someone special. Yet such was not the case.

St. Luke tells us that, after the Annunciation and with the
departure of Gabriel, "Mary set out, proceeding in haste into
the hill country to a town of Judah, where she entered
Zechariah's house and greeted Elizabeth" (Lk 1:39-40). Mary
had been told of Elizabeth's good news: that she would have a
son in her old age. Mary went in haste to be with Elizabeth in
order to help her with the pregnancy. She did not mention her
own good news, but was totally concerned about Elizabeth. It
was Mary who went to Elizabeth and wanted to know how she
could be of service. Mary did not wait for Elizabeth to come to
her. Mary did not tell Elizabeth that her role in salvation-
history was most important. Mary came in order to be of
service. Her son, Jesus, would in time tell the disciples that he

is among them as one who serves (Lk 22:27). The prenatal influence of Mary on Jesus cannot be doubted. She was and is the woman for others and the mother of the Man for others. This woman who was a servant of the Lord and of her neighbor was also the mother of the One who shows us the depth of service — the Cross. Luke closes the episode of the Visitation with these simple words: "Mary remained with Elizabeth about three months and then returned home" (Lk 1:56). The visit of Mary, her service and departure, were done without fanfare. Mary quietly did what was required.

The call to priesthood is the call to be among God's people as one who serves. Priesthood is not a position of status, honor, or power. Priesthood places on the one called the responsibility to be in the community as a servant of the servants and the one who washes the feet of the people. The priest must follow the example of Mary and make haste in searching out those in need. The priest knows how to be among people as one who shares their joys, feels their pain, and stays with them as a fellow companion who understands. The priest does not proclaim himself or his separateness from the community, but he tells the stories of God and rejoices in the many gifts of the Spirit for the common good. The priest must be ever mindful that his vocation is the result of God's grace. The words of Mary's Canticle give poetic expression to this deep truth: "For he has looked upon his servant in her lowliness. . . God who is mighty has done great things for me . . ." (Lk 1:46, 49).

The temptation is always present to fight over titles, places of honor, and to be among the people as one who is served. Clericalism did not die at the Second Vatican Council. And priestly arrogance is not the special flaw of the right or the left. Conservatives can fall into the trap of wanting to be served and seeing the priestly vocation as privilege. Priesthood becomes an exalted status, in which power and control reign. Liberals often fall into the trap of intellectual arrogance and moral superiority. In the name of tolerance, liberals can be most intolerant. If one does not agree with a certain position or program, one is labelled unenlightened or morally insensitive.

Mary's visitation of Elizabeth teaches us that the true privilege is the call to serve. It is not an arrogant service of superiority or a manipulative service which comes from trying to control others. The kind of service given by Mary is simple, respectful of persons and their freedom, and one filled with joy. The priest people turn to is one who makes himself available and whose "being proclaims the greatness of the Lord."

Prayer for a Spirit of True Service

O Lord, before whom every heart is open,
>   grant us the grace to forget ourselves.
Allow us to remember your many gifts and
>   grant us the generous spirit of sharing with others.
Help us to be strong and wise enough to let
>   others share their gifts with us.
Let us realize that each person whom we serve
>   is precious in your eyes and is your
>   precious gift to us as well.
In our service as priests, let us follow the example
of Mary, who experienced true joy
>   in rejoicing with others.
Let us imitate Jesus who lived in our midst
>   as a servant and who told us to follow
>   his example.
O Lord, let us experience the call to priesthood
>   as an invitation to holiness;
a holiness which touches you in others.

The Wedding at Cana: Faith in Times of Transition

The Gospel of John does not use the term "miracle" for the works of Jesus, but rather the term "sign." "Miracle" can be a misleading term in that it conveys a sense of magic and superstition when wrongly understood. Jesus comes to be presented as a magician or wonder-worker seeking popularity and power. By contrast, the term "sign" is used so as to indicate that what Jesus does *points beyond* the event to the loving will of the Father. Signs are not hitching-posts, but indicators of the God who is at work in the world. Signs lead us, when viewed through faith, beyond the event and to the glory of the Father through Jesus. Jesus comes to do the will of the Father. All glory goes to the Father whom Jesus has been sent to reveal. The Fourth Gospel lists seven signs: the changing of the water into wine at the wedding at Cana (Ch. 2); the cure of the royal official's son (Ch. 4); the cure of the sick man by the Sheep Pool (Ch. 5); the multiplication of the loaves and fishes (Ch. 6); the walking on the Sea (Ch. 7); and the culmination of the signs with the raising of Lazarus (Ch. 11).

The first sign seems simple enough on the face of it. Jesus, Mary, and the disciples were attending a wedding and the wine ran out. This could have caused great embarrassment to the couple and their families. What should be done? Mary told Jesus of the problem. At first, Jesus did not wish to be concerned with such a matter. He was a guest and not the host. However, Mary, exercising the prerogative of a Jewish mother (she probably had some Irish, as well), simply instructed the attendants to "do whatever he tells you" (Jn 2:5). We know that the water became wine. In fact, it was the best wine that had been served at the wedding. The head waiter wanted to know why the best had been saved for last.

The simplicity of this story and sign should not obscure its rich meaning and profound consequences. Neither should we overlook the manner of Mary. The sign at Cana is the first revelation of Jesus' glory and occasions the belief of the disciples, however imperfect (v. 11). The changing of the water into wine indicated that Jesus and the Father shared the same glory. The Word is God and now that Word had been made visible. The curtain now starts to rise on the true identity of Jesus and we see his glory, "the glory of an only Son coming from the Father, filled with enduring love" (Jn 1:14). The first of the signs is profoundly Christological in nature and began the process of the revelation of Jesus' glory which would culminate on the Cross. It was on the Cross that the full glory would be revealed. That is, God's very nature would be shown to all as suffering, enduring love for all humankind.

Secondly, the sign at Cana is an eschatological sign. That is, it signals the coming presence of the Messiah. Also, the sign is performed within the context of a wedding which itself is associated with the end time. The abundance of wine and the setting of a wedding serve to highlight that God was now at work in a definitive manner in revealing his glory, fulfilling Israel's history, and that the Messiah was in their midst. The Old Testament is replete with references (Am 9:13; Is 29:17; Hos 2:24; Jr 31:5) linking the abundance of new wine with the coming salvation by God. The prophet Joel provides us with these words:

> And then, on that day,
>   the mountains shall drip new wine,
>   and the hills shall flow with milk;
> And the channels of Judah
>   shall flow with water;
> A fountain shall issue from the
>   house of the Lord, to water the Valley
>   of Shittim. (Jl 4:18)

Finally, the sign at Cana signalled a break with the past and the superiority of Jesus over the traditions of Judaism. With the person of Jesus, the new covenant had replaced the old. Only by turning in faith to Jesus as the Son of God can one worship in spirit and truth. Only in the Word made flesh does one come to know eternal life (Jn 17:3). The sign at Cana clearly contrasted the precious wine which Jesus had given with the water used for Jewish rites of purification. The water was obsolete and must be replaced with the abundant wine provided by Jesus. The law would be replaced by grace in the person of Jesus: "For while the law was given through Moses, this enduring love came through Jesus Christ. No one has ever seen God. It is God the only Son, ever at the Father's side, who has revealed him" (Jn 1:17).

The simple story at Cana contains the seeds of the most profound of changes — the old covenant of Law was being replaced by the new covenant of Grace in the person of Jesus,

the Son of God. The old creeds, codes, and cults are like water
when wine is called for — lacking and in need of replacement.
The sign at Cana is the first of the dramatic episodes which will
invite all people to believe that Jesus is the Son of God. The
familiar ways of worship and the security provided by the great
traditions and structures of Judaism must make way for the
One who is Truth and Life and Light. None of this would be
easy. Much would be required. The pull of the past is strong
and the lure of the future must always contend with the timidity
of the human heart. Yet this is what is now being required. The
only true temple of worship is Jesus' own body (Jn 2:13) and
only those who are born again of the Spirit can enter God's
Kingdom (Jn 3:5).

Catholics have experienced their own Cana with the
Second Vatican Council. The Holy Spirit blew in ways which
called for updating, renewal, and even replacement. Much
was being asked of the Church as the People of God. The Spirit
was at work reminding us that we are a pilgrim people who
cannot afford to become too comfortable or complacent with
what is. We must also move toward that goal where Christ
Jesus reigns on high. Our once fruitful structures and traditions were being pruned so that the branches could become
more intimately related to the True Vine (Jn 15:1). But pruning
is painful and all growth exacts a price. Natural birth happens
amidst pain, sweat, tears, suffering, and the shedding of
blood. It is no different with our spiritual rebirth. There is the
pain of birth but also the joy of new life. In the words of Jesus:

> When a woman is in labor she is sad that her time has
> come. When she has borne her child, she no longer
> remembers her pain for joy that a man has been born into
> the world. In the same way, you are sad for a time, but I
> shall see you again; then your hearts will rejoice with a
> joy no one can take from you. (Jn 16:21-22)

As I mentioned in the Introduction and the opening
chapter of these reflections, the priesthood (and priests lest we

forget the human in our desire to focus on the structure) has undergone significant changes since Vatican II. There has been a profound pruning of the Church as a whole and the priesthood in particular. At times, this process has been quite painful, but there is also the joy which comes with new life. Exciting new ways of being Church and priest have been born in the last two decades. The priest has been called to renew the biblical roots of priesthood along the models of servant and herald. Such models do not conflict with the liturgical aspects of priesthood; rather, they help complement and enrich what it means to be a priest of Jesus Christ in the service of the Gospel and the Church.

How do we as priests respond to our time of transition? How do we grow through the pain so that the joy of new life will be born in us? How do we continue to be born again in our priestly ministry? The words of Mary are for us: "Do whatever he tells you" (Jn 2:5). These are not the words of arrogance or presumption. They come from the heart of a woman who knows how to trust. These are the words of a woman who is at peace amidst the tensions of everyday life. In the face of a shortage and a time of transition, Mary was able to trust and be at peace because Jesus will provide. There is still the need to turn to Jesus. There is still the need for using what is available (water). Human effort must join with grace. However, there was no fear or frantic action by Mary. She just trusted that Jesus would bring forth the best from what was at hand.

The shortage of priests in a time of transition is not a time for fear, panic, or frantic action. It is a time for prayer, serious reflection on the priesthood in light of the signs of the times, and a courageous trust that Jesus will bring forth the best from what is at hand. We need to have the confidence of Mary: "Do whatever he tells you." Jesus is speaking through the Spirit. The real challenge confronts us: "Are we prayerful enough to listen? Are we courageous enough to ask? Are we hopeful enough to believe that the best will be brought forth from what is at hand?"

Prayer for Faith in Times of Transition

O Lord, at times we find ourselves facing a
    crumbling world where all our
        certainties melt into air.
We are afraid and fear moves us into greater
    darkness as we act by our demons and
        ignore our finer angels.
Fill us with your renewing Spirit and change
    our hearts of stone to flesh.
    Give us the courage to be born anew and
        accept the pain that comes with
        all growth and new life.
Daily we see the world as we know it passing away.
    The Church of our youth has changed many times over.
    The priesthood of our ordination has
        passed into the priesthood of today.
O God, open our eyes to see in all passings
    and changes your loving Providence.
Grant us a spirit of serenity to live for You
    and our neighbor in this passing world,
        with our hearts set on that
        world which never ends.
In the midst of all that is dying and being replaced,
    let us be one with Mary in believing
        You will bring forth what is best.
Let us do whatever You tell us, knowing that
    in doing Your word we shall know true Peace.

The Foot of the Cross: Faithful Love

From the perspective of the Fourth Gospel, it is on the
Cross that the glory of Jesus is revealed and the Father's name
is revealed as suffering, enduring love. It is at the foot of the
Cross, as well, that we witness faithful love. John tells the story
with a restraint that befits the occasion:

Near the cross of Jesus there stood his mother, his
mother's sister, Mary the wife of Clopas, and Mary Mag-

dalene. Seeing his mother there with the disciple whom
he loved, Jesus said to his mother, "Woman, there is your
son." In turn he said to the disciple, "There is your
mother." From that hour onward, the disciple took her
into his care. (Jn 19:25-27)

The Mary of the Annunciation, Visitation, and wedding
at Cana is also the Mary who must fulfill the words of Simeon,
"you yourself shall be pierced with a sword — so that the
thoughts of many hearts may be laid bare" (Lk 2:35). Mary is
not spared or excused from suffering. In fact, because Mary
loves so deeply and is so committed to Jesus, her pain is all the
more acute. To love is to know suffering. To love is to feel the
hurt of others and to keep company with the fallen. Mary did
not speak beneath the Cross. It is the eloquence of all that has
gone before and the power of her silent vigil that speaks down
through the ages. Long ago, the will of the Most High was made
flesh in her. The will of the Father was once again being
accomplished. No doubt Mary found herself deeply troubled.
Yet once again, as servant and disciple, she surrendered to the
will of God. The work of continuing the revelation of God would
not stop. It passed into the community of faith symbolized by
Mary and the Beloved Disciple. Even beneath the shadow of
the Cross, there was the message of hope; the Paraclete would
guide the community in truth (Jn 16:13; 19:30). With his death
on the Cross, Jesus' work of revealing the Father was completed. Jesus handed on the Spirit.

Priestly existence is lived under the Cross. There can be
no growth in priestly holiness apart from the Cross and the
need to be tested by suffering. The school of suffering is often
lacking in students, especially in a culture which believes that
life is to be enjoyed and we should only do what feels good. It
cannot be stressed enough that Jesus' suffering and death did
not remove these from the human condition. Jesus' passion and
death changed the *meaning* of these consequences of sin.
Jesus experienced our sufferings and died a real death. In so
doing, he robbed them of their ultimate claim on us. Jesus'

passion and death are the signs of his total love for us. It is not
the sins of Jesus that put him on the Cross, but our sins which
he accepted out of love. St. Paul, writing to the Romans, is
caught up in the depth of this love:

> At the appointed time, when we were still powerless,
> Christ died for us godless men. It is rare that anyone
> should lay down his life for a just man, though it is barely
> possible that for a good man someone may have the
> courage to die. It is precisely in this that God proves his
> love for us: that while we were still sinners, Christ died
> for us. (Rm 5:6-8)

The sufferings of most priests are often hidden from view
and shared with few. There is the pain of loneliness, single
meals, and, all too often, an absence of clerical support. There
is the cross as well as the charism of celibacy. The absence of a
family of one's own cannot be replaced with an empty room of
one's own. Each priest has experienced the pain of being
misunderstood and often written off as too idealistic, too lib-
eral, too progressive, or worse, irrelevant. How often are the
times when the well-prepared sermon fails to move the spirit?
Who has not known the frustration of working on a project,
preparing a class, or organizing an activity, only to have it
undermined by indifference, rivalry, and the pettiness of
which we humans are so capable? At times, the priest is
assailed by doubts and questions his vocation. Most of what
consumes our day consumes us with feelings of despair. We
can feel that we don't make a difference. The absence of God
can be more of a reality than his presence. The Cross is much
with us.

What to do? Again, we turn to Mary as a model for priestly
holiness through suffering. We must do what the world finds so
astounding, namely, we must treasure all these things and
reflect on them in our hearts (Lk 2:19). Yes, even, and most
especially, the Cross. It is the ultimate revelation of God's love
and our hope of glory. The Cross comes to each priest in the
particularity of his vocation. The Cross fits into his situation.

Like Mary, we are challenged to let God's will be done; to grow in love through suffering; and keep faithful watch with the God whose faithful love sets us free. Our own particular cross, when united with the Cross of Jesus, does not eliminate the suffering. However, it does change the meaning. Our cross is not a sign of punishment, but an invitation to grow in holiness.

Prayer to Grow in Holiness Through the Cross

O Lord, You are Holy and call us to be holy as well.
    This invitation fills us with fear
        for we are all too human;
    we fall short of Your glory.
In the depth of our being, we hear the call
    of the Holy Spirit to be conformed
        to Your love.
    Again, we are afraid. We know that
    growth in holiness requires of us
        a willingness to suffer.
We are hesitant to be tested in the fire;
    we may be destroyed in the crucible;
        we may flee the chalice.
Yet we want to do Your will and be your
        priestly servants.
    Help us to be one with Mary and the
        Blessed Disciple. In our own cross
        let us minister in the shadow of Your Cross.
For when we surrender our spirit to You
    we are renewed. We are tired, but
    Your grace spurs us on. We are faint,
    but we shall not stop. We are weak,
    but You lift us up on eagles' wings.
O Lord, You are holy.
Help us to be an image of Your holiness. Amen.

Pentecost/Assumption: Mary Our Hope

The Cross of Jesus Christ must always be understood in relation to the joy of Easter. The death of Jesus needs to be experienced within the horizon of the hope of resurrection. In dying to ourselves and sin, we hope to rise to new life. This is not a hope based on our merits, but on the gracious will of God at work in Jesus. The story of the Cross continues on to the next chapter which tells us that he is risen! The One who died now lives. The One who rose is now alive at the right hand of the Father. Yet Jesus does not abandon us, but sends the Holy Spirit (Mt 28:18-20; Jn 20:21-23; Ac 2:1-4). The story of the death and resurrection of Jesus must continue in history through the Church. And we find Mary not only at the foot of the Cross, but also at the start of the Church's history:

> After that [the Ascension] they [the Eleven] returned to Jerusalem from the mount called Olivet near Jerusalem . . . Entering the city, they went to the upstairs room where they were staying . . . Together they devoted themselves to constant prayer. There were some women in their company, and Mary the mother of Jesus, and his brothers. (Ac 1:12-14)

On that first Pentecost, the Holy Spirit liberated them from fear and sent them forth to proclaim the good news about Jesus. The heart of Mary, which had known its share of suffering, was now filled with the renewing presence of the Spirit. No doubt Mary did much to contribute to the life of the early Church and the quality of its life. Again, we turn to Acts:

> Those who believed shared all things in common; they would sell their property and goods, dividing everything on the basis of each one's need. They went to the temple area together every day, while in their homes they broke bread. With exultant and sincere hearts they took their meals in common, praising God and winning the approval of all the people. Day by day the Lord added to their number those who were being saved. (Ac 2:44-47)

We see clearly that Mary was a woman of the Church. She has contributed in a lasting way to the community of faith. The

Church has honored her throughout the generations and called her blessed (Lk 1:48). The Catholic community joyfully celebrates the Assumption of Mary, that is, Mary being received into heaven without undergoing bodily corruption. Through God's grace, Mary anticipates the effects of Jesus' death by her Immaculate Conception and the effects of Jesus' Resurrection in her Assumption. At the first and the last of life, she was full of grace. At the edges of life, she was the servant of the Lord and was received into the unbounded love of God. Mary's total centering in the Lord, her life of holiness, culminated with her being taken in the presence of the God who is holiness itself. Mary anticipates our destiny and offers encouragements as we make our pilgrimage. When we look at Mary, we see a fellow human being through whom God has done wondrous things. So it is with us. When we look to Mary, we can hope. We can look at the Cross and know that there is the resurrection. We can look to Mary and know with blessed faith that her Assumption is offered to us as an encouragement. In Mary, we see the victory of Jesus. It is a victory not simply for her, but for all humankind. From the beginning, Mary believed, loved, and hoped, and she was not disappointed.

The priest is a man of the Church, a man whose life witnesses to hope in Christ. The holiness of the priest contains the tension of the here and not yet; the everyday concerns of this world while pointing to the new Jerusalem. What Mary teaches the priest, Christian, and Church as a whole is this: God is faithful to his promises and his grace can do mighty things through us. Holiness comes through suffering and a willingness to serve and keep vigil in the shadow of the Cross. At times, our life and ministry may seem to be crashing all around us. We find ourselves deeply troubled over what the Lord is asking of us. The witness of Mary tells us to hold on and hope. Every cross united with the Cross of Jesus gives way to the joy of Easter. The God who called us to be priests is the same God who inflames our hearts to preach the Gospel, celebrate the Eucharist, and build up the Body of Christ. This same God also waits to receive us, when our earthly days are

done, into that fellowship of the Spirit with Jesus, Mary, and
the community of saints.

A Prayer of Hope to the Holy Spirit

O Holy Spirit, liberate us from fear and give
    us the courage to proclaim the Gospel.
Set our hearts free so that we may boldly go forth
    and witness to the great things
        God has done for us.
Let us not be arrogant or filled with a sense
    of self-importance. Let us follow the
    example of Mary and turn humbly to You
        in all our joys and seek You
        in all our sufferings.
Let Your gifts be used in us for the good of
    the Church. Over all Your gifts,
    let us show love which unites and
    perfects all gifts for the common good.
O Spirit, enlighten our minds, enliven our
    imaginations and warm our hearts so we
    may better serve like Jesus and Mary.
Help us when doubts assail to know that You
    are waiting to receive us into the
    eternity of Your Unbounded Love.

A Life Worthy of Your Calling

As a second year college seminarian, I was privileged to
participate in a retreat conducted by then Father Bernie Law
(who has since gone on to become Cardinal Law of Boston).
The theme of his retreat was taken from the words of St. Paul to
the Ephesians:

> I plead with you, then, as a prisoner for the Lord, to live a
> life worthy of the calling you have received, with perfect
> humility, meekness, and patience, bearing with one
> another lovingly. (Ep 4: 1-2)

His conferences centered around the call of Jesus to follow him as priests in the service of the Gospel and the Church. This call was directed to us personally and was a sign of Jesus' love for us. Father Law stressed the importance of God's call as the invitation to a life of holy service. All that we would do as priests would bear fruit if we humbly served in the name of Jesus. A priestly spirituality which follows the example of Mary is humble, meek, patient, and loving. To live a life worthy of our calling, to be a holy priest, is to experience the grace of that hope given by our call. In the midst of many temptations, divisions, and uncertainties, the word of God remains constant. God's word is always YES. It is YES to our call; YES to our ministry; and YES to our hope in him who never disappoints.

Mary discloses to the priest a spirituality which is open to the Word; serves others in a selfless manner; trusts in the Lord during times of transition; keeps vigil with the Crucified God; and hopes for the new creation. Such a spirituality is not mastered in a day or obtained through various techniques. What is required is the whole of one's heart, over a lifetime, centered in doing the will of God. In growing into such a priestly spirituality, we live a life worthy of our calling.

CHAPTER TEN

PETER:
The Priest as Leader

"Where are the giants?" is a question which each generation asks and must seek to answer. Both society and Church
are in need of men and women of vision without whom we
perish. Every community needs leaders in order to grow and
tell the next generation. Leadership is a perennial need, but
never more so than during times of uncertainty and periods of
transition. There is a special need for men and women who
know how to draw from tradition those insights which steady
the present and light the future. There is a need for a leadership which is able to enliven the imagination and encourage a
prudent walk into tomorrow. The leadership people turn to
during times of change is a leadership which knows how to
balance comfort with challenge; the need to take care with the
need to take a risk. In these post-Vatican II days, we have
witnessed our share of change and have felt the need for
leadership. At times, we have known the pain which comes
from being without a vision and a shepherd to guide the way.
Yet we must also be sensitive to the exciting new ways of
exercising leadership through the creative presence of the
Spirit. But that is getting ahead of our story. For now, we must
turn our attention to Simon-Peter as the disclosure model for
leadership in the Church.

    Why Simon-Peter? Simon-Peter is so attractive and so
powerful a figure because we see in him Every Christian and

the full range of complexity which confronts those called to lead. Simon-Peter is anything but a simple, plastic, carbon-copy figure of some Madison Avenue success factory. Simon-Peter is complex and inconsistent to such a degree that he is the hobgoblin of small minds. He does not fit neatly into our categories and he refuses to conform to our clear and distinct ideas about leadership. Simon-Peter is so attractive because he is so thoroughly human. We are able to see ourselves in the various faces of Simon-Peter. And, to the credit of the Gospel writers, they do not try to cover up his faults or exaggerate his virtues beyond reasonable proportion. In the Gospels, there is no cover-up or stonewalling it. When Simon-Peter is weak, fails, sins, and simply says things before he thinks, we see ourselves and we love him the more. We can risk being honest with our own limitations because in Peter, we see God's grace shining through human weakness. The flaws of Simon-Peter make his virtues all the more inspiring. For not only is there the Simon-Peter who tries to keep Jesus from going to Jerusalem, and denies he knows the Lord, but there is also the Simon-Peter who declares Jesus to be the Messiah, and the fisherman who three times affirms his total love for Jesus.

In this chapter, we will explore the crucial issue of leadership within the Christian community. As previously mentioned, Simon-Peter will serve as our disclosure model. To be specific, I will focus on important aspects of Simon-Peter's life and relate these episodes to the issue of priestly leadership within the parish. I will conclude this chapter with a brief reflection on priestly leadership within the horizon of the contemporary parish.

The Call of Simon

The public ministry of Jesus had begun with the preaching of the Kingdom of heaven (Mt 4:17). He began to gather around his person and message those disciples who would follow him. Jesus called a fisherman named Simon and his brother Andrew: "Come follow me and I will make you fishers of men" (Mt 4:19). This call was simple, direct, and open-minded. At the center of the invitation was the *person of Jesus*. There was no offer of glory, money, power, fame, or a life free from empty nets. There was only the offer of Jesus himself. From then on, the meaning and destiny of their lives would be intimately related to Jesus. All of their future success as well as their coming crosses would be understood in light of this initial call. The former ways of making a living, securing a reputation, and providing for the future were rendered obsolete.

Being fishermen, the first disciples were curious men and had an instinct for finding the big catch and telling the good story. Jesus knew whom to call. To be a successful fisherman, one has to be patient as well as alert to seize the moment; one has to be gentle as well as strong; and one must know the power of the lure in catching fish. A good fisherman knows how to work with others and is able to read the signs offered by nature. To misread the current or the wind is to miss out on today's catch. The fisherman must learn to live with uncertainty, complexity, and forces beyond his control. In theological terms, the fisherman must become at home with grace. Life on land and at sea is filled with ambiguity and the unexpected. Grace lurks everywhere ready to surprise us. Yet we can easily miss it because we are busy looking elsewhere or simply miss reading the signs of grace which abound.

Fishermen take chances in hope of gaining the one big catch which will establish their reputation and provide security for the future. The disciples took a chance that day along the Sea of Galilee. Matthew tells us that they left their boats, nets, and father in order to follow Jesus (Mt 4:20, 22). They took a chance and responded to the person of Jesus to follow him. No doubt they did not fully comprehend what was being offered or what lay in store. What is crucial was their willingness to risk and to accept the invitation of Jesus. They may have thought they made the catch of their lives. They may have thought their future would be secure. Time would prove just how much their willingness to risk following Jesus would pay off. To be sure, the payoff would come not in the ways they expected. They would be rewarded with a share in Jesus' Cross so as to have a share in his glory. Their names would be written in the book of eternal life.

Every man called to be a priest finds himself in the situation of Simon-Peter and the other disciples. Namely, Jesus' call comes as the invitation of grace to lead others to the person of Jesus Christ. And this call is extended *within* the everyday concerns of life. The call of Jesus to follow him grows out of tending our own nets. The call may come early when one is first considering a life's work. The call of Jesus may come during the middle or later years when significant projects have already been completed. Regardless, the call comes to follow Jesus and lead others to follow him as well. In order to accept the call, one must surrender to the Lord unconditionally and journey with him. Such a surrendering to the person of Jesus is not easy and it involves the cost of discipleship. We must be willing to let go of our own nets and use the ones supplied by Jesus. We must be willing to empty ourselves so that Jesus can fill our hearts, enlighten our vision, and sustain us in priestly ministry.

Priestly leadership is centered totally in the person of Jesus. It is Jesus who calls and it is Jesus to whom we respond. That's what it means to be a fisher of others for the Kingdom. The priest reveals in his life the saving power of Jesus' love. This saving relationship with Jesus is more than an idea or a pious thought. Relationship with Jesus Christ is at the heart of priestly existence and leadership. The priest people turn to is one who knows Jesus and leads them to know Jesus as well. In the twelfth chapter of John's Gospel, some Greeks came to Philip with this request: "Sir, we would like to see Jesus" (Jn 12:20-21). Philip and Andrew told Jesus of their request. Jesus responded: "The hour has come for the Son of Man to be glorified" (Jn 12:23). Each time someone seeks Jesus, in spirit and truth, the glory of God is revealed. The priest is entrusted with that leadership ministry, that is, taking the requests of others to see Jesus because the priest sees and loves Jesus. The

American Bishops' document on pastoral ministry captures the need for the priest to foster this relationship with Jesus:

> Those who answered his call were more than pupils gathered around a rabbi. They were disciples, that is, followers closely adhering to Jesus in a personal relationship that deepened into true friendship. To be accepted into personal fellowship with Jesus was his gift and He gave it only to those willing to surrender themselves to Him in faith and love. They were called to be with Jesus, to see his works, to listen to his words, and to live like Him so that through their own lives, words, and works they could witness to the initiation of the reign of God in the person of Jesus the Lord. (*As One Who Serves*, p. 9)

Leadership, Paradox, and the Scandal of the Cross

If fishing is filled with ambiguity, uncertainty, and the surprise of the unexpected, so is following Jesus, as Peter would soon find out. Jesus did not fit into the neat categories of the time. He was not the kind of Messiah that they had expected or wanted. Jesus challenged the too neat answers that were being uncritically offered to the deepest questions of human existence. To accept the invitation to follow Jesus meant that one was accepting the call to paradox. The Jesus and Messiah one would help people see was one who exclaimed:

> I solemnly assure you, unless the grain of wheat falls to the ground and dies, it remains just a grain of wheat. But if it dies, it produces much fruit. The man who loves his life loses it, while the man who hates his life in this world preserves it to life eternal. (Jn 12:24-25)

Talk about paradox! Peter would encounter this paradox head on.

One day, Jesus and the disciples were making their way to Caesarea Philippi. Jesus inquired among the disciples as to

the latest speculation concerning his identity. Answers filled
the air: Jesus was really John the Baptizer, Elijah, Jeremiah,
or some prophet. Jesus was interested in something deeper
than small town gossip or clever speculation. He turned to the
disciples and asked, "Who do you say that I am?" (Mt 16:15).
Simon-Peter, as he was in the habit of doing, spoke for the
group, "You are the Messiah, the Son of the living God!" (Mt
16:16). Jesus blessed Simon and declared him to be the
"Rock" on which the Church would be built. It is not a Church
built on the person of Peter, but on the revelation given to Peter
concerning Jesus as the Messiah. (Unfortunately, the failure to
keep this distinction in mind has caused trouble for the
Church.) Furthermore, Peter was *entrusted* with the keys of the
Kingdom of heaven. Peter did not own them. They were placed
in his hands as a sacred trust that he would wisely exercise
authority. Such a wise leadership of the community always
involves the true revelation of Jesus as Messiah.

At this point, all seems well. However, Jesus went on to
tell the disciples that "he must go to Jerusalem and suffer
greatly there at the hands of the elders, the chief priests, and
the scribes, and to be put to death, and raised up on the third
day" (Mt 16:21). All of this became too much for Peter. He
took Jesus aside and tried to protect him from himself. "May
you be spared, Master! God forbid that any such thing ever
happen to you!" (Mt 16:22). Jesus, who had just blessed Peter,
now rebuked him sharply: "Get out of my sight, you Satan! You
are trying to make me trip and fall. You are not judging by
God's standards but by man's" (Mt 16:23). Satan was always
looking for ways to get Jesus to abandon his mission and reject
the will of the Father. Satan even used those closest to Jesus to
try to accomplish this task.

Simon-Peter could accept the Jesus who is the glorified,
exalted Messiah. Simon-Peter could follow with little trouble
the Jesus who cured the sick, expelled demons, left the crowd
spellbound with his preaching, confounded the Pharisees, and
fed the four thousand, but he had great difficulty with the Jesus
who was rejected, suffered, died, and was a scandal. Simply

put, to follow Jesus means that one must be in relationship with a suffering Messiah who points to a Crucified God. To accept the invitation of Jesus to follow him means that one must be willing to take up one's cross and lose one's life for the sake of the Gospel. Only then can one come to know the unsurpassing glory of God. The Lordship of Jesus is one which exists within the necessary tension of this paradox: in loving one's life for the Gospel, there is eternal life; in the Cross, there is victory; and in being received into the earth, an abundant harvest comes forth.

Priestly existence and leadership must struggle daily with this paradox. We lead others to see Jesus but we lead them to a Messiah who is both/and. Jesus is both Suffering Servant and Risen Lord; rejected Messiah and the Holy One of God. The Lordship of Jesus cannot be separated in order to make his ministry and message more acceptable. We cannot divide what God has joined so perfectly in the person of Jesus. To follow Jesus and to exercise priestly leadership means that one has to walk with this paradox. At times, the scandal can be a heavy burden. The Apostle Paul tried to use worldly wisdom as a way of making Jesus and the resurrection more believable. He met with disaster. Finally, Paul came to realize that the Cross must be preached in all its offensiveness so that the power of God's saving love can shine forth. Paul wrote to the Corinthians:

> The message of the cross is complete absurdity to those who are headed for ruin, but to us who are expecting salvation it is the power of God. . . For God's folly is wiser than men, and his weakness more powerful than men. (1 Cor 1:18, 25)

The challenge for priestly leadership and those entrusted with the welfare of the Church is to resist the temptation to suppress the paradox of Jesus as Messiah and the scandal of the Cross. This is especially true as we become more aware of the social justice dimensions of the Gospel and the mission of the Church. The Crucified God reminds us that our Lord stands in solidarity with victims and those who are despised, rejected, lonely, suffering, dying, and deemed of no account. Jesus on the Cross is one with the wretched of the earth. The Cross of Christ is the symbol throughout history that the ongoing stories of victims and the blood of the innocent have meaning and destiny. Jesus' own victimhood and innocent suffering transforms the meaning of all who are crucified through the ages. The witness of victims is not lost but taken up into God's unbounded love and healed: in the end, there is the hope of victory. Jesus on the Cross tells us that the history written by victims becomes the history of hope through Jesus' resurrection. The scandal of the Cross becomes the saving power of God. Jesus teaches that history is written by the victims who refuse to despair and continue to hope beyond all hope. Priestly leadership proclaims a Jesus who is Messiah and Lord. Priestly leadership points to its Messiah as the Man of Sorrows and the Abandoned One of God.

Pastoral leadership that is true to the person and mission of Jesus is one which constantly helps the community to ask and answer Jesus' question: Who do you say that I am? Answers which seek to soften or eliminate altogether the Cross and the cost of discipleship are the work of Satan and the agenda of the world. A cheerful Gospel is not the good news of Jesus Christ. An interesting Jesus falls short of the scandal and paradox of the Messiah. There is much in daily parish life which brings one in contact with the Cross and its radical demands: the need to develop loving forms of shared ministry; confronting the challenges of decision-making in the parish; the call to witness to social justice; the opportunity to preach a Messiah who stands with the hurting and broken within the parish community; and to live the message of hope that the Crucified God is also the Risen Lord of Easter joy.

Leadership with a Human Face

What we find most attractive and believable about those we encounter in the Bible is the willingness of the writers to let the full range of the human condition shine through. There is no attempt to idealize them beyond who and what they were. The Bible writers allow us to see even the most revered in their moments of greatest weakness and even sin. The story of David's sin (2 S 11) and his confrontation by Nathan (2 S 12) is but one example of the candor of biblical authors. Peter is no exception to the rule of biblical candor.

The Peter who is Rock and the one entrusted with the keys of the Kingdom is also the Simon who would deny his Lord three times. All four Gospels contain the story (Mt 26:29; Mk 14:66; Lk 22:54; Jn 18:15, 25). In the words of Simon-Peter, "I do not know him" (Lk 22:57). These words came from the same mouth which only a short time before had declared to Jesus, "at your side I am prepared to face imprisonment and death itself" (Lk 22:33). Jesus knew the willingness of the spirit and the weakness of the flesh. In addition to foretelling Peter's denials, Luke presents Jesus doing much more. Jesus prays, "Simon, Simon! Remember that Satan has asked for you, to sift you all like wheat. But I have prayed for you that your faith may never fail" (Lk 22:31-33). There is one thing more. Even though Peter would deny his Lord, God's grace would have the final word. Peter must strengthen the community. He must be a *wounded healer* who learned much from his own pretensions and weakness. Jesus did not love Simon because he was perfect, but because he was so human. Jesus did not choose Simon-Peter to be the one to strengthen others because he was strong on his own, but because through Peter's weakness, God's grace could become visible.

The human limitations of our condition are not erased at ordination. If we are lucky, we become more keenly aware of our thorns in the flesh and how much of a vessel of clay we are. Both clergy and laity can easily fall under the influence of the ego-ideal and the tyranny of unrealistic expectations. There are times when the congregation can expect a level of service and ministerial performance that even Jesus would have difficulty providing. Many priests, because of poor self-image, or because of an unrealistic view of ministry, try mightily to meet everyone's needs and expectations. This often results in frustration, conflict, resentment, and burnout. Both priests and parish need to value the human, and help each other to establish mature limits and expectations. If this can be done, there is less chance for disillusionment and feelings of betrayal. The priest as the one who serves must also be wise enough to let others serve him in his humanity. Jesus let others show him hospitality and meet his needs. A crucial aspect of priestly leadership is helping others to appreciate their humanity and to share their humanity with others. Peter would not be nearly as attractive without his human limitations. He became a good shepherd and true leader *after* the denials and the illusion of invincibility was broken. Peter was able to strengthen the community because he had matured through weakness and amazing grace.

In recent times, we have witnessed a number of scandals within the Catholic and Protestant communities involving priests and ministers. Such scandals deeply wound the Body of Christ and invite people to attack the Church with glee. Talk-show hosts and book publishing houses are engaged in battle for the exclusive interview or the rights to the story. There are large amounts of money to be made with religious scandal, especially when sex is a central theme. The temptation is great for fellow clergy and members of the faith community to engage in moral posturing, self-righteousness, and ministerial bashing. Somehow, if we outdo the secular press or outsiders in condemning the wayward clergy, we can feel morally superior as well as give the appearance that we are not soft on sin. Lost in all the media hype and judging is the value and spiritual need of the priest who also stumbles.

Peter committed a great sin; he denied the Lord. He did not deny Jesus once, but three times. Jesus did not condemn Peter to take back the keys of the Kingdom. Jesus prayed for Peter and indicated that he would play a crucial role in the life of the community of faith. In the Gospel of John, we read that the resurrected Jesus came to Peter, not to condemn, but to rehabilitate and renew him with the message of Easter hope and joy. Simon-Peter could begin again. Denial and the tears

of contrition will give way to the three affirmations of love and
the joy of feeding the followers of Jesus (Jn 21:15-19). Peter
was no longer the arrogant, self-assured fisherman who was
certain of his own power to make it through any situation. Peter
had become a true disciple and shepherd who would follow
Jesus through humble service and the Cross. The Peter who
denied Jesus was then entrusted with feeding and protecting
the disciples of Jesus. Sin is never so deep that God's grace is
not deeper still.

The story of Peter is crucial for the priest and congregation. Those entrusted with positions of leadership and authority are given much and much is expected. But the total suspen-
sion of human frailty is not a realistic expectation. Priests do
and will fall short of the glory of God. Priests do and will deny
and betray the vision of discipleship presented by Jesus.
Simply put, priests are in need of God's mercy because priests
sin. If the humanity of the priest is ignored by the congregation, and denied by the priest himself, there will be a great deal
of neurotic guilt, repression, and harmful moralizing. Furthermore, if the humanity of the priest is denied, we will feel the
need to rewrite chapter 21 of John. We will want a Jesus who
confronts and condemns. We will demand a Jesus who grabs
back the keys and gives them to one more deserving. Yet
chapter 21 stands as it is because there is no one more
deserving than Peter who had been matured by what he
suffered.

None of what has been said above is meant to condone
sin, nor is it to be taken as a defense of fellow clergy. Sin must
be confronted and a change of life is required. But Jesus
showed us, in dealing with Peter, that confronting sin must be
done with prayer and not gossip. Confrontation of sin must be
met with the greater message of hope and new life for the
sinner. Even the one who denied Jesus was given the chance to
reaffirm his love. Long ago, a brash fisherman asked Jesus how
often he was required to show forgiveness. Jesus indicated that
forgiveness was always in season. Simon-Peter finally knew
just what Jesus meant. The priest who is aware of his sinfulness

and weakness can be a priest people turn to for understanding
and compassion. Such a priest is able to lead others to God's
saving grace because he has been touched by that grace. In the
words of Hebrews:

> Every high priest is taken from among men and made
> their representative before God, to offer gifts and sac-
> rifices for sins. He is able to deal patiently with erring
> sinners, for he himself is beset by weakness and so must
> make sin offerings for himself as well as for the people.
> (Heb 5:1-3)

A Word of Summary and Transition

What portrait of priestly leadership emerges from what we
have said so far? In the life of Simon-Peter, we find a man who
encountered Jesus within the context of his everyday work.
Jesus called Simon while he was tending his nets and made
him an offer he would have been crazy to refuse: "Follow me.
Come and see where I stay and maybe, just maybe, what you
are seeking will be found in my person, message, and mission.
Not only will you sit on thrones judging the tribes of Israel but
you will have abundant share in my Cross." The call of Jesus
was addressed to Simon as he was. The vices and virtues of
Simon were accepted by Jesus and empowered for the work of
the Kingdom. From the first moment of that encounter at the
Sea of Galilee, Jesus was Peter's ultimate concern. Even in his
denial of the Lord, there could be little doubt that Jesus was the
center of Peter's being. The Gospel of Luke tells us that after
Peter denied Jesus, "he went out and wept bitterly" (Lk
22:62). Priestly leadership, even in episodes of denial and
betrayal, is most authentic when it leads others to Jesus.

In the life of Simon-Peter, we see a man who had to
struggle with the paradox and scandal of the Lordship of Jesus
Christ. Peter found much that was appealing about a glorified
Messiah, but much that was appalling about a rejected and

crucified Lord. Yet, as Simon-Peter continued to journey with Jesus, he came to see that both the humiliation of the Cross and the glory of Easter are parts of the one story of grace over sin. In time, Peter would come to carry his own cross into death and eternal life. Priestly leadership is one which holds up to the congregation and world the Crucified God who is in solidarity with all victims and the Risen Lord who is the hope of salvation.

Finally, we see disclosed a shepherd and leader who embodies the full range of humanity. We never doubt for a moment the humanity of Peter as well as the grace of God shining through that humanity. We are privileged to see the transformation of a man who at the beginning is self-assured, arrogant, and overly confident of his own powers. However, in time, Peter would mature through an awareness of his weakness and the reality of sin. Peter denied his Lord. Yet Simon-Peter was a man of character. He accepted the invitation of Jesus to be reborn and affirmed his love of the Risen Lord. Priestly existence is a call to develop one's own humanity and to lead others to an appreciation of their humanity. Priestly leadership is one which only matures when the priest and congregation rejoice in human weakness so that God's grace can be strong. The community of faith is desperately in need of a priestly leadership which affirms all that is human to the glory of God.

From Simon-Peter, we have disclosed to us a priestly leadership which is motivated by total commitment to the person of Jesus; a willingness to proclaim a Lord who must suffer and die so as to be raised to life; and the humility to celebrate a humanity accepted and redeemed by Jesus. This threefold vision of priestly leadership cannot be frozen in time but must continue throughout the history of the Church. The Second Vatican Council and contemporary theology have done much to continue this kind of priestly leadership. It is to the current situation of priestly leadership that we now turn our attention.

Priestly Leadership: The Signs of the Times

Pope John XXIII convened the Second Vatican Council as a response to the signs of the times. The renewal of the Catholic Church was motivated by the commission of Jesus to preach the Gospel to the whole world (Mt 28:19). In the years following the Council, we have witnessed many troubling as well as exciting changes in the Church. From all that has unfolded, one thing remains clear: the pastoral mission of the Church has been embraced with enthusiasm and a new style of leadership has emerged throughout the Church. This new style of priestly-pastoral leadership is one which is empowering, collaborative, and which guides through service.

1. Priestly leadership demands more than the ability to give orders and get things done. The priest people turn to for leadership is one who is expressive, empowering, and enabling. The days of Father doing everything and controlling the parish in an absolute manner are fast fading. Priestly leadership is less and less about giving orders and administration, and more and more about fostering mature relationships in love. The priest is expected to be the leader in the ways of true Christian love and concern. The parish looks to the priest for guidance in how to forgive, reconcile, and be renewed in body and spirit. The priest must disclose in his life the ability to love, forgive, reconcile, and heal, so his preaching, teaching, and celebrating will be credible. Such a priest is turned to not because he gives orders and gets things done (though certainly someone must make decisions so things will get done), but because he is friend, lover, comforter, challenger, and God's man of hope.

Priestly leadership is not about Father doing all the work and having all the responsibility. The Catholic community in the United States has come of age educationally, economically, professionally, and in terms of the ability to think critically about Church and world. Within each parish, there are many gifts from the Holy Spirit. Priestly leadership is being challenged to lead in much more complex and exciting ways

than simply giving orders. Parish priests are being challenged
to recognize, call forth, and unify the many gifts of the Holy
Spirit for the common good. Far from a parish not needing
priestly leadership, the contemporary parish requires men of
vision and maturity who are able to blend the many into the one
community of faith. St. Paul faced a similar challenge at
Corinth. He wrote to the community the following:

> There are different gifts but the same Spirit; there are
> different ministries but the same Lord; there are different
> works but the same God who accomplishes all of them in
> everyone. To each person the manifestation of the Spirit
> is given for the common good. . . But it is one and the
> same Spirit who produces all these gifts, distributing
> them to each as he wills. (1 Cor 12:4-7, 11)

Paul went on to indicate that the greater gifts, which each
follower of Jesus and the community as a whole must seek
after, are the theological virtues of faith, hope, and love. The
greatest of the gifts is love (1 Cor 13:13). It is the gift which
binds all other gifts together for the good of the community. If
love is absent, then gifts become selfish possessions and
sources of conflict. The priest people turn to is one who knows
how to love each person for the gift he or she is. Such a priest is
the wise lover who knows how to appreciate each gift in relation
to the gifts of the whole community. Priestly leadership is
about the power of love and not the love of power.

2. Joseph Gremillion and Jim Castelli conducted an
extensive research project concerning Catholic life since the
Second Vatican Council. In their chapter on leadership within
the parish, they write:

> In the postconciliar American Catholic parish, leader-
> ship is a plural noun — both by necessity and design.
> While the pastor is still central to parish leadership,
> many other people, most of them laity, share responsibil-
> ity for the operation and direction of the parish. This has
> happened by design through efforts to implement the

sharing of ministry among ordained and non-ordained
persons stressed by Vatican II. It has also happened
because the declining numbers of priests, particularly in
proportion to the size of the Catholic population, has
made it impossible for priests alone to run a parish.
(*The Emerging Parish*, p. 99)

Msgr. Gremillion and Mr. Castelli confirm empirically
what we have known all along, namely, the role of the laity has
been greatly enhanced in the past two decades. Priestly leadership in the post-Vatican II parish requires the avoidance of
two dangers: the passive pastor who is content to let the lay folk
run the show and the autocratic pastor who feels threatened by
all these lay people "trying to take over the parish." Once
again, virtue lies in the middle. Effective priestly leadership is
exercised by the pastor who prudently unites gifts for the
common good. Such a pastor has a vision which he can share
with the community and make them feel a real stake in its
outcome. Such a pastor is one who welcomes the contributions
of the laity and sees their efforts as a furthering of the Gospel.
Far from being threatened, the pastor is able to recognize the
gifts of others and help those gifts mature. When conflicts
arise, as surely they will, priestly leadership is exercised
through mutual respect, love, listening, prayer, and the confidence to make decisions based on the common good under the
guidance of the Spirit.
    3. Priestly leadership is best exemplified through
service in imitation of Jesus for the People of God. The priest
as one who serves is always motivated by the example of Jesus.
This is the unique dimension which the Church and the priest
brings to service — the person and message of Jesus Christ.
Such priestly, Christ-centered service is one which enfleshes
God's love for all people, especially the poor. Priestly leadership as service risks touching lives and becoming involved in
the hurts and hopes of the faith community. Service requires
that the priest allow himself to be drawn deeply into the
mystery of human existence, the lives of those whom he serves,

and the unbounded love of God. If any of these are missing, priestly leadership through service will be less than what Jesus demonstrated and expects of us.

Naturally, a heavy responsibility for the formation of priests falls to the seminary. We can no longer be satisfied with the training of a few good men for one-dimensional lives in a one-dimensional parish. The demands on the priest are enormous and complex. Seminary training cannot be satisfied with education from the neck up. The priest-to-be must be a man of imagination and creativity. He must be able to move hearts as well as minds; involve others as well as get things done himself; and he must be able to rejoice in the many gifts of the Spirit for the common good. He must be a man of hope who daily confronts despair in himself and others. He must be a man of faith in the midst of a world which recognizes no Lord except the ones of its own making. He must be a man of love who is able to drive out the fear which prevents us from responding to the Holy Spirit. As a priest who works in a seminary, I believe the seminary is up to the challenge. But at the same time, I must say to my Lord, "I believe. Help my unbelief."

An Example I Leave You

The issue of leadership within the faith community is not new. The night before Jesus was to show the disciples the depth of his love, they shared a last supper. No doubt, they knew what it meant to go up to Jerusalem. In all probability, Jesus would be arrested and maybe even killed. What was to become of the community? Who would be in charge and make the decisions?

Not only the issue of leadership, but also conflict over leadership is not new within the community of faith. Luke tells us that, while they were sharing this last meal, "a dispute arose among them about who should be considered the greatest" (Lk 22:24). Perhaps it would be Simon-Peter, since he had been the first one called and the one who received the keys of the Kingdom. Maybe John, since Jesus loved him so much and seemed to confide in him at key moments. Each disciple advanced his qualifications for the role of leader. We can only imagine how Jesus felt. Finally, when Jesus could take no more, he told them what would be required of the one who would be shepherd of the little flock: "Let the greater among you be as the junior, the leader as the servant" (Lk 24:26). The standards of the world cannot be the standards by which the community of faith takes the measure of leadership. The world looks for the external symbols of power and clout. It cannot be that way with us.

Authentic leadership, a leadership of service, is one which continues the example of Jesus. Throughout their three years together, Jesus has been among them as a servant. Jesus has been the man for others who constantly told them about the importance of humility. He even went so far as to indicate that the Kingdom is made up of those with child-like trust and faith. Jesus had dwelled among them as one who served. True greatness is for those who allow the needs of others to become their own. Jesus knew that more than eloquent words would be required. Jesus must enflesh what it means to be a servant-leader. In a most dramatic and moving fashion, Jesus gave them an example of what it means to be Lord and Teacher.

The second division of the Gospel of John, the Book of Glory (Chs. 13-21), opens with the washing of the disciples' feet by Jesus (Jn 13:1-17). The hour of Jesus' glory, his revelation as the Son of God on the Cross, began with this "parable in action" (Father Bruce Vawter). Jesus assumed the role of the humblest servant by washing the disciples' feet. So shocking was this action that Simon-Peter initially refused (notice the connection with Peter's unwillingness to let Jesus go to Jerusalem after Jesus predicts his passion). Jesus was their Teacher and Lord. It was they who should wash his feet. It was they who should serve him. This parable brings about a transvaluation of values. The greatest is the servant. The Lord washes the feet of his followers. The Teacher meets the most menial needs of his disciples. What can all this mean?

The words of Jesus are clear: the titles of Teacher and Lord applied to Jesus are true. What Jesus wants them to understand is the *deeper* meaning of these terms. To be a Teacher with authority and a Lord who is followed, one must be schooled in humble service. The Christian community is a community of fraternal love and humble service. Fellow members of the Body of Christ are to wash the feet of one another. These would be just pious words or spiritual exhortation but for one thing — Jesus washed their feet. He gave the example and invited them to do the same. It is only by such loving, humble service that the community will experience happiness and peace.

The need to understand what Jesus did by washing the disciples' feet is essential for priestly leadership. If the parish or community is to grow in fraternal love and follow Jesus, the need for priests who wash feet is crucial. Such a priest does not lord it over those whom he serves, but follows the example of his Lord who served with generosity and love. Such a priest does not covet titles and places of honor, or live within the community as one who expects to be served. The priest people turn to is the priest who knows that love is a verb; an action word. The priest people turn to knows Jesus because such a priest *does* love through humble service. To such a priest and community, Jesus speaks the following: "Once you know all these things, blest will you be if you put them into practice" (Jn 13:17).

CHAPTER ELEVEN

LUKE:
The Priest and Women

In a less complex age of the not so long ago, a reflection on women in the life of the priest would have been short and direct: avoid them. To include the subject of women under the topic of priestly holiness would have been viewed as a classic example of an oxymoron. Women were viewed (and, unfortunately, they may still be so viewed) as real and present dangers to priestly commitment, that is, celibacy. Women, it was thought, were constantly looking for some poor priest to lead astray. Women were vamps and priests were too naive to know what was happening to them. This was hardly a realistic view of women or priests. But such images do not die easily. Seminary training and a subsequent priestly spirituality called for control of the eyes, training of the thoughts, denial of impure feelings, and a double-check of intentions when it came to sex and women. In other words, avoid it and them in thought, word, and deed.

I do not want to deny the human capacity for self-deception, pride, and rationalization. Relationships between priests and women do contain special tensions and built-in temptations which only a fool would ignore or deny. The relationship between the celibate priest and women is in need of mature reflection under the guidance of an experienced spiritual director. Such relationships require the first of the cardinal virtues, prudence, so that scandal can be reasonably avoided and false impressions not given.

While I grant the dangers of friendships between priests and women, I all the more want to affirm the richness which such relationships can bring to the priest and his ministry. The old spirituality of denial, repression, anger, and guilt may have been safe (though not as safe as some believe), but it was a safety bought at a terrible price. The counsel to avoid women left priests highly fearful of a significant part of their own personality, the feminine, and highly defensive when being "forced" to "deal" with women. The normal male response of finding a woman attractive and the subsequent feelings must be denied and quickly controlled. Even the most innocent moments of intimacy were viewed with suspicion. To have sexual desires and erotic thoughts was to be declared impure; it was an infallible sign that one's vocation was in trouble. One could easily be left with the impression that ordination removed the priest from the human family and that he was required to turn in his humanity at the chancery office.

The priest people turn to is one who desires to be fully human in the manner of Jesus and who desires to serve *all* of the People of God. Friendship with women can be a source of grace in the development of the priest as a person and for his ministry as God's man of love and hope. The days of defensive ministry and viewing all women as dangers to priestly holiness are long past. The Church needs men who are strong enough in their commitment to love, serve, and respect all members of the human family. In their reflections on the pastoral dimensions of the priesthood, the American Bishops wrote:

> Women today properly seek and claim the prerogatives and responsibilities of full personhood for themselves in all spheres of human and Church life. Such insights call for a deepening sensitivity on the part of the priest in his relationship with women.
>
> Too often, some stress has been placed on avoiding relationships with women. Such a negative emphasis

often effects a defensive style when the priest relates with women either socially or in ministry. Such style is particularly inappropriate today when the priest is expected to interact on a regular basis with women as co-workers as well as in social situations. (*As One Who Serves*, p. 65)

In what follows, we will examine what women have to teach priests, drawing on three major themes contained in the Gospel of Luke. Women play a prominent role in his Gospel-narrative and the stories of three women have much to offer the priest. Next we shall reflect on the contemporary situation of women in the Church. To be specific, we shall explore the presence of women in the Church and their contribution to the Church's ministry and mission. I will then try to ground these reflections in my own life as a priest. We shall conclude our reflections with a consideration of the pastoral letter by the American Bishops on the role of women in the Church. For now, we turn our attention to the Gospel of Luke and three major themes which emerge from the stories of women: Burdens to Blessings; Rejection to Reconciliation; and Fear to Fidelity. Each of these themes, and the lives of these women, have much to teach the priest. These are themes and lives of grace.

Burdens to Blessings

Elizabeth, Mary, and Anna are not blessed with burdens but they turn their burdens into blessings through God's grace. Elizabeth is sterile and advanced in years (Lk 1:7). Mary is deeply troubled over the announcement that she is to be the mother of Jesus (Lk 1:29). Anna is quite old and has lived as a widow for some time (Lk 2:37). Each of these women must confront a burden which has all the potential for being a curse and not a blessing. Each burden touches on a crucial aspect of priestly existence.

Unlike our own age, in Elizabeth's time, to be without

children was considered a disgrace and a punishment from God. Elizabeth was advanced in years and sterile as well. However, both she and Zechariah "were just in the eyes of God, blamelessly following all the commandments and ordinances of the Lord" (Lk 1:6). Into this lifeless and barren situation, a messenger of grace came, announcing that a son would be born to them and he was to be called John. This good news of new life evokes from Elizabeth words of praise: "In these days the Lord is acting on my behalf; he has seen fit to remove my reproach among men" (Lk 1:25). The child was born and all of Elizabeth's neighbors and relations gathered to rejoice with her and give praise to the Lord who extends mercy and brings forth new life in sterile situations.

The story of Elizabeth speaks to the hearts of all priests who must struggle in barren and sterile situations of ministry. What priest has not had the experience of putting forth great time, effort, and prayer in a project, only to have it stillborn? What priest has not had to struggle with feelings of inadequacy and failure over an assignment or even the whole of one's priestly life? What priest has not faced situations which seemed hopeless? What priest, at one time or another, has not had to face the reproach of others for failing to bring forth the expected harvest from a ministry? In such situations and times, it is so easy to allow our burdens to embitter us. We find it impossible to sing the Lord's praises. We become silent as resentment fills our hearts. We no longer trust that God's grace is at work, even in this situation, at this moment. Our burdens become curses.

Elizabeth speaks to the heart of each priest so afflicted. Elizabeth's story is one of God's life-giving grace at work in the face of great obstacles. Elizabeth did not allow the limits of law and reason, as well as the opinion of others, to limit her capacity to trust and hope in grace. Elizabeth would not be defeated. In the beautiful simplicity of faith, Elizabeth praised God for his deliverance. Into that sterile, barren, and lifeless situation, a son would be born. And this son, John, would be the herald of the Messiah!

Priestly existence knows its share of barrenness and each priest experiences episodes of sterility, when the Spirit seems to be elsewhere. Elizabeth invites us to keep looking and hoping for the messengers of grace who announce new life, for it is in the very depths of what seems so lifeless that conception occurs. It is in those moments of barrenness that, below the surface, the miracle of birth unfolds. It is in the sterility of our hearts that a place has been cleared for God's grace to burst forth with an abundant harvest. Like Elizabeth, we must continue to hope and be open to the surprise of grace. The Lord who long ago extended his mercy to Elizabeth extends that same life-giving mercy to us.

Mary's burden runs in a different direction. She was not married, but she would soon be a mother. Mary's burden was further complicated by the fact that she lived in a small town and was a devoted follower of Judaism, with its strict sexual morality. As if that were not enough, the conception of this child would take place through the Holy Spirit (Lk 1:35). Luke, in a classic display of biblical understatement, tells us that Mary was "deeply troubled by his words, and wondered what his greeting meant" (Lk 1:29). Troubled indeed! The annunciation to Mary of her role in salvation-history breaks all the norms of human reason and challenges her to move into the realm of divine wisdom, grace, and love. This challenge is not merely verbal or propositional, but profoundly existential. God's total involvement in our human condition requires that Mary give herself totally to the Lord. This she does with her words of receptivity to the word and will of God: "I am the servant of the Lord. Let it be done to me as you say" (Lk 1:38).

The call to the priesthood, as well as fidelity to priestly commitment, has its "deeply troubling" aspects. It is a fearful (awesome) thing to be called by God to proclaim the Gospel, gather the community for Eucharist and prayer, and dwell in the midst of others as one who serves and is servant of the Lord. How can this be, since we are sinners? How can such a work be entrusted to us who are limited and nothing but poor earthen vessels (2 Cor 4:7)? Why would God choose men so weak and beset by thorns in the flesh for the harvest of the Kingdom? Why indeed. Because God's grace is at its most powerfully loving when it shines through human weakness. It is in our weakness and limitations that God can be strong, and human boasting is replaced by humble adoration. The call to the priesthood is a gift within the total gift of human existence. For the gift of life and vocation, we can only echo the words of Mary: "God who is mighty has done great things for me" (Lk 1:49).

Fidelity to priestly commitment and letting God's word be done in us has its deeply troubling aspects as well. We can be afflicted with doubts as to whether we are doing ministry for the glory of God or for our self-glory. We can be troubled about the decisions we make as priests and bishops concerning the lives of others. We can suffer from doubts as to whether we are using our talents fully for the Kingdom of God. At times, we are very unclear as to what God is asking of us and what is the most prudent way to proceed. We may find ourselves brought low by some sickness or sin which causes us to doubt our worth and priestly vocation. We may even experience persecution and feel that we are left to fight alone. In these moments, the angel Gabriel says to us, "Rejoice . . . the Lord is with you."

Even in the midst of being deeply troubled, Mary could hear the words of comfort and grace. She would not allow herself to become self-absorbed into her own feelings to the exclusion of what was being asked of her. Her doubts, fears, and questions were real. But the Really Real was asking her to entrust all such concerns to the Lord with whom nothing is impossible. Mary was able to declare herself the servant of the Lord who is ready to let God's will be done in her.

In the midst of the call and the commitment to priestly life, there are troubling moments and deep fears. Doubts are present to cloud judgment and weaken the will. But more present and abundant is grace. The troubles do not magically cease. The fears do not vanish like a summer shower. And the doubts will persist until we see God face to face. Yet through grace, we can continue to hope, trust, and have confidence in the God who is worthy of our total dedication. Such a God is totally committed to us and will not abandon us. Even though deeply troubled, we can also make Mary's words our own: "Let it be done to me as you say." These are not the words of a muscular Christianity or a defiant stance in the face of fate. These are the words of a receptive heart in whom God can do infinitely more than we ever imagined.

Finally, there is the prophetess and widow, Anna. Advanced in years, she had been a widow for some time, as her husband had died only seven years after they were married. To be a widow is to be alone and without the necessary support and protection which are enjoyed by the married. To be a widow is also to know one's share of loneliness and the pain of abandonment. No doubt Anna experienced her share of suffering, exploitation, and feelings of emptiness. It would have been easy for her to turn to a life of pleasure or to try to fill up the lonely days with superficial relationships. The pain of loneliness can be intense and move people to seek comfort in all the wrong places.

Anna rejected such destructive mechanisms of coping. She devoted herself to growth in the Lord. Luke tells us: "She was constantly in the temple, worshiping day and night in fasting and prayer" (Lk 2:37). The Lord rewarded her fidelity by allowing her to see the child-Messiah who would deliver Jerusalem. Although she was advanced in years and burdened as a widow, she was blessed. There was no bitterness, anger, resentment, or self-pity. Anna was an ordinary woman of extraordinary faith and devotion. Her prophetic ministry had borne fruit in her old age. She had been granted the grace to recognize, praise, and proclaim the liberation of Jerusalem.

The senior years of priestly ministry can be a time of integrity or a time of bitterness. So much of ministry is evaluated in terms of activity, building, and a general up and doing approach. It is easy to feel useless when the winged chariot of time slows the walk and the general pace of one's ministry is not what it used to be. The get up and go got up and went. And with it one's self-worth may take flight as well.

Bitterness can set in and the pain of loneliness and abandonment can be acute.

Anna teaches the priest in his senior years that ministry
need not end but can fruitfully change for the betterment of the
Church. While the activist ministry may slow down, the contemplative and prayer-full ministry can move front and center.
Anna teaches us that prayer, worship, and fasting are essential
for recognizing the Messiah in our midst. The senior priest can
devote himself to such a contemplative ministry which will
enrich his priestly life, transform his loneliness into holy
solitude, and allow him to contribute to the spiritual mission of
the Mystical Body of Christ. Far from being obsolete or useless, such a priest serves as a powerful symbol of God's abiding
grace. Such a priest has much to teach those in the so-called
active ministry about the need for prayer, worship, and fasting.
Both the younger clergy and the senior pastor are called to
continue the prophetic ministry of Anna. That is, they are to
give praise to God and talk about Jesus as the Redeemer of
humankind.

Rejection to Reconciliation

Not all of the women presented by Luke and touched by
grace are found worshiping in the temple. God's grace, especially from the perspective of St. Luke, is for the lost sheep, the
misplaced coin, and the child who travels to a distant land after
breaking relationship with the loving parent (Lk 15). St. Luke
tells the story of two women who pass from rejection to reconciliation. One is unknown, the other has been honored down
through the ages. Both share a common narrative of the reality
of sin overcome by the greater reality of God's saving grace.
Both women have much to teach the priest about the ministry of
reconciliation, a ministry for which the priest is the very
ambassador for Christ (2 Cor 5).

The first woman we encounter will remain anonymous.
All we do know about her is that she was a sinner (Lk 7:37).
And her reputation for being a sinner was well known through-

out the town. Luke goes on to tell us that Jesus accepted an invitation to dinner at the home of Simon the Pharisee. This woman found out about Jesus attending the dinner, so she showed up as well. Not only did she show up, but "she brought in a vase of perfumed oil and stood behind him at his feet, weeping so that her tears fell upon his feet. Then she wiped them with her hair, kissing them and perfuming them with the oil" (Lk 7:37-38).

Simon the Pharisee was shocked by such a display. In his heart and thoughts, he berated Jesus for not knowing what kind of woman she was, and he judged this woman as being unworthy of associating with the good folk like himself. Jesus confronted Simon with a little parable which contained a big lesson. Two men owed money to a moneylender. One man owed five hundred coins, the other fifty. Neither man could pay. The moneylender forgave both debts. Jesus wanted to know which man was more grateful. Simon responded, "He, I presume, to whom he remitted the larger sum" (Lk 7:43). Jesus indicated that Simon had answered properly. Unfortunately for Simon, his answer was purely intellectual and academic. He knew little about forgiveness and gratitude. His answer lacked existential credibility. He failed to recognize the dynamics of forgiveness, love, and gratitude taking place in his home with this woman. His false judgments distorted his vision.

Jesus went on to remind Simon that he did not show Jesus the basic courtesies of a good host. Simon gave Jesus no water with which to wash the dust from his feet. Simon did not greet Jesus with the kiss of peace. Simon did not anoint Jesus with the oil of gladness. Yet this sinful woman provided water by her tears and used her hair as a towel. She had kissed Jesus' feet and anointed them with perfume.

Why had she done all this? Jesus provided the answer: "because of her great love" (Lk 7:47). Yes, she was a sinner. Yes, she had a bad reputation around town. Yes, she had looked for love in all the wrong places with all the wrong faces. But now this woman, because of her great capacity to love, had been reborn through the loving forgiveness of Jesus. Forgiveness liberates one to extravagant love and overflowing gestures of gratitude. The power of the past had been broken. Public opinion and town gossip mattered not at all. What was important were the words of Jesus: "Your sins are forgiven" (Lk 7:48). Jesus did not excuse her sins nor did he pretend that they did not exist. Yes, she had sinned. However, it was for the sinner that Jesus came and heaven rejoices. Her actions showed that amazing grace was at work in her. Jesus sent her forth with, "Your faith has been your salvation. Now go in peace" (Lk 7:50).

What does this unknown woman have to teach Simon the Pharisee and the priest? Her actions provide us with an eloquent statement about the God we dare to call our Father. This woman tells a story, by her actions, of a God who is loving, tender, compassionate, forgiving, and so understanding of his children. This woman reveals in this episode with Jesus a God whose grace and forgiveness call forth in us the capacity to love, forgive, show gratitude, and know the peace which comes from being saved. The story of God which emerges is one which balances the God of strict justice and fierce judgment. The God who is demanding and who will ask for an account of our stewardship is also a God whose finger tips the cosmic scale on the side of mercy. Simon's God is one-dimensional — stern, exacting, and only for the (self) righteous. The God of this unknown woman is the one Jesus came to reveal. It is the God who knows well the destructive power of sin but who knows more the healing power of grace upon grace.

One of the more significant dimensions of priestly ministry is that of reconciliation. The Church and the priest are entrusted with the mission of seeking the lost and helping to bring home with joy those gone astray. In the words of St. Paul:

> . . . if anyone is in Christ, he is a new creation. The old order has passed away; now all is new! . . . I mean that God, in Christ, was reconciling the world to himself, not counting men's transgressions against them, and that he has entrusted the message of reconciliation to us. This

makes us ambassadors for Christ, God as it were appealing through us. (2 Cor 5:17, 19-21)

The ministry of reconciliation must be carried on in the
name of the God revealed in the life of this woman. Her story of
God is one that invites forgiveness and love. It must have taken
great courage to do what she did. Yet that is the way it is with
grace. Grace liberates the sinner to live in a new way, the way
of peace which only Jesus can give. The ministry of reconciliation by Church and priest is one which continues to extend that
peace of Christ. The ministry of reconciliation is one which
washes the feet of the wayward sinner; extends the kiss of
peace to those who have known only conflict; and anoints the
prodigal with the oil of gladness because the lost has been
found and the dead returned to life. All of this is a scandal to
Simon and his story of the stern God. To Jesus and this
unknown woman, all this is cause for celebration on earth as it
is in heaven.

The second woman is well known and one I have already
written about previously in these reflections — Mary of
Magdala (see Chapter Four, "Mary Magdalene: The Priest and
Self-Image"). The story of the unknown penitent woman just
discussed ends with Jesus sending the woman forth forgiven
and at peace. But what is the rest of the story? What happens
after one encounters Jesus and is forgiven? Mary Magdalene
helps to answer these questions, for she, too, was sinful. In
fact, she was possessed by seven devils until Jesus drove them
out. The story of the penitent woman ends chapter seven in
Luke and chapter eight opens with the woman who assisted
Jesus and the disciples.

Jesus and the Twelve journeyed about preaching the good
news of the Kingdom of God. Also included in the mission of
Jesus was a group of women who had been liberated from sin.
Jesus did not merely cure and dismiss, but allowed each
person to contribute to the works of the Kingdom according to
their means and ability. These women did not merely take from
Jesus and then go off and forget what happened. These women

have a ministry and Jesus is wise enough to accept their generosity. To go forth in the peace of Christ is to live in a new way by showing others the generosity that has been shown to us by God. To be healed by Jesus is to be challenged to move beyond the self into some larger horizon of service. To be reconciled to God is to be liberated for service and love.

The ministry of reconciliation is more than following the correct matter and form of the sacrament. Reconciliation is the meeting of the sinful soul with the healing love of God. The spiritual well-being of the person must be front and center. Reconciliation calls for the one reconciled to live in a new way. The reconciled one is not forgiven and forgotten, but reconciled and remembered as a child of God with unique gifts for the community. The ministry of Jesus would have been more difficult without the generosity of Mary and the other women. Jesus told Mary and the others that sin did not have the last word. God has a dream for everyone's life and everyone can make a difference for the Kingdom. In fact, sinners who repent have a special place at the Lord's table and in his ministry.

Mary Magdalene and her companions remind us of the need to make welcome those who have been separated from the Church. How many are they who experience the pain of alienation because of abortion, divorce, abuse, changes in the Church, not enough changes in the Church, and the pain of guilt from past sins. None of these hurts will be healed overnight. But love is patient. Love is kind. Jesus healed and welcomed these women into his community. Can the Church which proclaims him as Lord do less? Can the priest who is his ambassador of reconciliation fail to creatively use the talents of all God's children? Of course not. God gives and calls forth the talents of all according to their means. Jesus accepted the generosity of these women. Jesus accepts the generous service of the sinners who dwell in the pulpit, rectory, chancery, and Vatican. We are all sinners for whom our loving Lord died. We are all the sinners whom Jesus grants a share in his ministry and destiny.

Fear to Fidelity

On that first Easter morning, St. Luke tells us that the women (Mary of Magdala, Joanna, and Mary, the mother of James) came to the tomb in order to minister to the body of Jesus. They did not find Jesus, but instead two angels reminded the women of all that Jesus had taught about his passion, death, and resurrection. The women proceeded to tell the Eleven who were hiding out of fear of the authorities. The disciples considered the women's story nonsense and refused to believe them (Lk 24:11). However, Peter went to see for himself. He found only the wrappings and left filled with amazement.

To proclaim the story of Easter is to risk looking foolish and being labeled unrealistic. The proclamation that Jesus is the Living One who offers forgiveness from sins and the hope of eternal life often brings ridicule. The disciples thought the women had spoken nonsense. Can we expect a better reception to the Gospel from the world? Hardly. Yet the minister of the Gospel must proclaim the message of Easter, with its hope of glory. The women had to know that their story would bring disbelief and rejection. No doubt they feared the opinions of others, especially the judgment of their significant others. But they had the courage to move beyond their fear in order to remain faithful to the One who remained faithful to them. These women would tell the Easter story, the story of grace over sin, because they experienced its reality long before that Easter Sunday. Granted they didn't understand it completely. Who does? What is important is the telling, even if it all seems like nonsense.

In the rush to be relevant, the priest can easily compromise the scandal of the Cross and the "foolishness" of the Easter story. We can be fearful of turning people off and of having the "cultured despisers" label our story nonsense. The pressure to conform is tremendous in a society so dominated by mass media and the emphasis placed on fitting in. The courage of the women on that first Easter reminds us that there is something more painful than public ridicule, namely, the failure to tell the story of Jesus as Crucified and Risen. The words of St. Paul are much to the priest: "Do not conform yourselves to this age but be transformed by the renewal of your mind, so that you may judge what is God's will, what is good, pleasing, and perfect" (Rm 12:2).

The lives of the women who appear in the Gospel of Luke speak to the heart of every priest who daily struggles to find blessings in burdens; who daily brings the ministry of Jesus' reconciliation to a broken world; and who, with courage and fidelity, proclaims the message of Easter to a skeptical and indifferent world. The lives of these women remind us of the power of grace working through earthen vessels. Their lives transcend time and space in bringing us the message of hope and courage. Once again, in our age, we see the working of the Holy Spirit challenging us to new understandings of ministry, Church, and the role of women within the one Body of Christ. The tensions and pains of this time result from the birth of something new. Tensions and pains can be a sign of deep caring and growth. Once again, the Spirit is blowing through the Church, empowering sons and daughters to prophesy; young men to see visions; and the senior members of the community to dream dreams (Jl 3). It is to the present community of faith, with its birth pains, visions, and dreams that we now turn.

Women in the Church

The role expectations of women in Western society have undergone dramatic change in the past few decades. The traditional role assignments of woman as wife and homemaker no longer define a woman's place as they once did. Dramatic changes have also occurred within the Church. Women are no longer limited to the Ladies' Altar Society or the Blue Army. Women are active in many phases of parish life. Once again the study of Catholic life after the Second Vatican Council by Msgr. Joseph Gremillion and Jim Castelli is worth noting.

Their study of contemporary parish life indicates that 58 percent of parish leadership positions (DRE, liturgy, music, adult education, youth, social justice ministries) are occupied by women. However, the presence of women in leadership positions does not translate into decision-making authority. That power still resides elsewhere. The authority structure is still male (due mainly to the presence of the clergy), and decisions are made by the inner circle controlled by men.

Father Andrew M. Greeley and his sister, Doctor Mary Durkin, have studied sociologically and theologically the presence of women in the Church. The title of their study highlights what they found the feelings of women to be, namely, *angry* (see Durkin and Greeley, *Angry Catholic Women*, published by Thomas More Press). This anger results from what women perceive to be more work than influence. Women continue to feel that their ministry, insights, talents, and presence are undervalued or ignored. Consider these conclusions from the Durkin-Greeley study:

- an increasing number of Catholics support the ordination of women;
- a growing number of Catholics find it acceptable for women to work outside the home and feel that children do not suffer from a working mother;
- these are issues which could be termed "feminist" and a growing Catholic population is becoming "feminist";
- only 40 percent of feminists go to Church weekly (between 1 and 1½ million Catholic women). These women tend to be college educated and from a home in which mother did not work and practices a strict Catholicism; and
- even women who attend Church regularly are angry, though their anger is not of sufficient intensity to drive them away. Such women stay and complain.

Are these findings cause for despair? Despair, no. But certainly cause for concern by the hierarchy as well as the parish priest. Yet there is a hopeful finding among the anger. Namely, even women who are angry and can be labelled "feminist" continue to attend Church and participate *if* they have developed a good relationship with a priest who understands. Such a priest listens with respect to the concerns of women and has learned to prudently integrate their talents within the parish structure. Such a priest also insures that women have a role in decision-making commensurate with the work they perform. Women who know such priests turn to them with confidence and trust. Women who find such priests, while still experiencing inner conflict about the Church, remain active, believing that the relationship with such a priest is cause for hope in the future. A priest who is confident about his vocation and the Church, respectful and open to women, and one who knows how to listen, can help to lessen the anger of women. And what is more, such priests are able to help women rethink their future with the Church. In the coming years, it is going to be increasingly important for priests to develop attitudes of genuine respect for the gifts of lay and religious women. Seminaries have no more important challenge than helping to form priests who are appreciative of the gifts of women and who know how to work with women as partners in the Gospel. An attitude of paternalism toward women must be replaced by one of mutual respect, trust, and responsibility for leadership and decision-making. This is not simply an issue of effective management, but a demand for justice.

A Personal Witness

St. Thomas Aquinas teaches that God comes to us through secondary causes. Grace is indicated through rumors of angels and signals of transcendence (Peter L. Berger). The secondary causes and angels of grace who helped develop and mature my vocation as a priest have been women. From my Irish mother (really!), to the women who have been colleagues within my various professional and academic communities, all have helped to make me a better teacher, human being, and priest. God has blessed me with the good fortune to be associated with two outstanding Catholic high schools: Mercy

Academy and St. Scholastica Academy. Both are all-girls schools and staffed by a significant number of lay women teachers and administrators. In addition, I teach courses in medical and legal ethics to classes which are comprised mainly of female students. My teaching in the seminary and my various pastoral ministries have been greatly enriched by my association with women.

I have come to value my association with women and the many ways they have enriched my spiritual life. Women have helped me to balance my male notions of God with important feminine aspects. My friendships with women have helped me to experience God as loving, compassionate, transforming, nurturing, challenging, and life-giving. Women have helped me to formulate a story of God which contains the masculine and the feminine. I have experienced the strength of God's grace as well as the supportive presence of God through women friends. Women have helped me to enrich many of my exclusively male notions of God and the spiritual life. I am in no way saying that the feminine is superior to the masculine or vice versa. Both are needed if we are to develop as human beings and formulate a spiritually rich story of God. It is in the unity of the masculine and the feminine (male and female) that we grow into the humanity given to us by God. It is the presence of sin which divides and places the masculine over the feminine. Through grace, we are healed of this division. We begin to befriend the masculine and feminine aspects of our personalities. We can experience God as Father and Mother (Julian of Norwich).

My friendships with women have helped me to grow intellectually as a priest. I am comfortable with and like to think in clear and distinct ideas. I respect propositional language and take delight in ideas and concepts. The abstract world holds an attraction for me. Unfortunately, it is easy for me to ignore the metaphysical, the narrational, the concrete, and the complexity of the historical particular. In other words, I often find myself forgetting that the Word became flesh. I forget that the Word needs to continue to become flesh in my

life and in my priestly ministry. I have been blessed with
women friends who have called me back again and again to the
concrete realities of human existence. They have helped me to
appreciate the complexity of life and the power of metaphor,
symbol, and story in gaining some insight into that complexity.
They have not allowed me to escape into some Platonic world of
ideas. They have helped me to see the need for balance in my
intellectual life. Ideas, propositions, and concepts are important. But they are not so important as to exclude metaphor,
story, and symbol. I believe that I have grown as a teacher and
preacher because of my friendships with women. These golden
friends remind me of the need to connect the head with the
heart.

In a similar vein, I have grown in my priestly ministry as a
counselor (especially in the area of making moral decisions).
Women friends have helped me to develop my feminine ways of
counseling and to speak of moral decision-making in a different
voice (see the work of Nancy Goldberger, et al, *Women's Ways of
Knowing* and Carol Gilligan's *In a Different Voice*). I have a
strong tendency to counsel in terms of providing answers and
solving problems. However, in the past few years, I have been
helped to counsel in terms of *empowerment*. That is, in my
experience with women, and in reading the literature written, I
have learned the wisdom of calling forth the gifts of others.
Solving problems and making decisions are often ways of man-
ipulating and controlling others. This is especially easy to do
when counseling women who are trained to be dependent on
men. It also gives men a sense of power over women and builds
their ego. Yet such an approach is not only unhealthy, it is also
un-Christian. Jesus did not try to manipulate or control others.
He did not try to have people become overly dependent on him.
Jesus liberated people from sin so that they could go forth and
live a new life. Jesus respected those whom he counseled,
healed, and forgave. Essential to that respect was Jesus challenging people to accept their healing and realize their own
talents and blessings. Jesus gave people a healthy sense of
self-respect by respecting them.

When I am called to counsel on matters ethical, I have a tendency to line up my moral principles and propose a course of action (or better yet, let the principles decide for me). While not wanting to minimize the importance of principles, I must confess that I easily overlook the H - Factor, the Human Factor, and the intricate social context out of which people's moral stories arise. It is very easy for me to make decisions and provide answers as if human beings were not involved. It is easy for me to make decisions as if these human beings floated above history, society, and the human condition. I constantly forget what that great feminist Aristotle (!) told me early on in his *Ethics*: ethics is *not* an exact science.

From women I have come (and still have miles yet to run) to appreciate the importance of connections and the contextual aspects of the moral life. Justice is not simply the balancing of the scales and being fair (equal treatment) with others. Women have helped me to see that, in the best biblical sense of the word, justice calls for compassion and a deep respect for the needs of the persons involved in every story. Moral principles are present to help us live more humanly and *hear* the special needs of others. None of this seeing or hearing diminishes the moral life. Rather, the ability to see and hear enables us to respond to the many faces of Lazarus. Women have experienced the acute pain of being ignored and rendered invisible. Women's pain is a source of challenge and grace for the whole Church. Through their suffering and strength, the witness of women provides the Church with a deep source of spiritual and moral insight (see Joann Wolshi Conn, *Women's Spirituality*, Paulist, 1986). Out of the chalice of their suffering, new life is emerging.

I would like to think that my experiences with women are not unique. I am sure that each priest counts himself blessed for the gifts of women who have enriched his priestly ministry. I believe that we are moving into a challenging and exciting new time of the Holy Spirit in the history of the Church. We are seriously and joyfully facing the presence of women in the Church. And we are prayerfully reflecting on what the Spirit is calling us to do and be as the community of faith in Jesus Christ. The American Catholic Bishops have turned their attention to the role of women in the Church. It is to their important reflections that we now turn.

Shepherds Speak

On March 23, 1988, the National Conference of Catholic Bishops released their first draft of the pastoral letter on women in the Church, entitled *Partners in the Mystery of Redemption* (A Pastoral Response to Women's Concerns for Church and Society). There are many things in the letter to praise and ponder. First, to the praise. The process for drafting the letter is itself important, for it signals a new way of addressing issues facing Church and society. The Pastoral invited a broad range of responses and viewpoints from women and men in dioceses throughout the United States. Such a democratic and grassroots approach signals the willingness of the bishops to listen and learn as well as to speak and teach. Also, women scholars served as consultants and staff persons to the ad hoc committee on women's concerns. The presence of women both in the preparation and writing phases of the Pastoral is crucial for the document's credibility and ability to speak to women's concerns.

Praise must be extended for the methodology used in writing this first draft. The writing process involved LISTEN-ING, REFLECTION, and RESPONDING. The bishops listened to the voices of women in terms of affirmation and alienation. They listened when women spoke of the ways in which they found the Church to be supportive of their concerns. Women also spoke of their sense of frustration, anger, and alienation over what they perceive to be the Church's indifference and injustice toward them. After this essential phase of listening, there was a creative attempt to unite the voices of women with the richness of the Catholic Story. The bishops and writers have done an excellent job of correlating the lived experience of women with the symbols, metaphors, teachings, and narratives which make up the Catholic heritage. This phase of reflecting on our tradition in light of human experience (and vice versa) is Catholic theology at its best. The final stage involves the bishops' teaching as shepherds entrusted with the pastoral care of the faith community. Their teaching is done with added authority since it comes through the creative synthesis of the Catholic heritage and the working of the Spirit in the lives of people today. The Pastoral is an excellent example of faith seeking understanding.

Praise is in order not only for the method but also for the content of the Pastoral. The bishops acknowledge the dignity of all women as human beings made in the image and likeness of God. Women are to be accorded the same respect, dignity, love, and honor that are extended to men. Each human being, male or female, is precious is God's eyes. The Church must recognize the equal dignity of women; acknowledge their talents; and welcome their presence as a source of deep enrichment for the faith-life of the Church. The Church needs to recognize the sinful presence of sexism and the exploitation of women both within and outside the Church. The Church calls society to respect all human beings and must also provide a living example of a community which honors and respects all of its members as children of God. The Church must live under the word it preaches and strive daily to put that word into practice.

The Pastoral goes on to acknowledge the alienating as well as the affirming ministry of priests in the lives of women. The bishops are quite candid in acknowledging the insensitivity (not to mention injustice) of the clergy in ministering to and with women:

> . . . many women experience in their relationship with the clergy attitudes that are patronizing, condescending, or self-serving. . . Instead of valuing women as peers and partners, some priests treat them as competitors or inferiors . . . Many women religious express frustration because they bring to the Church a full time, lifelong

commitment, often combined with advanced training,
only to meet with nonacceptance on the part of the clergy
. . . Single women, too, have the energy and expertise
needed to share in church ministry but find fewer opportunities offered to them by the clergy than to married
women or members of religious congregations. (*Partners
in the Mystery of Redemption*, p. 67)

When priests affirm the dignity of women, welcome their
gifts, and minister in mutual respect, the finest aspects of our
biblical Catholic tradition are practiced. To affirm women and
welcome them into the total life of the Church is not a fad,
whim, or an act of charity. We as a Church are following the
example of Jesus and helping to let the mighty waters of justice
flow like an unfailing stream (Amos).

Finally, the Pastoral leaves us things to ponder. Chapter
four, *Partners in the Church*, raises the issue of the ordination
of women to the ministerial priesthood. The Pastoral reminds
us of the constant practice and unbroken tradition of calling
only men to the priesthood. Such a tradition is normative in the
life of the Church. The Pastoral quotes the position of the
Sacred Congregation on the matter: "the Church, in fidelity to
the example of the Lord, does not consider herself authorized
to admit women to priestly ordination" (*Inter Insigna*, a *Declaration on the Question of the Admission of Women to the
Ministerial Priesthood*). The Pastoral goes on to recognize that
some Catholic scholars have challenged the reasoning advanced in the Congregation's Declaration. The Pastoral addi-
tionally invites scholars to ponder further the role of women in
all phases of Church life, and, in so doing, help all God's
people to discern what the Spirit is calling us to do and be.

The Pastoral also challenges scholars to help the whole
Church ponder the possibility of having women admitted to the
office of deacon. Such a question for reflection was recom-
mended by the Congregation for the Doctrine of the Faith (*Inter
Insigna*, 24). This study is needed since many of the functions
associated with the diaconate are now being performed by

women. Also, the practice of women being excluded from certain aspects of service at the altar should be discontinued. The Pastoral recommends that women be allowed to "participate in all liturgical ministries that do not require ordination" (p. 75). The Eucharist is a sign of our unity in Christ. The celebrating of his death and resurrection should not be a cause of division.

The presence and role of women in the Church is a reminder of the diversity of gifts through the Holy Spirit. The years ahead will test our capacity to think and to love. We are being invited to take part in the dazzling adventure of the Spirit who makes all things new by creatively transforming what has been and what is into what will be. There will be tensions, conflicts, misunderstandings, and wrong turns. In other words, there will be signs of life within the Church. These signs need not destroy or embitter. They can bless us in ways not yet imagined if we have but the courage to hope and the wisdom to love in greater measure than we fear and hate.

CHAPTER   TWELVE

JESUS:
Priest, High Priest and Priest To Turn To

Throughout these reflections on the Catholic priesthood, I have turned to various disclosure models contained in Scripture to highlight important aspects of priestly life and ministry. In this final reflection, I want to turn to *the* disclosure model for the Catholic priest: Jesus Christ who is the Way, the Truth, and the Life. It is in the Person of Jesus that the call, ministry, and destiny of priesthood finds its full expression and ultimate fulfillment. To be specific, I want to prayerfully reflect on Jesus as the Priest, the High Priest, and the Priest we turn to. In order to guide these reflections, I want to employ some of the deepest images provided to us by the Fourth Gospel. That is, Jesus is the Priest who pastorally guides the community as the Good Shepherd. Secondly, Jesus is the High Priest who reveals the glory of the Father through his death and resurrection. Finally, Jesus is the Priest we turn to because he empowers us to be courageous and hopeful through the indwelling of the Paraclete.

Jesus as Priest: The Good Shepherd

In chapter ten of John's Gospel, Jesus tells two pastoral parables using the metaphor of the sheep gate and the good shepherd. The metaphor of the sheep gate or door has rich roots in Old Testament imagery. The door or gate is a symbol of the Savior who leads the just into the presence of the Lord. In Psalm 118, we read: "This gate is the Lord's; the just shall enter it" (v. 20). Jesus is the True or Exclusive Gate to the Father. All others are thieves and marauders. These others try to lead the community astray by claiming to show members the way to God, but in fact are only out for their own gain. No one can come to the Father except through Jesus. There is an intimacy between Jesus, the community, and the Father. The community hears the voice of Jesus and follows him because they know (experience) his voice and believe he will lead them to the Father. Jesus calls his followers by name, so great is their degree of intimacy. Jesus knows them because he loves them and wants to lead them to the one source of eternal life. The community knows (experiences) Jesus as the True Gate or Door which leads to heaven. Jesus does not exploit the community, but comes "that they might have life and have it to the full" (Jn 10:10).

The pastoral image of Jesus as the True Gate or Door leading to abundant life in the Father is a powerful image for those entrusted with priestly ministry in the parish. The priest is called to continue the work of Jesus by leading the community to the Father through Jesus. The pastor must accept such a calling in the face of many who try to lead the community astray. We live in a culture which does not acknowledge the Lordship of Jesus Christ and rejects the Gospel. Materialism, consumerism, hedonism, and pan-sexualism all promise they are the true doors to the abundant life. They promise that all one need do is own enough, buy enough, experience enough pleasure, and engage in sex for fun without fidelity, and total happiness is theirs. The principalities and powers of this world proclaim an anti-gospel which is also anti-life. In the end, those who follow such a message come to ruin. The priest, and the Church as a whole, must provide a clear (but not arrogant) telling of the Gospel and a visible commitment to the Person of Jesus Christ.

We must honestly acknowledge that we cannot continue the pastoral ministry of Jesus as the True Gate if we within the community do not hear and follow his voice. Words are necessary, but not sufficient. The priest must dwell in the community as a man who knows (experiences) Jesus and the abundant life he offers. Such a priest must not simply know about Jesus. He must be intimate with Jesus so as to lead the community to the One alone who gives life in abundance. The priest must never become so self-absorbed that he forgets he ministers in the name of Jesus. The priest must never come to believe he is the gate or the door which leads to the Father. It is Jesus who is the Way to the Father. If such self-absorption and confusion arise, the priest becomes, in the imagery of John, a thief and marauder who ends up destroying himself and hurting the community. The priest people turn to is one who knows them by name and calls them to follow his example of loving Jesus as the Way to the Father.

Jesus progresses from the image of the sheep gate to that of the good shepherd (Jn 10:11). Once again, we encounter in the shepherd an image and symbol with rich roots in the Old Testament. In chapter thirty-four of Ezekiel, we find the parable of the shepherds. The prophet contrasts the unworthy rulers of Israel (bad shepherds) with the worthy shepherd that will be appointed by the Lord. Such a shepherd will be a messianic Davidic king who will reign over the restored Israel leading the people in the ways of the Lord. An important Old Testament theme is added by the prophet Zechariah to the metaphor of worthy shepherd. Namely, the shepherd who is chosen by God, leads the people into the ways of righteousness, and is faithful to the sheep even to the point of self-sacrifice. At times, the shepherd may even have to give up his life. However, through the death of the shepherd, a new way of life develops. We read in Zechariah:

> Awake, O sword, against my shepherd,
> against the man who is my associate,
> says the Lord of hosts.
> Strike the shepherd that the sheep may be dispersed,
> and I will turn my hand against the little ones.

In all the land, says the Lord, two-thirds of them
shall be cut off and perish,
and one-third shall be left.
I will bring the one-third through fire,
and I will refine them as silver is refined,
and I will test them as gold is tested.
They shall call upon my name, and I will hear them.
I will say, "They are my people," and they shall say,
"The Lord is my God." (Zc 13:7-9)

The metaphor of the Good Shepherd is applied to Jesus. However, the understanding of Jesus as the Good Shepherd requires some essential clarification. Jesus is *not* a shepherd who rules with the force of earthly power, nor does he surround himself with the trappings of worldly status. Jesus is the Good Shepherd "who lays down his life for the sheep" (Jn 10:11). Jesus clearly shows that he is the True and Good Shepherd by his willingness to sacrifice his life for the community. Unlike the person who is active in the community for money, personal honor, or power, Jesus is a True Shepherd because he loves the community with a total love. In the face of danger, and when the forces of death gather, the person who is simply "a hired hand" runs away and allows the community to be scattered and destroyed. The Good, True Shepherd is a Faithful Lover who will give his life so the community may live. There is no greater union and intimacy between shepherd and community than the willingness to die out of love. Through such a free, loving act of self-sacrifice, new life comes forth in abundance.

Jesus is the Good Shepherd who offers the perfect sacrifice. Jesus freely and lovingly offers himself to the Father on behalf of the community. No one takes his life from him (Jn 10:18), but out of total love, Jesus gives up his life for the community. The sacrifice of Jesus on the Cross also brings others into the community of faith. This sacrifice on the Cross leads to the glory of the resurrection. Jesus says, "I lay down my life to take it up again" (Jn 10:17). The death of Jesus is not the end, but a new beginning. Through the death of the Good Shepherd, the words of Zechariah have come to pass. The little flock which proclaims Jesus as the Son of God and lives in fraternal love will be the community of God's new people.

Each priest and bishop is called to continue the pastoral ministry of the Good Shepherd. The priest as Good Shepherd is one who loves and serve the community in the way of total love. The priest must daily lay down his life for the community. How? By lovingly caring for and pastoring the members of the community. The priest must die to himself in order to take up a new life of Christian and priestly existence. This dying to self is not a call to compulsive, workaholic, manipulative "service." Rather, we die to that egoism which keeps us from meeting the real needs of the community. Dying to self is not a negative self-hatred which fills us with bitterness. The dying required of each good shepherd is one which is motivated by a love grounded in freedom. The priest freely serves the community and, through his service, he helps to empower the community to serve one another freely in love.

The priest as good shepherd is on intimate terms with the community. The priest is a friend and a man of love who reveals the ways of love to the community. In the quality of relationships enjoyed by the priest, the community comes to know (experience) what it means to love as Jesus loved. This love is not love in the abstract but a daily caring for the needs of others and a keeping company with the hurting members of the community. The priest is willing to enter the lives of those whom he serves in order to learn as well as lead. The priest risks becoming involved in the lives of those whom he is called to serve. Jesus did not care for people at a distance, but lovingly touched them as he brought the grace of healing. The community hears the voice of the priest because they recognize him as "friend." The Eucharist is a celebration of Jesus' love for the disciples through the gift of himself. Jesus asked us to *do* this in remembrance of him. Jesus asked us to gather and celebrate his love for us and receive the spiritual food which empowers us to love one another. The priest can celebrate this love at the table because he is found among the community as the friend among friends.

The priest as good shepherd is a man of hope. The love which moves Jesus to lay down his life is also the love which brings forth new life. The attack of the wolf is a frightening experience. Life is lost. The tranquility of the community is never quite as secure as it once was. Yet when the shepherd faces the wolf, he sends a signal that the fearful attack of the wolf can be withstood and even bring forth new strength. The priest faces the attack of the wolf on many fronts. But because he serves out of love, and not the desire for money, the priest is able to strengthen the community with a vision and a hope. The vision which brings forth new life is contained in the Gospel. The hope of glory is offered to all who believe that Jesus is the Son of God and who live in fraternal love.

The reaction of the crowd to these pastoral parables offers another example of Jesus coming to his own but finding only rejection (Jn 1:11).

The crowd was sharply divided. Many claimed: "He is possessed by a devil — out of his mind! Why pay any attention to him?" (Jn 10:20). Why indeed. The words of the crowd continue to echo down through the ages into our time. The priests and bishops, in proclaiming the Gospel, are often labeled (and libeled) as being crazy, or worse, unrealistic and irrelevant. The cultured despisers of our age wrap themselves in a worldly wisdom which seeks to nullify the Gospel and render the good news foolishness. Yet the Good Shepherd, and those who continue to be good shepherds, will not be scared off. And the Father loves us for this (Jn 10:17). We know with the Apostle Paul, "that we preach Christ crucified . . . For God's folly is wiser than men, and his weakness more powerful than men" (1 Cor 1:23, 25).

Jesus as High Priest: Consecrated in Truth

Chapter seventeen of John's Gospel is referred to as the "High Priestly Prayer" of Jesus and is one of the most beautiful in all of Scripture. This prayer of Jesus shows a substantial relationship with the Jewish liturgy for the Day of Atonement (the day on which Israel was cleansed of all its sins and once again made a holy people). The Day of Atonement was the most important of festivals since it renewed the covenant relationship between Israel and Yahweh. It was the time of forgiveness when all the sins of the people were thrust on the sacrificial animal and sent into the desert away from the community. The Day of Atonement indicates that renewal and new life are possible.

Jesus assumed the traditional posture for one at prayer, by looking up to heaven and addressing the Father. The theme of glory dominates these opening verses (Jn 17:1-5) and refers to the mission of revealing the Father's name to the disciples. Jesus reveals the glory of the Father, makes the Father's name known, as Suffering, Faithful Love. The Father is Love. The unbounded love of the Father was made manifest at creation, the Incarnation, and would be fully revealed on the Cross. The Cross would reveal the glory of God as Love. The "I am" of Mount Sinai is the Love made visible by Jesus on Golgotha. Jesus had been faithful to the mission given by the Father. The disciples had become the friends of God because they had had the glory of the Father revealed to them. To accept the revelation of God as Love and Jesus Christ as the Son is to experience eternal life. The knowledge which brings eternal life is not academic but existential; it is not frozen in ideas but made visible through the Word made flesh. André Feuillet writes:

> Revealing the Father's name to men means communicating new knowledge to them. If we look at it as the Bible does, this "knowledge" is not of a theoretical kind but calls upon all of man's powers and is intended to bring him into communion with the very life of God. The revelation of the Father's name concerns two points: It teaches men that God is the Father of Jesus Christ in a totally unique way, and it teaches them that God wants to become their Father in a wholly new manner. (*The Priesthood of Christ and His Ministers*, p. 64)

Jesus, ever the Good Shepherd, then prayed for the

community which must remain in the world so as to continue the work of proclaiming Jesus as the Son of God and revealing the Father's name as Love. The world will arise in opposition to the community in the same manner that it arose in hostility to Jesus. It is only the name (the very essence of God as Love) of the Father that will protect them from the evil one. The community must remain in the world but also it must avoid becoming of the world. The gift of the Paraclete will strengthen the community to proclaim the truth about Jesus and withstand the false claims of the forces of evil (Jn 15:26-27).

The revelation of the Father's glory as Suffering Love and the knowledge that Jesus is the Son of God does not come through cheap grace. Jesus proclaims the truth that is consecrated, made holy, through his sacrifice on the Cross. Truth comes at a dear price. It is precious. The community of believers must remain in the world as the community made holy by the blood of Christ on the Cross. They remain in the world so that the world will know the name of the Father (Love) and Jesus Christ as the Son. The community receives the truth about the Father and Jesus and *does* the truth in love.

Finally, Jesus looked down the ages and prayed for all who would believe in him as the Son of God. Jesus prayed for a unity in love and belief between the Father, himself, and the community in the power of the Paraclete. Such a unity of love and belief provides convincing testimony that Jesus is the Word made flesh and sent by the Father to make known his name: "I have given them the glory you gave me that they may be one, as we are one — I living in them, you living in me — that their unity may be complete. So shall the world know that you sent me, and that you loved them as you loved me" (Jn 17:22-23). The world does not know Jesus or the Father. The world refuses to be open to revelation and only grows deeper in hostility and hatred for Jesus and the community. It is through the world's hatred that the revelation of God as Love would reach its climax on the Cross. This total revelation of God as Love would live in the disciples and be proclaimed to the world down through history.

Each priest, taken from the human family, is consecrated in the holy truth of Jesus Christ as the Son of God and entrusted with the revelation that God is Love. Such a truth is not simply propositional or frozen in some creedal statement. The truth about the Father and Jesus is the dynamic reality which dwells, through the Paraclete, in the heart of the disciple and the community. To believe in spirit and truth that Jesus is the Son of God calls for the disciple to love as Jesus loved. The distinguishing public witness of the community which follows Jesus is fraternal charity. The priest must be the leader, good shepherd, and servant who provides the molding for the discipleship of love. The priest must be the man of prayer for the community of prayer, leading the people into greater unity with the Father, the Son, and the Paraclete. The spiritual life of the community requires this intimate relationship of love and belief. Without living in Jesus, the community dies spiritually. Jesus drew on the Old Testament metaphor of the vine to express this deep truth: "I am the vine, you are the branches. He who lives in me and I in him, will produce abundantly, for apart from me you can do nothing" (Jn 15:5).

The danger is always present that the community will seek to withdraw from the world in order to remain holy. Jesus clearly indicated that such is not the mission of the community. Jesus was sent by the Father into the world to tell the world of the Father's love and to call the world to respond in love to Love. So Jesus sent the disciples forth into the world to proclaim the truth about Jesus, the Son of God. Love is extending and reaches out to others in calling forth new life. Holiness cannot be purchased at the price of withdrawing from the world. There is a social dimension to love, holiness, and belief in Jesus as the Son of God and knowing the Father's name as Love. Rudolf Schnackenburg writes:

> . . . the Johannine community did not succumb to the
> danger of encapsulation and isolation from the world. The
> prayer bears witness to a concentration on what is essen-
> tial and a reflection about what has been given to the

community by God through Christ, namely, life in God and in his love that is filled with inner glory. This call to the inner life, to inner recollection and to unity with God and within the community, is still significant even in our own age, which is so characterized by external activity. On the other hand, we also encounter in this prayer the risk and limitations of this Christian attitude and these can only be avoided by a community that is conscious of its mission to the world as a permanent task. (*The Gospel According to John*, Vol. 3, p. 202)

The mission to the world as a permanent pastoral calling was given new impetus with the Second Vatican Council. The Church is to be a pastoral Church, hearing and healing the hearts of the world with the saving message of the Gospel. The priest people turn to is one who leads the community in holiness while ministering to the world community in the name of Jesus Christ. The mission to the world is not a call to give up what is distinctive about the Christian life. The pastoral care of the human family is anything but a call to become less holy. The mission to the world is one given to the Church and the priest by Jesus himself. It is a mission to proclaim a holy truth consecrated through the Cross so that all people will be drawn to salvation.

Jesus: The Priest To Turn To

The public ministry of Jesus involves more than the mission to reveal the name and show forth the glory of the Father. Jesus called Twelve disciples to be his friends and stand by him in his moments of acceptance and rejection. The sharing of the public ministry with the Twelve was an intense and intimate experience. The time for farewell and departure is a time of sadness and pain. Jesus was leaving them and their hearts were troubled. The disciples were fearful as they must continue the mission of Jesus in the face of a hostile world. Long ago, they left everything to follow Jesus. Now he was leaving them and their sorrow was acute: "Truly, truly, I say to you, you will weep and lament . . . and . . . you have sorrow now . . ." (Jn 16:20, 22). Jesus was returning to the Father from whom he came. The Son had been faithful to the will of the Father. Jesus would now go back to the Father and claim the glory they shared from eternity. The disciples did not focus on the glory of Jesus but on their own sense of loss. Their pain narrowed their vision and dulled their senses to the need for Jesus to go back to the Father so the Paraclete could be sent.

Jesus took seriously their pain and offered them words of comfort and hope: "your sorrow will turn to joy . . . and . . . I will see you again and your hearts will rejoice and no one will take your joy from you" (Jn 16:20, 22). This joy and peace did not mean that they would never experience conflict, hostility from the world, or tribulation. The community would experience all of these. But Jesus assured them that hope, not despair; love, not fear; light, not darkness; and grace, not sin, would carry the day. Why? Because Jesus made known the Father, freely laid down his life out of love, and is to return to the Father in order to send the Paraclete. It is the indwelling Paraclete who will strengthen, comfort, and guide the community until God brings forth the new heavens and new earth. Jesus concluded his dialogue with the disciples in these stirring words: "be of good cheer, I have overcome the world" (Jn 16:33).

Jesus challenged the disciples to look through their pain and sense of loss to the victory of the Cross and the glorification of the Son. Jesus' departure was not a desertion. Jesus was going to return to them through the indwelling of the Paraclete. Jesus' victory, departure, and sending of the Paraclete is offered in order to encourage the disciples for what lies ahead. There would be tribulations and crosses to bear. But they were not left orphans, without the protection of their loving Father. The Paraclete would guide, strengthen, and counsel them in the days to come. Jesus' victory was their victory. His glorification was their hope of glory. Jesus did not minimize their sense of loss, nor did he allow them to fall into self-pity. Jesus extended a vision which faced the reality of opposition and the hope of victory through the power of the God who is Love.

In my initial reflection, I indicated that the priesthood had faced (and would continue to so face) its share of tribulation in these post-Vatican II decades. For some, this tribulation has been a time of abandonment without a sense of hope or a vision which gives life in abundance. The past decades, for some priests, have been the worst of times, and there is no relief in sight. Their pain and sense of loss are real. The importance of their contributions and what they have yet to give is too precious to be dismissed. Hurting priests do not need lectures, ridicule, or pity. Priests who feel left behind by the Church need what Jesus offered to his disciples: a vision of victory brought forth by love and the hope that out of every departure, there is a return more abundant than we can imagine. Simply because many once valuable forms, structures, symbols and stories undergo change or even elimination does not mean that Jesus has left us orphaned. The Paraclete continues to indwell with the community and within the heart of each disciple. The indwelling Paraclete gives us courage in times of tribulation and transition. The strengthening words of Jesus are for all priests who find their faith shaken and despair outrunning hope: "be of good cheer, I have overcome the world."

The priest not only accepts this message of hope and joy, but he extends it through his priestly ministry within the community. The priest is a man of vision and hope who invites hurting members to be healed. The priest speaks words of courage to those who are growing weak. To the despairing, the priest incarnates hope in Jesus Christ raised from the dead. To those who feel the burden of sin and the prison of guilt, the priest extends the peace which comes to us through the Cross of our Crucified God. The priest people turn to is one who leads them in love to Christ who alone is the Priest, the High Priest, and the Priest we all turn to.

A Concluding Word

It is fitting that we end these reflections with the Person and Priesthood of Jesus Christ. All that the priest does and hopes to become only makes sense in light of Christ. Apart from Jesus, we can do nothing and the most spectacular of achievements do not last. Jesus is not only the One who calls the priest to follow him, but he also sustains that call. This means that at the heart of priestly existence is daily meditation on the Person of Jesus. Priestly existence can only be sustained and strengthened by the priest contemplating the unbounded love of God shown through the call to the priesthood. Such meditation and daily spiritual renewal are not luxuries but are among the essentials for priestly growth in holiness. The call to follow Jesus as a priest reveals God's continuing love for the community of faith.

There is much talk today about the crisis and problem of the Catholic priesthood. Much of this talk is wrapped in the language and spirit of gloom and doom. The problems are familiar: decline in vocations; the loss of identity for today's priests; the number of priests who have left the active ministry; the refusal of priests to recruit young men to the priesthood. The list goes on and on. Yet if all we see are problems, then all we have are problems. Our future becomes not one of hope but one of despair. However, despair is the one response to life's challenges in which the Christian cannot indulge. Ever since Jesus arose from the dead, the Christian community is committed to hope, life, and the unfolding story of the new creation. In the midst of what seems most desperate, fatal, and lost, the Christian looks for signs of life, new birth, and hope. To the natural eye, Jesus' abandonment and death on the Cross was the ultimate defeat of grace by sin. To the eye of faith, the Cross of Jesus is the hour of glory and the time of grace when God is revealed as LOVE. To see rightly is crucial.

The challenges facing the Catholic priesthood are real and only a fool would minimize their seriousness. At the same time, these challenges will not be met by a loss of nerve and a

collective abandonment of the vision which grounds our hope
— the Crucified and Risen Lord. This is the same Lord who
consoled the disciples before his departure to the Father. This
is the same Lord who walked the road to Emmaus with disciples who had lost hope. Jesus stayed with them and their hearts
burned with love. This is the same Lord who sent the Paraclete
and offered the gift of peace. This is the same Lord who dwells
among us in the Spirit with the invitation to "Come and see . . .
Come follow me."

FURTHER READING

In addition to the books and articles mentioned previously, the following works would be of help in enriching these reflections.

Bernardin, Joseph Cardinal, *In Service of One Another: Pastoral Letter on Ministry* (Chicago: Chicago Catholic Publishing Co., 1985).

Brown, Raymond E., *Priest and Bishop: Biblical Reflections* (New York: Paulist Press, 1970).

Coll, Regina, ed., *Women and Religion: A Reader for the Clergy* (New York: Paulist Press, 1982).

Cooke, Bernard, *Ministry to Word and Sacraments. History and Theology* (Philadelphia: Fortress, 1976).

Durkin, Mary, *A Feast of Love* (Chicago: Loyola University Press, 1986).

Farley, Margaret A., *Personal Commitments* (San Francisco: Harper & Row, 1986).

Goergen, Donald, *The Sexual Celibate* (New York: Doubleday/ Image, 1979).

Haring, Bernard, *The Sacraments and Your Everyday Life* (Liguori, MO: Liguori, 1977).

Kane, Thomas A., *The Healing Touch of Affirmation* (Whitinsville, MA: Affirmation Books, 1976).

Kelsey, Morton T., *Prophetic Ministry. The Psychology and Spirituality of Pastoral Life* (New York: Harper & Row, 1984).

Mitchell, Nathan, *Mission and Ministry: History and Theology in the Sacrament of Orders* (Wilmington, DE: Michael Glazier, 1982).

Polcino, Anna, *Intimacy: Issues of Emotional Living in an Age of Stress for Clergy and Religious* (Whitinsville, MA: Affirmation Books, 1978).

Power, David, *Gifts That Differ: Lay Ministries Established and Unestablished* (New York: Pueblo, 1985).

Provost, James H., ed., *Official Ministry in a New Age* (Washington, D.C.: Canon Law Society of America, 1981).

Rahner, Karl, *Concern for the Church* (New York: Crossroads, 1981).

An Interesting Thought

The publication you have just finished reading is part of the apostolic efforts of the Society of St. Paul of the American Province. The Society of St. Paul is an international religious community located in 23 countries, whose particular call and ministry is to bring the message of Christ to all people through the communications media.

Following in the footsteps of their patron, St. Paul the Apostle, priests and brothers blend a life of prayer and technology as writers, editors, marketing directors, graphic designers, bookstore managers, pressmen, sound engineers, etc. in the various fields of the mass media, to announce the message of Jesus.

If you know a young man who might be interested in a religious vocation as a brother or priest and who shows talent and skill in the communications arts, ask him to consider our life and ministry. For more information at no cost or obligation write:

Vocation Office
2187 Victory Blvd.
Staten Island, NY 10314-6603
Telephone: (718) 698-3698